# the beats

# the
# beats

From Kerouac to Kesey, **an Illustrated Journey through the Beat Generation**

## Mike Evans

RUNNING PRESS
PHILADELPHIA · LONDON

This 2007 edition published by Running Press, by arrangement with
Elephant Book Company Limited,
14, Dryden Court, Renfrew Road, London, SE11 2NH, United Kingdom.

9   8   7   6   5   4   3   2   1
Digit on the right indicates the number of this printing

Library of Congress Control Number: 2007923123

ISBN-13: 978-0-7624-3048-2
ISBN-10: 0-7624-3048-6

Editorial Director: Will Steeds
Project Editor: Laura Ward
Designer: Paul Palmer-Edwards, Grade Design Consultants, London
Picture Research: Sally Claxton
Index: Sandra Shotter
Production: Robert Paulley
Color reproduction: Modern Age Repro House Ltd, Hong Kong
Maps by Grade Design Consultants, London
Cover design by Grade Design Consultants, London

Running Press Editor: Jennifer Leczkowski

This book may be ordered by mail from the publisher.
Please include $2.50 for postage and handling.
*But try your bookstore first!*

Running Press Book Publishers
2300 Chestnut Street
Philadelphia, PA 19103-4371

Visit us on the web!
www.runningpress.com

Special thanks to Carolyn Cassady whose interview with the
author is featured throughout. Also thanks to Carolyn Cassady
and Brian Patten for access to various items of archive material
from their personal collections.

**Cover picture:** Jack Kerouac photographed
by Elliott Erwitt, New York 1953.

**Page 181:** Bob Dylan and Allen Ginsberg
at the grave of Jack Kerouac, in Lowell,
Massachusetts, November 3, 1975.

# contents

# introduction

Most of the profound cultural and social changes characterizing the latter half of the 20th century, often identified as having been triggered in the liberated atmosphere of the 60s, had their roots firmly in the post-war years of the late 40s and early 50s. This manifested itself in innumerable ways in an otherwise largely conservative society, particularly in the US; from the first stirrings of the Civil Rights struggle to the spawning of rock 'n' roll, from Method acting to abstract expressionism. Significant in this was the literary movement that became known as the Beat Generation, whose influence went far beyond its impact in poetry and prose.

But what was Beat? Well, it had a lot to do with attitude. Indeed, Jack Kerouac (while at the same time invoking a religious connotation) talked of "Beatitude." Earlier, John Clellon Holmes had been the first to refer to a "Beat Generation." Kerouac put it in its historical/social context when he defined the term for an entry in the *Random House Dictionary*: "Members of the generation that came of age after World War II, who, supposedly as a result of disillusionment stemming from the Cold War, espouse mystical detachment and relaxation of social and sexual tensions." Though a rather more broad-based interpretation than that which would link it directly with a particular group of writers and their immediate followers, he described the Beat phenomenon as a precise response to circumstances, which in many ways it was.

In the immediate aftermath of World War II, under the Presidency of Harry S. Truman, followed by that of Dwight D. Eisenhower, the US enjoyed unprecedented affluence. Fed by a consumerism the scale of which the world had never seen before, industry boomed. In the expanding suburbs, every family owned at least one car, while items that had previously been seen as luxuries—washing machines and air

conditioning, for example—became the norm. Radio, which had united the country culturally in the 20s and 30s, was quickly being replaced by TV as the premier mass medium. On the home front, all was comfortable, but with the new prosperity came a deeply orthodox outlook on the part of most citizens of the US.

With its great wealth, mainstream America was largely insulated from the rest of the world. Notwithstanding the Korean conflict from 1950–53, as World War II gave way to the Cold War, and the accompanying nuclear arms race between the Western allies and the Soviet bloc, the country was gripped by a paranoia in the early 50s that was reinforced by the anti-Communist witch-hunts conducted by Senator Joe McCarthy and HUAC—the House Un-American Activities Committee.

McCarthyism spread like a cancer through all sections of society, most virulently in the creative and media world, where radical—and therefore suspect—attitudes were considered most prevalent. Writers and artists of all kinds were hauled in front of the Committee and questioned as to their political associations, and those of friends and colleagues. It was this last "naming of names" that led to numerous, often famous and eminent individuals being constrained in their activities or even losing their jobs, particularly in the journalistic world and Hollywood.

In this highly censorious atmosphere the Beat Generation was born, and as Kerouac suggested, in many ways it was a reaction to the right-wing orthodoxy and narrow-mindedness of society at large. But it was not just a question of political attitudes. Strait-laced sexual conventions were challenged in the Beats' liberal attitude to sex outside marriage, homosexuality, and promiscuity. And their almost evangelical advocacy of drug use as a positive aid to the creative process was likewise taboo in the postwar US.

It was less than surprising, therefore, that the Beats attracted high-profile publicity, most of it derogatory, in the late 50s. The tag of "beatnik" was coined, the "nik" having a direct association with the Russian sputnik, the Communists' surprise contender in the burgeoning space race. But the Beats' notoriety in the sensationalist media was balanced with genuine success in their literary output, in both commercial and critical terms.

With the release of *On the Road* in 1957, after years of trying to place his book with a publisher, Jack Kerouac—possibly surprising himself as much as the publishing world at large—had a best-seller on his hands. Likewise, Allen Ginsberg saw his debut collection, *Howl*, reprinted six times in the two years following publication (against the background of a highly publicized obscenity trial that eventually ruled in the book's favor). And when it appeared in 1959, initially in an otherwise-banned edition that was published in Paris, France, William Burroughs' masterwork *The Naked Lunch* was greeted with critical acclaim.

Other Beat names—John Clellon Holmes, Gregory Corso, and Lawrence Ferlinghetti among them—experienced similar success and the celebrity that came with it, though fame often came at a price. As the glare of the media spotlight fell on Beat enclaves in Greenwich Village, San Francisco's North Beach, and elsewhere, as tourists swarmed the streets on the lookout for "genuine" beatniks, many of the real writers and artists began to distance themselves from the ballyhoo. Others basked in the novelty of being fêted by the same cultural establishment they had previously, and very publicly, decried. And some, Kerouac among them, fell victim to the disreputable image that they themselves, albeit inadvertently, had often helped promote.

The period of the Beats' preeminence spanned less than a decade, from the mid-50s to the early 60s, but their presence has been felt in literature—and other areas of the arts and popular culture—ever since. In the 50 years since *On the Road* was first published, the major works of the Beat Generation writers have become accepted as classics, while the circumstances of their genesis, as spelled out in these pages, are now recognized as having been a turning point in our cultural history.

# beginnings

"Wisdom is not finally tested in the schools,
Wisdom cannot be pass'd from one having it
to another not having it, Wisdom is of the Soul . . ."
Walt Whitman

The oldest institution of higher learning in the State of New York—Columbia University —was founded by Royal Charter in 1754, before the US had even come into being. At that time it was known as King's College, in deference to the ruling British monarch King George II, but even then the institution harbored voices of dissent.

Not least of which was Alexander Hamilton, a radical Scotsman, who wrote anti-British leaflets and who would figure strongly in the upcoming Revolutionary War. It was after Independence that the College was renamed, moving from its original site on Lower Broadway to midtown Manhattan, eventually settling in its present uptown location in 1897. The grandiose complex of redbrick buildings straddles a campus area between Riverside Drive and Morningside Park, up between 114th and 120th Streets and just west of Harlem.

As well as two US Presidents—Theodore Roosevelt and Franklin Delano Roosevelt—Columbia counts among its alumni the songwriters Richard Rodgers, Oscar Hammerstein II, and Lorenz Hart, singer Art Garfunkel, and the composer Béla Bartók. Writers who have passed through its portals include J.D. Salinger and Isaac Asimov, and the poets Langston Hughes and Federico García Lorca. And it was Columbia University that would be the catalyst in the coming together of the three major literary figures of the Beat Generation: William (Bill) Burroughs, Jack Kerouac, and Allen Ginsberg.

Although they would go on to constitute a "movement" in modern letters, in their creative output the triumvirate was fiercely individualistic and independent of each other—kindred in spirit though certainly not in style. And before their paths first crossed in the early 40s, the backgrounds and early experiences that brought them to that point were equally diverse.

## William Burroughs: the early years

The younger of two sons of a well-to-do St. Louis, Missouri, family, William Seward Burroughs II was born on February 5, 1914. The first William Seward Burroughs, his grandfather, was founder of the Burroughs Adding Machine Company, having invented and patented the first key-operated recording and adding machine in the late 1880s. The company went on to make a fortune, but by that time the inventor had sold most of his stock, so his children and grandchildren would never see the great wealth that the enterprise might have generated for the family.

Nevertheless, young William grew up in a comfortable, middle-class household on Pershing Avenue, St. Louis, complete with a staff of maid, nanny, cook, and gardener. For a time his father, Mortimer, ran a plate-glass company before becoming the proud proprietor of an antique and gift store in St. Louis, known as Cobblestone Gardens. His mother, born Laura Hammon Lee, was the daughter of a church minister whose family claimed to be descendants of Civil War Confederate General Robert E. Lee.

Despite this cosseted upbringing—or perhaps, in part, because of it—"Billy," as the family called him, was something of a loner as a child. With the combination of a pasty, unhealthy-looking complexion, sinus problems, and a spindly frame, he was regarded as something of an oddball, and was shunned by many of the neighborhood children (and, as often as not, by their parents, too). The father of one of his schoolfriends even described him as "a walking corpse." His older brother—Mort—on the other hand, was the more conventionally attuned sibling, ending up at Princeton University, where he studied architecture before embarking on a lifelong career with General Electric. But Billy never lacked attention from his parents: his mother adored him, doting on his often-weird sense of humor. His father, meanwhile, initiated him in the use of firearms for hunting, and read to him avidly, nurturing the youngster's vocabulary by setting him the target of having to learn five new words a day. Taking into account the idiosyncrasies already evident in his behavior, they knew he was a "clever" child.

At age eight Billy produced his first work of fiction: a ten-page adventure about a wild animal that had lost its mate and was subsequently killed by a grisly bear. He named his book *Autobiography Of A Wolf*, and when his parents suggested the title should be a "Biography," he insisted it was to be an "Autobiography"—and continued to do so when famously retelling the incident in later life.

**Previous pages:** St. Louis, Missouri, 1940.

**Right:** William Burroughs' grandfather, William S. Burroughs Sr., c. 1897.

**Far right:** William Burroughs in 1927, on the porch of the Big House at the Ranch School in Los Alamos. Before he became a regular student there, Burroughs spent several summers attending the school's summer camp.

**Below:** Students reading in the Ranch School Lodge, c. 1940.

**Opposite:** The imposing Low Memorial Library at Columbia University.

"As a boy I was much plagued by nightmares. I remember a nurse telling me that opium gives you sweet dreams, and I resolved that I would smoke opium when I grew up."

William Burroughs

As Billy approached adolescence, two major preoccupations became apparent: a fascination with weaponry, and guns in particular, and an insatiable appetite for reading. The latter, seemingly laudable, pastime was dominated, however, by a love of pulp fiction. At age 13 he came across *You Can't Win*, the autobiography of Jack Black, a down-and-out drug addict and self-confessed thief. Although the book was intended as a warning against the criminal life, its colorful cast of petty crooks, con men, drunks, and drifters attracted the young Burroughs. From there on in, it seemed the die was cast: Bill Burroughs was never going to fit in with the conventionalities and social niceties of the mid-West bourgeoisie. As if to confirm just that, he began to produce short stories while still at school—grim tales, worthy of the goriest newsstand crime fiction, full of murder and mayhem, but always with an edge of equally dark humor.

It was while he was attending the John Burroughs School in St. Louis that he had his first work published, at age 15. It was an essay titled "Personal Magnetism," which appeared in the *John Burroughs Review* in 1929. Most of his remaining high school days, though, were spent at the private Los Alamos Ranch School in New Mexico. The experience was, if nothing else, certainly formative. While learning the macho arts of rifle-shooting and knife-throwing, Burroughs' inner turmoils began to surface through the pages of confessional diaries, as he formed an erotic attachment to a fellow student. Although he did his best to keep this a secret, he couldn't disguise his infatuation from his sniggering peers, whose taunts and whispered innuendos soon became unbearable for him.

Around the same time he got into some serious trouble after drinking (in the company of another student) some chloral hydrate, which he'd purchased in a local Santa Fe drugstore. It nearly killed him, and although the school concluded that he would never try anything similar again, it was his earliest instance of a lifelong history of chemical experimentation. With his parents' support, as always, he dropped out of Los Alamos just two months before graduation, finishing high school at Taylor School in St. Louis, from where he managed to get onto an English Literature degree course at Harvard starting in September 1932. There, he became even more of a malcontent, reacting immediately against the Ivy League stuffiness of its class-bound manners and traditions. He would spend most of his leisure time on campus locked in his room with the live ferret he kept as a pet, but once he experienced his first proper sexual "awakening," he began to make forays into the homosexual underground of New York City. There, he would visit gay bars, lesbian clubs, and so forth in the multiracial bohemia of Greenwich Village and

Harlem, usually in the company of Richard Stern, a wealthy friend from Kansas City. Stern almost became a victim of Burroughs' obsession with firearms when the latter brandished and inadvertently fired his .32 revolver in his college room, not realizing it was loaded. It was a harbinger of things to come.

Burroughs' main academic interest at Harvard was focused on English literature, where he was introduced to the works of Thomas de Quincey and Samuel Taylor Coleridge, both of whom described the psychedelic effect of opium on their writing. But Burroughs himself was yet to be in a position to explore these mind-altering experiences.

Graduating in English in 1936, once again he was able to rely on the financial security provided by his ever-sympathetic parents. They decided to give him a monthly allowance of $200, which he would receive for the next quarter century, allowing him not to have to rely on paid employment to survive. Later, he would acknowledge his privileged position when he wrote in his first published novel, *Junkie*, that were it not for his heroin addiction, he would never have to worry about supporting himself. As he had no prospect of any immediate career move, Mortimer and Laura also gave their son a year's trip to Europe as a graduation present.

There, he experienced firsthand the darkening shadow of Nazism against the decadent background of the gay scene in Austria, Hungary, and Yugoslavia. And it was in the Austrian capital, Vienna, that he decided to stay and study medicine to pursue a long-lived interest in psychoanalysis. But all around there were those—particularly Jews, and to a lesser degree the homosexual community—who were increasingly anxious about the rise of the Far Right, many sensing they should not remain in Germany or Austria any longer than they had to.

One such was Ilse Klapper, a 35-year-old Jewish woman, who became friends with Burroughs and married him in 1937. But it was a marriage of convenience on both sides, strictly to facilitate Klapper's emigration to America. Contrary to his parents' concerns, when she got to New York Klapper never sought any money and the couple were eventually divorced in 1945, though they remained friends for many years afterward.

Still with the long-term plan of studying psychoanalysis in mind, between 1938 and 1942 Burroughs studied Anthropology and Psychology at Harvard and Columbia universities, though he never completed either course. Now ensconced in New York, it was after this that he formed his first regular relationship with a man, Jack Anderson, with whom he had a turbulent affair, which at one stage resulted in Burroughs amputating the tip of one of his own fingers in frustration at his lover's infidelity.

Early in 1942, soon after the bombing of Pearl Harbor, Burroughs enlisted in the US Army, where he trained as a glider pilot. But he was discharged as mentally unfit after just a few months and moved to Chicago, where he held a variety of jobs, including one as an insect exterminator. He soon became acquainted with the city's notorious North Side and its sleazy street life; he also met up with an old friend from St. Louis, David Kammerer, and his young companion, Lucien Carr. Kammerer was obsessed with Carr, though the latter—he was not homosexual, like Kammerer—didn't reciprocate physically. And when the two moved to New York early in 1943, Burroughs followed them.

**Opposite left:** A copy of *Dime Mystery* magazine, one of the many "penny dreadfuls" that were part of Burroughs' formative literary diet.

**Opposite right:** Pulp magazines featured a lurid mix of sex and crime, graphically evoked on this cover of *Spicy Mystery* from 1935.

**Left:** Coast Guard Certificate confirming Burroughs' brief spell in the service.

**Far left:** A portrait of the student Burroughs from the Harvard yearbook.

**Opposite:** Jack Kerouac's birthplace at 9 Lupine Avenue in Lowell.

**Opposite below:** Lowell's textile mills on the banks of the Merrimack river, when the town was still a thriving center of the industry in the early 20th century.

**Right:** Jack's mother Gabrielle (left) with his sister Caroline.

## Jack Kerouac: the early years

Lowell, Massachusetts, had once been the hub of New England's textile industry, but by the early 20s it was in economic decline. In more prosperous days it had attracted immigrants from the Canadian province of Quebec, among them Leo-Alcide Kerouac and his wife Gabrielle-Ange (née Levesque). Born Jean-Louis (Jack) Lebris de Kerouac on March 12, 1922, their third child was six years old before he spoke any English. Like many other *Québécois* of their generation, the Kerouacs spoke French as a first language, and *Ti Jean* ("Little Jean") as he was known to the family, was brought up speaking the Quebec French *joual* dialect.

Jean had an elder sister (Caroline, born 1918), and a brother (Gerard), who was five years older. Their mother Gabrielle was a strict Catholic, and among Jack's earliest memories of home were the crucifixes, devotional candles, and other religious artifacts that filled it. They had an added dynamic in that Gabrielle was preoccupied with administering to the ailing Gerard, who was born with a rheumatic heart and contracted rheumatic fever when he was seven. Gerard was seen as an "angel" by those around him—not least little Jack—stoically accepting, as he did, that his physical decline was the will of God (Gerard even claimed he had visions of being transported to heaven by the blessed Virgin). In Jack's eyes, his elder sibling was a saint, and when Gerard died age nine, in 1926, to the four-year-old he was indeed a martyr.

Her favorite gone, Gabrielle transferred her stifling attentions to Jack, cosseting him in unhealthy proximity until he was an adolescent, even letting him share the bed where her husband should have been sleeping. Leo, meanwhile, quit his job on a local newspaper to strike out on his own as a jobbing printer, a badly timed move in the light of the burgeoning recession. As his fortunes declined, so his drinking and gambling increased: Leo's flamboyant but unreliable lifestyle was in stark contrast to the strict and stable influence of Gabrielle.

Jack's first school was the St. Louis de France Parochial School, a severe Catholic establishment run by nuns, followed by an equally draconian academy, St. Joseph's School, administered by Jesuits. Little wonder his childhood would seem in many respects a solitary one, in which he retreated into his own fantasy world inspired by comic-book characters, Saturday cinema serials, and a radio mystery series introduced by a character called "The Shadow." A keen student who achieved good grades, his apparent lack of verbal communication skills—not helped in class by the fact that English was his second language—was offset by an enthusiasm for the written word.

Moving to Bartlett Junior High School in 1933, Jack was an avid reader of pulp fiction magazines featuring larger-than-life heroes such as "The Green Hornet" and "Phantom Detective," and soon he was creating his own stories, encouraged by the school librarian, Miss Mansfield, who ran an after-school discussion group and writing club. The first story he produced, written longhand in the spiral-bound notebook he'd begun to carry everywhere, was a lurid piece titled "The Cop and the Beat."

At Bartlett he formed his first real friendships, the most important being with Sebastian "Sammy" Sampas. The extrovertly confident Sampas would also figure a few years later in Jack's life, as part of the Young Prometheans literary and political debating group in Lowell.

By his early teens, Jack—now a strong and muscular youth—also developed an enthusiasm for sport in general and for baseball, athletics, and football in particular. In 1936 he graduated from Bartlett to Lowell High School, where his prowess on the football field was soon noticed by the team coach. Scoring several touchdowns in his first season with the school team, he quickly became something of a local hero; a status that didn't go unnoticed, along with his good looks and shy charm, with the young girls of Lowell.

**Opposite left:** Jack Kerouac in full football outfit at Columbia.

**Opposite center:** The respectable-looking student at Horace Mann School.

**Opposite right:** Mary Carney, who Kerouac later celebrated in his novel *Maggie Cassidy*, written in 1953.

**Opposite below:** The school clock at Lowell High.

**Right:** A pulp detective magazine, typical of the genre which influenced Kerouac's early literary ambitions.

It was at a New Year's Eve dance on December 31, 1937, that he met the first love of his life, Mary Carney. A tall, pretty Irish-American redhead, she was a regular, small-town girl who wanted nothing more than to settle down in Lowell with an equally regular type of guy, while Jack's horizons seemed to broaden by the day. Alongside sporting interests, his passion for literature continued unabated, his taste taking in work as disparate as the poetry of Emily Dickinson, short stories by Damon Runyon, and Dan Parker's baseball column. He had also developed a growing love of jazz music. But, in the short term at least, any incongruity between his burgeoning ambition and Mary's limited aspirations was forgotten as the two fell in love, beginning a relationship that was to continue for the next couple of years.

Physically, it would be what one writer has described as a "fumbled" romance, for Mary Carney was a good Catholic girl in the strictest sense, and on dates that meant kissing, even some "heavy petting," but never anything more than that. The chastity of the affair would prove too frustrating for Kerouac, who was to secretly embark on a more sensuous liaison with another Lowell girl, Peggy Coffey, while still dating Mary. The extrovertly sexy Coffey, who nurtured an ambition to leave small-town life to become a jazz singer, seemed to have far more in common with Kerouac, whose own sights were increasingly focused on the beckoning metropolis of New York City.

It was Jack's potential as a star football player that proved to be the initial key to his moving to Manhattan, when both Boston College and Columbia University offered him athletics scholarships. But it didn't take long for him to make a choice, what with Boston being only a few miles from Lowell, while Columbia was right in the middle of New York City, and all it promised. His eventual entry to Columbia was preceded by a year at its

"Forget this writing stuff, Jean, it'll never pay. You're such a good student—sure you'll go to college, get a job. Stop dreaming!"

Leo Kerouac to son Jean (Jack)

preparatory school, the Horace Mann School for Boys, where he arrived in the fall of 1939.

Given his route of entry into Horace Mann, football was an immediate priority as far as Jack and the school were concerned. He was immediately recruited into the school team, scoring spectacular touchdowns that had the sports columns buzzing with excitement, and within and outside the team, the normally shy Kerouac quickly made friends. Among them were two Dixieland jazz fanatics, Peter Gordon and Bob Olsted, who took him to innumerable New York bars and clubs. It was also at Horace Mann where Jack got involved with two characters who would significantly influence the course of his future: Seymour Wyse and Henri Cru.

Wyse was a London-based jazz enthusiast, who introduced Kerouac—already a fan of the then fashionable Swing—to the new Bebop music emerging in such places as Harlem's Apollo and the Savoy Ballroom. It was in Wyse's company that he first heard the classic Count Basie Orchestra featuring avant-garde tenor sax player of the era, Lester Young. The budding writer immediately recorded his new-found enthusiasm for modern jazz in the school newspaper, the *Horace Mann Record*, justly claiming years later to be one of the first scribes to have "discovered" Young.

Cru came from a well-off French family in Massachusetts, who had emigrated early in the century. A couple of years after they left Horace Mann, he was to be responsible for introducing Jack to Frankie Edith Parker, destined to become his first wife.

For Jack it was an exploratory time in more ways than one. As well as his school newspaper contributions, during his year at the college he had two short stories ("The Brothers" and "Une Veille de Noel") published in the *Horace Mann Quarterly*. On one of his frequent trips to Manhattan he smoked marijuana for the first time, and there also he lost his virginity with a prostitute in December 1939.

Graduating from Horace Mann the following June, Jack couldn't afford the obligatory formal white suit for the official ceremony, so he listened to the speeches stretched out on the lawn outside the assembly hall while reading, as he would later recollect, Walt Whitman. He failed two of his courses (Chemistry and French), the latter something of a disappointment to him as he had long regarded himself as bilingual. He'd never anticipated that the French-Canadian patois on which he had been brought up, bore little relation to the more formal French language taught in the classroom.

In summer 1940 Kerouac returned to Lowell, ostensibly to study the two failed courses, but he was easily distracted by his continuing relationship with Mary Carney, by the alternative attraction of full-blown sex with Peggy Coffey, and by the reappearance of the flamboyant Sebastian "Sammy" Sampas. By this time Sampas had become something of a local eccentric, taken to reciting Shelley and Byron in public, often from a café tabletop, and he involved Jack in the Young Prometheans, an earnest literary-political group, the motive of which was nothing less than the betterment of society.

The effeminate Sammy, whose influence was understandably viewed by Gabrielle and Leo Kerouac with some suspicion, adored Jack. The feeling was reciprocal, though it seems there was never any sexual relationship between the two. Crucially, Sampas introduced him to the work of two writers who would inspire his literary ambitions: William Saroyan and Thomas Wolfe. Saroyan's use of language in his short stories energized Jack's own approach to writing, while Wolfe's eulogies to the mythical, open spaces of America directly influenced his decision to go on the road in search of literary stimuli and subject matter. For the moment, though, Columbia beckoned.

In September 1940, Jack began as a freshman at Columbia. Unlike during his Horace Mann days, he no longer had to commute from Brooklyn, where he had lodged with Gabrielle's stepmother; instead he had a room right on the campus. At least

**Opposite:** During his time at Horace Mann, Kerouac excelled at football. This picture—of a game between Horace Mann and Maryland-based Tome School—in a local paper was captioned "Kerouac Getting Off a Punt In Tome Encounter."

**Right:** A 1939 poster advertising the Count Basie band, one of the first jazz names to excite the teenage Kerouac.

**Below:** And it wasn't just at football that Kerouac excelled: here he strikes out for the school baseball team.

initially he threw himself into the student persona with gusto; adopting a sports jacket, smoking a pipe, listening to classical music on the radio, and working at his studies. Similarly, he embroiled himself in football training and was picked by the college team coach, Lou Little, to play wingback.

Disaster struck with his second game for Columbia when he injured his leg in a match against St. Benedict's Preparatory School. Though forced to limp off the pitch, his trainer diagnosed his injury as no more than a sprain and, in increasing discomfort, Kerouac continued with training for a week or so. What galled him more than the injury itself was being accused by Little of faking it, especially after an X-ray revealed he had a hairline fracture. Kerouac's leg had to be put in plaster for the rest of the season, and his football ambitions were over.

Absence from the football field gave Kerouac more time to investigate the joys of New York City, however: from art museums and movie theaters to the jazz clubs of 52nd Street and Harlem—especially Harlem. Less than a mile from the august halls of learning at Columbia, it was there he also acquired a taste for the black prostitutes who hung out in those very same clubs. At that time he had a predilection for sex with hookers, an enthusiasm in which he would also indulge accompanied by his cronies from Lowell when they visited on weekends.

Summer 1941 saw him back in Lowell for the vacation, dating Mary Carney again, and occasionally hitchhiking to Boston with Sebastian Sampas, who in term time was now studying at the city's Emerson College. Although it was only a 25-mile journey, hitching to the Massachusetts capital conjured up images in Jack's mind of crossing the US coast-to-coast in the same fashion. It was a vision inspired in part by one of his favorite writers—Jack London—who, at the end of the 19th century, explored America's vast frontier by hopping on and off freight trains, his adventures feeding the short stories and novels for which he was to become famous.

In September 1941 Kerouac returned to Columbia, but his stay was to be short-lived. Confident of being selected for the varsity football team, when he wasn't chosen by Little, a stand-up row ensued and a disgusted Kerouac stormed out. He packed a suitcase and was soon on a Greyhound bus heading south for Washington DC, having dropped out of college. This was a break that had more to do with his wish to strike out on his own as a writer than a mere fit of pique over football.

"That was the most important decision of my life," he would later write. His feelings at the time were more accurately summed up in a letter he wrote to Sebastian from the cheap hotel he'd booked into in Washington, in which he admitted he was too afraid to face his parents and too proud to go back to the team. But go home he did, or at least to West Haven, Connecticut, where his parents had recently moved. Once there, he explained to them his reasons for leaving. His father, in particular, was furious and at the end of September he escaped the bad-tempered atmosphere by going to stay with a friend in Hartford, Connecticut, where he managed to find a job in a gas station that gave him a chance to read and work on some short stories.

At the end of November his parents moved back to Lowell, where their prodigal son joined them, the tension between father and son having eased somewhat. He found himself a job as sports reporter on the *Lowell Sun* but then—following the Japanese bombing of Pearl Harbor on December 7, 1941—war was declared. To everyone's surprise, Jack decided to enlist in the Navy and while awaiting his papers, he once again traveled to Washington DC, where he visited an old Lowell buddy, G.J. Apostolos. G.J. was working on a huge construction site in Arlington, Virginia, which was to become the Pentagon military command complex, and Jack also worked there for a few weeks before being fired for continuous absence. It seems he preferred to spend his time contemplating the surrounding countryside. Before moving on further south, he briefly worked as a short-order cook in a diner, but eventually decided to return to Lowell.

There, he wrote an apologetic letter to Lou Little, asking if he could return to Columbia. But failure in his first-year chemistry course meant his scholarship was withdrawn, and he certainly couldn't afford the $400 to pay his fees until it was reinstated. A chance meeting one night in a bar suggested a solution to his financial difficulties: a merchant seaman with whom he fell into conversation told him shipping companies were paying as much as $2,000 to seamen prepared to make the five-month round trip to Russia.

So, Jack made for Boston, where he applied for a passport and membership of the National Maritime Union. He then joined the daily line at the Union Hall, waiting to be allocated a ship. In early July, 1942, his chance came when he was hired as kitchen scullion on the *SS Dorchester*, setting sail for Greenland. The trip was nothing if not eventful—twice the ship was attacked by German U-Boats, and it was also the scene of what was probably Kerouac's first homosexual experience when, as he put it years later, he was "buggered . . . by a lecherous fatso cook."

When the *Dorchester* arrived back in New York harbor in late October 1942, Sebastian Sampas was there to meet him. The two had a wild couple of days around the bars and clubs of Manhattan before returning to Lowell, where a telegram from Lou Little offering Jack his place back in the Columbia football squad greeted him, and so he went back, but not for long. Despite promising him a place on the team, Little passed on him when picking his squad for a big game against the Army. Once again Jack decided to quit college, this time saying he felt there were more important things for him to do for the war effort, specifically in the Merchant Marine.

> "Henri Cru and I were rather involved and he wanted to make an impression on me, and said he had a very wonderful genius friend and he would like me to meet him, so he arranged for us to have a luncheon. We went to the New York Delicatessen and Jack joined us, and I immediately ate six sauerkraut hot dogs, and from that time on Jack said he was madly in love with me."

Edith (Edie) Parker, 1988

Before he left Columbia once again, he was reunited with Henri Cru, his old Horace Mann friend, and it was through him that he became acquainted with a vivacious young student (and heiress) by the name of Edith "Edie" Parker. Like Jack, Cru had just ended a spell of duty at sea and was casually dating the sexually liberated Edie, who had arrived in New York in late 1941. When Cru was recalled for his next trip, in January 1943, he suggested Jack should "look after" his girlfriend while he was away. But Jack was smitten, and embarked on an affair with Edie as soon as his friend set sail.

But it seemed war would wait for no man and in March, 1943, Jack received his summons to boot camp training with the US Navy in Newport, Rhode Island. Inevitably, perhaps, the discipline there proved too much for the rebellious Kerouac, who on more than one occasion downed his rifle while on parade to head for the camp library. He was eventually discharged for running naked through an inspection line-up. On his way back to New York, he resumed his relationship with Edie, who confessed to having had an abortion in his absence, though she was not clear as to whether she was pregnant by him or Cru. However, he still had the sea in mind—he'd even begun a novel based on his time in the Merchant Marine titled *The Sea Is My Brother*—and in September 1943 he joined the crew of the *SS George Weems*. The trip would take him to England, visiting Liverpool and London.

Before he left on his Atlantic crossing, Edie Parker, who since starting college had lodged with her grandparents on West 116th Street, had moved. She was sharing an apartment with her friend Joan Vollmer Adams at 421 West 118th Street, just a block away from Columbia. Returning in October 1943, Jack headed straight for there, and so began a far more serious stage in their relationship. Over the next year and a half, the sixth-floor apartment would be the scene of the birth of the Beat Generation.

**Above:** Harlem's 125th Street in the early 40s, home of venues such as the Apollo (in the background), which Kerouac first visited as a student.

**Right:** Photo-booth portrait of Allen Ginsberg during his time at Paterson East Side High.

**Below:** The Ginsberg family c. 1936 in Woodstock, NY. Left to right: family friend Mendel Levy, Allen's brother Eugene, Allen, his mother Naomi, and father Louis.

**Opposite left:** A portrait of the innovative (though initially misunderstood) American poet Walt Whitman (1819–92) taken during the last years of his life.

**Opposite right:** *The Shadow,* whose adventures on radio and in print captivated the young Ginsberg.

## Allen Ginsberg: the early years

Unlike Kerouac and Burroughs, who both grew up in conventional, conservative households (the former basically working class, while the latter was solidly bourgeois), Allen Ginsberg was born and raised in a politically radical and artistic Jewish environment, which would define more directly the course his life would take.

Married in 1919, Louis, a Democratic Socialist, and Naomi Ginsberg, a card-carrying Communist Party member, were very much of the Left. Naomi worked as a schoolteacher, teaching disadvantaged children, while Louis was a modestly successful published poet. Though they lived in Newark, New Jersey, the couple was well known on the bohemian poetry scene based around Greenwich Village.

Even before her marriage, Naomi was showing early signs of the schizophrenia that would blight her later life, though these subsided for a time after the birth of her two sons. Eugene, named for the famous labor organizer, Eugene V. Debs, was born in 1921, and Irwin Allen five years later, on June 3, 1926. From early on, Allen and his elder brother were conscious of the ideological and aesthetic values of their parents. At times Naomi would burst into song, praising the revolutionary spirit of the working classes, or read bedtime stories where, as Allen later recalled, "the good king rode forth from his castle, saw the suffering workers, and healed them." Louis would routinely recite Shelley, Keats, Dickens, Poe, and Milton to his boys and the house (in a run-down Jewish neighborhood in Paterson, New Jersey, where they'd moved when Allen was a newborn) was alive to the sound of Beethoven, Leadbelly, and Bessie Smith. Their parents' socialism meant Allen and his brother were brought up with no religion: Allen wasn't given a Bar Mitzvah or taught Hebrew, and English was the only language spoken at home.

When Allen was just three, his mother suffered a severe bout of schizophrenia, as a result of which she signed herself into a sanatorium, leaving the boys in their father's care. From then on, Naomi would be in and out of psychiatric institutions for much of her life, suffering relapses characterized by a paranoid fantasy that Louis—after a time in league with Hitler, Mussolini, and President Franklin D. Roosevelt—was trying to control her mind. Outbursts at home were accompanied by increasingly strident declarations of her Communist beliefs and an insistence she put a long-held sympathy for naturism into practice. She frequently wandered around the house naked, to the particular discomfort of young Allen, who was often kept off school to look after her on bad days. Indeed, witnessing the various manifestations of his mother's mental illness throughout early childhood was to have a profound effect on his developing sensibilities.

At the same time, of course, he had the normal experiences of any child. He found math difficult, but could memorize by heart long passages of poetry. A bit of a loner, nevertheless he had friends, with whom he would, on occasion, get into trouble, and he was an avid follower of radio adventure series such as *Flash Gordon* and *The Shadow*. Despite their difference in age he was close to Eugene, though like all brothers the two argued endlessly. They shared a bed and while Allen wanted to cuddle up, the adolescent Gene would push him away, embarrassed. Later he would recall being conscious, even when he was as young as seven, of what he called "baser emotions." When he was eight he had a crush on a kid called Earl, leader of a neighborhood gang. "Prince of Peterson," he was to call him, in a poem written in 1963, in which he recalled how, while fantasizing about the youth, he pulled down his pants and exposed himself to passing motorists from the porch of the family home.

" . . . and still remember her black-dressed bulk seated squat behind an English class desk, her embroidered collar, her voice powerful and high, lilting Whitman's very words and shafts of sunlight through school windows that looked down on green grass."

Allen Ginsberg recalling his teacher Frances Durbin (1978)

In 1935 Louis was forced to commit his wife to Greystone State Mental Hospital in New Jersey, where she remained for a year. Returning, her paranoia continued, and she was convinced her doctors had inserted wires into her head and sticks in her back. Allen and Eugene, meanwhile, led a disrupted home life with their mother's periodic absences and returns, though when Naomi was away, Louis tried to retain some semblance of normality by making sure his sons attended family get-togethers. Sadly, just three weeks after Allen's eleventh birthday, on June 24, 1937, Naomi locked herself in the bathroom of their home and tried to commit suicide by slashing her wrists. She was interrupted when Louis broke down the door, but this latest breakdown led to a two-year commitment to Greystone.

By this time Allen had started to keep a private journal. In the written word he found a way to express his inner feelings, and to record some of the urges and anxieties of his earlier childhood years. He recalled incidents such as the time when he was five, when he was sent to a local store to buy a stamp for a letter. Not having been told otherwise, he stuck the stamp at the bottom rather than the top of the envelope, to the obvious amusement of others in the store; the humiliation he felt at that moment was to haunt him for the next few years.

In the leather-covered diary, which could be locked with a key, he set down his ideas and dreams, and his developing political views. Not unexpectedly, he was virulently anti-Nazi, but there were also colorful accounts of movies he'd seen, and of conversations and arguments he had had with his father and brother. In addition, he recounted in laborious detail, but undoubtedly a labor of love, a continuing narrative of his mother's mental deterioration, and its effect on his own development.

Allen graduated from junior high school in June 1939, moving to Paterson Central High, where he became much more involved in school activities, academic and extra-curricular, than ever before. He joined numerous school clubs, including the debating society, and in May 1940, at the end of his first year,

he took part in the school's annual stage show—including an appearance as a comic ballerina, complete with tutu. In early 1941 his first work appeared in print when two pieces were published in the school magazine, the *Spectator*.

Meanwhile, in fall 1939, a relatively stable Naomi returned home. While she vigorously continued to preach the virtues of the Communist way, an increasingly politicized Allen had his mind set on a more immediate issue: the war in Europe. He was appalled his country remained isolationist while the forces of Fascism were on the march, and with his brother Eugene he actively campaigned for the US to declare war on Hitler, Mussolini, and Franco.

In September 1941, the Ginsbergs were informed that a bureaucratic mistake had placed Allen in Paterson Central High when he should have been in Paterson East Side High. After moving, and as at his previous school, he soon found his niche, quickly becoming a leading light in the debating and drama societies (he was elected president of both); he also excelled in his English classes, where he was inspired by his teacher Frances Durbin, who introduced him to the work of Walt Whitman.

Back home, Naomi's return to normalcy proved to be short-lived. One of the most traumatic incidents, in the winter of 1941, involved 15-year-old Allen accompanying his mother on a nightmarish bus journey after she insisted he take her to a rest home in Lakewood, New Jersey; the episode resulted in Naomi being committed to Greystone for a further two years. Allen described the event in his epic autobiographical poem "Kaddish," which he dedicated to his mother and completed in 1961.

During his last year at East Side High School he developed a crush on a fellow student, Paul Roth, though nothing was spelt out verbally, let alone reciprocated. When Roth won a scholarship to Columbia University, over the Hudson in New York City, Ginsberg was determined to follow him. He applied successfully and enrolled in a pre-law course, planning to become a labor lawyer, in September 1943.

**Opposite:** Flash Gordon was another childhood hero of Ginsberg, on radio, in comic strips, and (as advertised here) in movie serials.

**Above:** The view down Market Street in Paterson, New Jersey, in 1937. Haunts such as the Manhattan Hotel and the Garden Theater would have been familiar to Ginsberg during his childhood years.

In December 1941, after the Japanese attack on Pearl Harbor, the US entered World War II and, like most institutions, Columbia University was obliged to adapt itself and its very fabric to the war effort. As far as Allen Ginsberg's arrival in September 1943 was concerned, it meant being lodged off campus, as the main halls of residence had been given over to V-12 naval cadets on a 90-day course prior to becoming officers.

Initially Ginsberg was billeted with two others in a large apartment on Morningside Drive, a block east of the main campus, before being moved, in December 1943, to the Union Theological Seminary on 122nd Street and Broadway, by which time he was otherwise settling into student life. Supported by a CIO (Congress of Industrial Organizations) scholarship and $100 grant from the University, the somewhat diffident 17-year-old freshman was acutely aware of the self-confidence exuded by most of his (generally older) fellow undergraduates. Anxious to fit in, he soon found his métier in the English department.

Under the tutelage of Raymond Weaver, Lionel Trilling, and Pulitzer-prize-winning poet Mark Van Doren, he threw himself into a daunting preparatory reading syllabus ranging from Aristotle to Zola, Sophocles to Shakespeare. Ensconced for hours in the University's Butler Library, he read copiously. At the same time his writing was published in the Columbia *Jester* humor magazine, and he became an active member of the Philolexian debating club. Previous plans to study labor law were soon put on the back burner, and subsequently forgotten altogether.

A few days before Christmas 1943, with most of the students away on vacation, the seminary was all but empty. Allen was still there, however, and as he wandered down the corridor of the seventh floor toward his room he realized he was not alone. From behind a door at the end he could hear the sound of music. Intrigued, he knocked, ostensibly to find out the composer's name. Lucien Carr, a student he recognized from Lionel Trilling's class, opened the door. The two had never spoken before. Allen was immediately struck by Carr's good looks—"the most angelic-looking kid I ever saw"—and, on being invited in, he was also charmed by the cultivated atmosphere of the room with its posters of Impressionist paintings and scholarly books on the shelves.

Over a bottle of burgundy the two young men fell into intense conversation, realizing at once they had much to talk about, and over the next few days and weeks a firm relationship was cemented. They discussed art, politics, life—all the typically serious undergraduate topics. It was a platonic friendship, but for Ginsberg it soon developed into an infatuation.

A year and three months older than Allen, Lucien Carr had been born on March 1, 1925. He was from a broken home—his parents had separated when he was five—but he had enjoyed most of the advantages of a wealthy family upbringing. He had attended the John Burroughs School, the best private school in St. Louis (William Burroughs had attended the same school a decade and a half earlier), and had been brought up by his mother. While in his early teens, Carr had begun to show signs of being the archetypal "difficult" adolescent, dropping out of school and so on. Much of his miscreant behavior seemed to have been caused by the attention paid him by one David Kammerer.

Sixteen years older than Carr, who was just 10 at the time, Kammerer was the latter's scoutmaster at a St. Louis Boy Scout group. A homosexual, he had developed an obsession for the boy, befriending him, and then following him through his teenage years as he moved from school to school, and then college, via Massachusetts and Brunswick, Maine, to the University of Chicago. Kammerer would take any menial job to "pay his way" on his odyssey but although he made sexual advances to Carr, they were never returned. Instead, Lucien quickly learned how to manipulate his always-compliant admirer who, while not necessarily his favorite person, was certainly a most constant friend. So, after he moved to Columbia in fall 1943, having dropped out of Chicago earlier in the year, David Kammerer was in tow as usual, with a job washing dishes in Greenwich Village, where he also rented an apartment on Morton Street.

It was at this ground-floor apartment that Allen Ginsberg first encountered the tall, red-bearded Kammerer, when Lucien Carr invited him to come down to the Village to meet some of his friends. For the far-from-worldly Allen this promised to be a journey into the exotic unknown, though his parents had treaded the very same bohemian streets many years before. It was also at this same apartment, a day or so later, that he was to come face to face with William Burroughs for the first time.

Burroughs had known Kammerer since his days in St. Louis, and he had witnessed first-hand his constant but unrequited pursuit of the much younger Lucien Carr. In 1942 he had come across the pair again in Chicago; he was leading a fairly rootless existence at the time, and when they made their separate ways to New York, it wasn't long before he followed suit. Seventeen-year-old Allen's first impression of Burroughs—29 at the time—was that he was old, very old. But with age came wisdom, and this was confirmed in their first, brief conversation when the strange-looking guy with sallow skin and a spindly frame casually quoted Shakespeare as if it were everyday speech.

**Previous pages:** Students gathered in front of Low Library, Columbia University.

**Right:** An edition of the Columbia *Jester* magazine during 1944—the year Ginsberg contributed to its pages—taking a typically satirical view of the students having to make way for the influx of wartime naval personnel.

**Far right:** Lionel Trilling, the eminent author, essayist, and literary critic, who taught in the English department at Columbia from 1931 up to his death in 1975 at the age of 70.

**Below:** The Japanese attack on Pearl Harbor proved to be a turning point in the lives of all Americans, including the nascent Beat Generation.

In the weeks following Christmas, 1943, Allen and Lucien saw more of each other. As well as his good looks, Lucien had another quality that attracted Allen equally strongly: the kind of "intellectual" attitude (as he put it in a letter to his brother Eugene) that he aspired to himself. The two debated endlessly, mutually confirming the need for a fresh approach to modern thinking, laying the basis for what they would come to call a "New Vision."

As well as the bars and other literary hangouts in Greenwich Village to which he introduced Allen, Lucien Carr also spent time in a Columbia University "local," the West End, a bar located on Broadway and West 113th Street. In this smoky watering hole he had got to know the strikingly attractive heiress Edie Parker, who attended the same drawing classes, and her friend, Joan Vollmer Adams, with whom she shared an apartment on West 118th Street on the other side of campus. Parker, along with many other women, was fascinated by Carr's flamboyant confidence and cultivated bonhomie. He was, in short, a charmer.

When Edie's boyfriend, Jack Kerouac, returned from serving at sea with the Merchant Marine in October 1943, there was initially a frisson of jealousy on the part of the comparatively unsophisticated seaman. But he soon fell for Carr's irresistible *joie de vivre*, and his enthusiastic knowledge of writers like Flaubert and Rimbaud. Before long, Jack was one of his growing circle of lively minds. For Carr, Jack represented the "real thing." Unlike himself, Kerouac was an actual writer, with working-class

credentials and a genuinely unaffected manner. And for Jack, Lucien's extolling of the virtues of the writer as visionary served to inspire his own literary ambitions.

Jack had moved in with Edie at 118th Street (in fact, he acted as co-signatory with Joan and Edie on the apartment's lease in August 1943). Before long, Lucien and his new girlfriend, Céline Young, would frequently be sleeping on the living-room couch, 118th Street providing a welcome bolt-hole from the seemingly incessant presence of David Kammerer. Jack and Lucien became firm friends, the fact that they were also drinking buddies helping to dissolve any differences of class or social demeanor. Often they would end up staggering home together from the West End, hardly able to stand, and singing bawdy songs. On one much-quoted occasion, Lucien rolled Jack down the street in a barrel! It would only be a matter of time before he introduced this "romantic seaman who writes poem books" to his other newfound friend, Allen Ginsberg.

The first actual meeting of Allen and Jack was hardly a momentous occasion, though. It was early 1944, and Lucien had given Allen the address of the 118th Street apartment, where he was greeted by a gruff-sounding Jack, dressed in a white T-shirt and chino pants, and eating a brunch of bacon and eggs. Offering his guest a beer, he grunted disinterestedly when the latter declined his hospitality; to an outside observer, the scene would have summed up the total opposites of the two characters:

"We were like ambassadors to the Chinese Emperor, making a delegation of ourselves to inquire into the nature of his soul. Quite literally and directly. Who is Burroughs? Why is he so intelligent? Will he be friendly or unfriendly?"

Allen Ginsberg, quoted in 1988

the no-nonsense man-of-the-world and nerdy neophyte. Jack recalled his first impression of the visitor as "this spindly Jewish kid with horn-rimmed glasses and tremendous ears sticking out, seventeen years old, burning black eyes, a strangely deep voice."

But a subsequent encounter in the grounds of Columbia campus proved to be far more revelatory for both young men, as they discussed a childhood fear of ghosts, and how they still wondered at the scale and infinity of the universe. For Allen this was a far more personal, spiritual discourse than the quasi-intellectual badinage with Lucien Carr, while Jack would declare, "Gee, I have thoughts like that all the time!"

West 118th was also the venue where Jack was to meet William Burroughs for the first time, when Burroughs was brought to the house by David Kammerer (who Jack had already met through Lucien). Carr had obviously enthused to William about Jack, much as he had to Allen. Equally, Jack was intrigued by the individual from St. Louis held in such thrall. Burroughs' excuse for the visit was to ask some questions about the Merchant Marine and Jack, wearing only a pair of chinos as he'd just showered, didn't quite know what to make of the quizzing he received.

It was apparent Burroughs was deeply intellectual and probably very well read, but Jack's first impression was that his visitor was "like a shy bank clerk with a patrician, thin-lipped, cold blue-lipped face." He concluded that both William Burroughs and David Kammerer were totally amoral, "the most evil and intelligent buncha bastards and shits in America," whom he nevertheless "had to admire in my admiring youth."

Any reservations Jack may have had about the moral integrity of Burroughs were forgotten after he and Allen visited the dour St. Louisian in his apartment at 69 Bedford Street in Greenwich Village, just round the corner from David Kammerer. The two younger men were fascinated by Burroughs' first-hand knowledge of pre-war Hungary, Yugoslavia, and Austria, his aristocratic bearing, and hugely catholic taste in reading matter. Generally skeptical of the older generation, from the start they viewed Burroughs with a certain amount of awe.

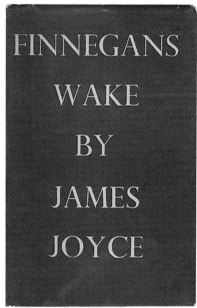

> "The new vision assumed the death of square morality and replaced that meaning with belief in creativity. I think we were quite moralistic in a way."

Allen Ginsberg

Both found themselves in immediate sympathy with the older man's conviction that only through experience of life's lowest depths could one feel totally fulfilled and qualified to express an opinion on such areas of existence. "Purity" of lifestyle, he argued, could only be attained by living outside the strictures and moral confines of conventional and essentially corrupt society. These attitudes were to become the cornerstone of Beat philosophy—ideas Ginsberg, Carr, Kerouac, and Burroughs would develop over the next few months as part of a "New Vision."

The concept of a "New Vision" grew out of innumerable and inevitably inconclusive conversations in the West End bar and the embryo Beats' various apartments. In early 1944 Allen moved out of the Theological Seminary and into a small 115th Street hotel, where Lucien now lived: the Warren Hall Residence Club. There, he and Lucien argued into the night about the meaning of "Art." A progressive at heart, Allen felt that art should ideally be in the service of mankind and that was its highest purpose. Lucien, on the other hand, held the view that art for its own sake was its ultimate justification. The debate rolled on, often lubricated by alcohol in the West End, where Jack put in his five cents-worth (that he didn't have a strong opinion either way) and Bill Burroughs (not for the first time) unhelpfully postulated, "art is a three-letter word."

Gradually the "vision" emerged from such abstract discourse, driven by a copious diet of books, most of which had never appeared on any reading list in the English department at Columbia. Crucial texts included such left-of-field works as W.H. Auden's *Age of Anxiety*, Franz Kafka's *The Trial*, and James Joyce's *Finnegans Wake*. French existentialists Albert Camus and Jean-Paul Sartre also figured, as did Jean Cocteau. When newly acquainted, William Burroughs had presented Allen with a copy of W.B. Yeats' *A Vision*, while Jack received a copy of Oswald Spengler's *Decline of the West*—the latter was to become a pivotal treatise in the birth of the New Vision. As spring turned to summer through the middle months of 1944, the New Vision gestated from a loose gene-pool of ideas and influences to nothing less than an unwritten manifesto of principles, which would ultimately represent the philosophical driving force of the Beat Generation.

Against the background of a world they felt was doomed to self-inflicted oblivion, the New Vision saw art as the highest state of man. Despite Allen Ginsberg's continuing conviction that it had a "political" role to play, "political in the highest sense—humanitarian," art was considered "above" conventional morality and therefore should be allowed to flourish unhindered by censorship or moral constraint. As a means to this end, the expansion of the creative mind via dreams, visions, or the use of hallucinogenic drugs was encouraged.

But then, amid all the high-flown rhetoric about art and morality, life, and death, something occurred which would bring the whole circle of young visionaries down to earth in a way they could never have imagined.

# on the streets of New York

For out-of-town, fledgling Beats (albeit in Allen Ginsberg's case, just across the Hudson in New Jersey), New York City was an exciting place to be. Visually, culturally, and socially it was arguably the most inspiring urban center ever. Certainly there's a case to be made that if they'd met anywhere else, the Beat Generation just wouldn't have evolved.

Even the architecture exuded modernity and progress. The oldest of the city's trademark skyscrapers had been standing for less than a half century; its most iconic buildings, the Chrysler and the Empire State (1929 and 1931 respectively) still seemed brand new. The economic power represented by these "cathedrals to capitalism" in the post-war boom was matched by a new confidence in the arts and popular culture.

The 40s saw the New York School of Abstract Expressionist painters like Jackson Pollock and Mark Rothko patronized by wealthy benefactors, galleries, and art establishment institutions. New York theater was at its most ground-breaking with writers, including Arthur Miller and Tennessee Williams, pioneering a new stage realism in hit productions on Broadway. Williams' *A Streetcar Named Desire* (1947) introduced the New York-based Method school of acting via the charismatic Marlon Brando. American popular music, too, long centered on "Tin Pan Alley," which comprised hundreds of song publishers between 50th and 52nd streets off Broadway, reached a turning point in 1944, with *Oklahoma!* heralding a golden age in the classic musical.

But it was in the bohemian enclaves of Greenwich Village, the smoky jazz clubs of Harlem and 52nd Street, and the seedier side of life around Times Square and on the Lower East Side, where the Beats would find particular inspiration. With its bookstores, small galleries, and numerous drinking places, since the turn of the century the Village had been something of an "artists' colony" in mid-Manhattan. It was hardly surprising that its bars, coffeehouses, and jazz clubs became a natural hangout for the young Ginsberg, Jack Kerouac, Bill Burroughs, and co. Similarly, Minton's, the Savoy Ballroom, and other Harlem jazz spots (a few blocks east of Columbia's hallowed precincts) were a magnet for the self-confessed thrill-seekers, as was "Swing Street," the midtown mecca of jazz in the 52nd Street stretch between Fifth and Sixth Avenues, with scores of venues featuring top names every night of the week.

Of course the Beats-to-be were drawn primarily by their passion for the music, but also the perceived "glamor," including drug pushers, pimps, and prostitutes. Following their newly honed credo that to have a real appreciation of life one had to experience its lowest depths, they sought out "real life" at street level, far removed from what they saw as the stuffiness of bourgeois academia and the frivolity of mainstream popular culture. It was this fascination with New York's underbelly that saw the unlikely crowd of students orienting toward the twilight world of gamblers, con men, and petty criminals wheeling and dealing in the shadows of the neon-lit gaudiness of 42nd Street adjacent to Times Square. The area had long been home to strip clubs, dive bars, "adult" bookstores, and sex cinemas—and it attracted a floating population of "unsavory" characters to match.

Places like the squalid Angle Bar (a.k.a the Angler bar) on the corner of 43rd and Eighth, a favorite of Manhattan low-lifes, were soon on the Beats' itinerary, with Columbia's West End bar and, a little later, the Village's San Remo. Burroughs instigated their forays into the "underworld," describing the Angler in his first novel, *Junkie*, as "a meeting place for 42nd Street hustlers, a peculiar breed of four-flushing, would-be criminals."

"They call it 42nd Street because you're not safe if you spend more than forty seconds on it."

Anon

The Lower East Side, including Little Italy and Chinatown, was considered even more disreputable. Once host to generations of immigrants, it was now one of the most cosmopolitan—and poorest—areas of Manhattan, notorious for street crime and gang warfare. West of the area, the Bowery was famous for the bums and down-and-outs who called it home. It was on the Lower East Side that Burroughs, ever slumming it, first came into the orbit of Herbert Huncke and his fellow junkies, whose exploits on New York City's mean streets (and Huncke's resulting accounts), would have a profound effect on the early Beats.

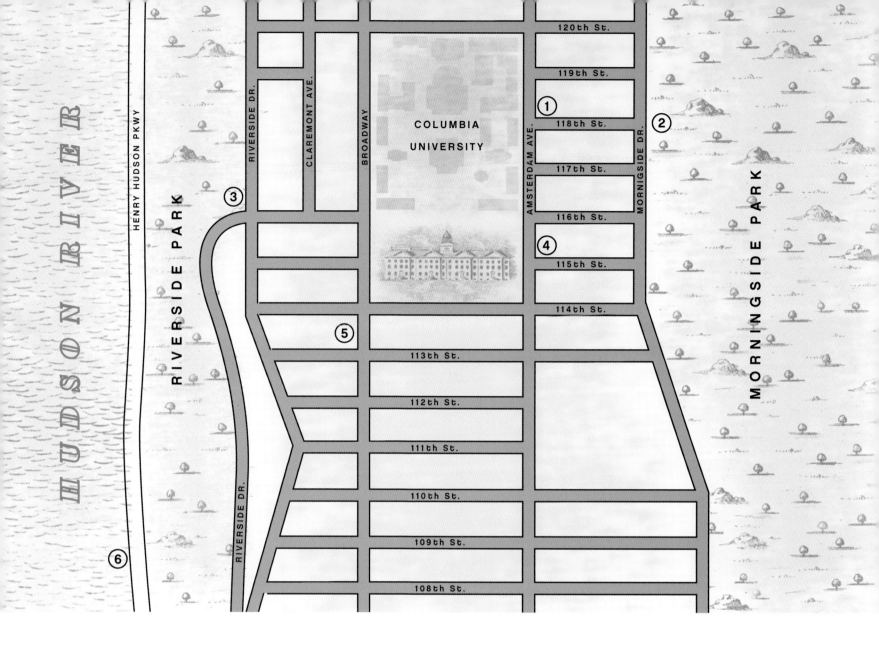

Although they were already living together, Jack's relationship with Edie Parker took an even more serious turn when they started to talk about marriage. Edie had already visited his parents, who were now living in Ozone Park in the New York borough of Queens, but despite her obvious "good breeding," they were not particularly impressed with her as a potential daughter-in-law. Certainly, had they known the details, they would not have approved of the couple's domestic arrangements, but to even contemplate marriage, Jack needed to earn some serious, and regular, cash.

With that in mind, in May 1944 he traveled down to New Orleans to find a ship for South America, but to no avail. The following month, things looked brighter when, in response to a synopsis he'd sent them, Columbia Pictures gave him a job as scriptwriter (with his own office and secretary) in their plush quarters in the Rockefeller Center. But the film-writing job only lasted a few weeks, and by early August he was once more contemplating the Merchant Marine as the only way of earning enough to marry Edie. It wasn't clear whether pressure from his

girlfriend may have contributed to his desire to set sail once again but when Lucien Carr also voiced a need to "get away" he was delighted.

Carr's incentive—to escape Kammerer's increasingly intolerable stalking—was much more straightforward. For years he had put up with the older man's attentions, indeed encouraged them to a degree, though not in a sexually explicit manner. But now, in New York, Kammerer was becoming more and more of a nuisance. At one point he had climbed the wall of Warren Hall to spy on Lucien while he was asleep, and had become aggressively resentful of his girlfriend, Céline. William Burroughs had warned Kammerer that his obsession was becoming dangerous, suggesting his friend take a trip abroad, but instead it was Lucien who decided that the only answer was to leave New York, for a while at least.

Jack and Lucien came up with an audacious plan to get jobs on a ship to France under assumed names so there was no way Kammerer would be able to follow them. The two aimed to jump ship when they docked at Le Havre and to make their way

# STUDENT IS SILENT ON SLAYING FRIEND

## Held Without Bail After He Listens Lackadaisically to Charge in Stabbing Case

Clasping a copy of "A Vision," a philosophic work by W. B. Yeats, under one arm, Lucien Carr, 19-year-old Columbia sophomore, listened lackadaisically to the proceeding as he was arraigned yesterday morning before Magistrate Anna M. Kross in Homicide Court. He was held without bail for a hearing on Aug. 29.

The pale, slender youth showed little interest as Detective James O'Brien presented a short affidavit charging him with homicide for having fatally stabbed on Monday David Kammerer, 33-year-old former instructor at Washington University, St. Louis, with whom he had been friendly. His attorney, Vincent J. Malone, told the court that the defendant had nothing to say.

### Court Asks Psychiatric Test

Magistrate Kross asked Mr. Malone whether he had any objection to having Carr sent to Bellevue Hospital for psychiatric observation at this time. Mr. Malone replied that he did object and would prefer to have the case follow the usual channels. Jacob Grumet, assistant district attorney in charge of the Homicide Bureau, also objected to the proposal, saying that that should be done in the Court of General Sessions.

Exclaiming that "we in the great State of New York still proceed under the early theory of eighteenth century justice," Magistrate Kross declared that this procedure would result in "a great loss of time." She said that the procedure she had suggested would be valuable in bringing out "the social background" of the defendant.

After ordering Carr held without bail, Magistrate Kross started for her chambers and motioned to Mr. Malone to accompany her. Mr. Grumet also started in but the magistrate informed him that he had not been asked. Mr. Grumet remained without but announced that he wanted it noted in the record that he objected to the court's conferring with defense counsel without the presence of a representative of the district attorney.

### Witness Held in $5,000 Bail

Later in the day John Kerouac, a 23-year-old merchant seaman and former Columbia student, who had been arrested Wednesday night as a material witness in the case, was held in $5,000 bail at a proceeding in the chambers of Judge John J. Sullivan of General Sessions.

Mr. Grumet told Judge Sullivan that after the slaying Carr went to Kerouac's room at 421 West 118th Street and told him what had happened. He said that Kerouac then went to Morningside Park with Carr and helped him bury Kammerer's eyeglasses.

"I only watched him bury the glasses," Kerouac interjected.

"You came very near becoming an accessory after the fact," the prosecutor replied.

Kerouac said that he and his fiancée had had blood tests taken and had planned to be married to-

HELD FOR HOMICIDE

*Lucien Carr as he was arraigned yesterday.* The New York Times

day. Appearing greatly concerned at the high bail set, he pleaded with Judge Sullivan to reduce it to a point that his parents, who live in Ozone Park, Queens, might be able to meet.

"They'll take very good care of you in the new city prison," Judge Sullivan assured him as he was led away.

---

to Paris in time for the Liberation. They found a ship, the *Robert Hayes*, but the scheme was stymied when a particularly unsympathetic chief mate threw them off the boat almost as soon as they boarded. Jack viewed the whole fiasco fairly dispassionately, but for Carr it was a bitter disappointment. David Kammerer, meanwhile, had got wind of his intention to set sail and vowed to follow him wherever he might go.

The following evening, August 13, Jack went to the West End to drown his sorrows with Allen, while Lucien had dinner with his mother, who now lived in Manhattan. Later that same night, Carr appeared in the West End, very much the worse for wear, and demanding whiskey. Jack was the first to leave, around midnight. On the way home, he bumped into David Kammerer and he told him that he would find Lucien with Allen at their usual haunt.

Leaving the bar soon after, Allen left Lucien and David locked in drunken conversation. Johnny, the barman, finally closed at 3 am and watched the pair lurch into the night, taking a bottle with them, in the direction of Riverside Park. There, on a grassy knoll overlooking the Hudson River, Kammerer made his familiar

demands and Lucien was too drunk simply to push him away. As the bigger man tried to overpower him, making sexual advances while threatening to hurt his girlfriend if he didn't comply, Lucien panicked and pulled out a small pocketknife. He stabbed Kammerer twice in the chest, fatally.

Terror stricken, and fearful someone would chance on the body, he used Kammerer's shoelaces and belt to truss up the corpse, before weighting it with rocks and rolling it down the bank into the river. When he could see the body was not going to sink, he stripped off and waded into the water, pushing it away from the riverbank until it began to float downstream.

His first instinct was to flee the scene, flee New York, even flee America. Then, when he thought it through a little more, he decided to seek the advice of the undisputed wise man of his social circle: Bill Burroughs. He caught a cab downtown, telling Burroughs bluntly, "I just killed the old man," adding he was sure he'd get "the hot seat" of the electric chair. Burroughs calmed him down, urging him to get a good lawyer, preferably the family lawyer, and then to do everything the attorney said.

"Clasping a copy of *A Vision*, a philosophical work by W.B. Yeats, under one arm, Lucien Carr, 19-year-old Columbia sophomore, listened lackadaisically to the proceeding as he was arraigned yesterday morning before Magistrate Anna M. Kross in Homicide Court. He was held without bail for a hearing on August 29th."

The *New York Times*, August 18, 1944

At dawn Lucien went up to 118th Street and told Jack what had happened. Kerouac managed to get Edie out of the room, suggesting she cook them some breakfast, then he and Lucien took a walk. While Lucien dropped the murder weapon down a subway grating, Jack acted as lookout, and then covered for him as he buried Kammerer's glasses in Morningside Park. A day or so later, accompanied by a lawyer, Lucien turned himself in at the office of the District Attorney, Frank S. Horan, telling his story to the Assistant DA in charge of the Homicide Bureau.

Initially, with no body discovered or missing person reported, the police thought he was crazy. Then, when Lucien offered to take them to the spot where he and Jack had buried the glasses *and* Kammerer's body turned up off 108th Street, they realized this was no crank they had on their hands. Lucien Carr was charged with homicide, with Jack Kerouac and William Burroughs booked as material witnesses because they had both known about the crime but failed to report it.

Burroughs' parents immediately put up the $2,500 bail required for their son's release, after which Bill traveled back to St. Louis with his father. But for Leo Kerouac the fact that Jack languished in the Bronx City jail simply confirmed previous misgivings about his son's lifestyle and the company he was keeping. As he saw it, being involved in something like a murder case brought disgrace on the whole family, and he refused to help with the bail money.

As part of a plea for leniency, Jack told the court he was due to be married on August 22 of that year. Whether this date had indeed been fixed isn't clear, but he and Edie had certainly been discussing marriage for some time. The prison situation now made it a *fait accompli*, as Edie's mother refused to loan them the bail money unless they were married. So, on the

22nd Jack was released from jail for one hour to marry Edie Parker in a brief ceremony in the Municipal Building, with two accompanying detectives acting as witnesses and Céline Young in attendance as the maid of honor.

Following his release a few days later, Jack and Edie traveled to Grosse Pointe, Michigan, to move in with Edie's divorced mother, Charlotte. They were met at the railroad station by a chauffeured limousine and driven to the grand Parker family home, where Jack immediately felt like a fish out of water. Almost as a defense mechanism he played up to Edie's family and friends as the uncouth "artist," which is how he described himself when asked what he did, while accepting a job in a ball-bearing factory arranged by Mrs. Parker, if only in order to pay off the bail-money debt.

Despite settling in to *some* aspects of life in the generally tranquil Grosse Pointe, such as spending much of his leisure time in a local bar when not locked in his room drafting a proposed novel or embarking on sexual adventures with a number of his wife's girlfriends, almost from the start Jack and Edie's marriage was doomed. Within a few weeks they had separated, with Jack back in New York City.

Lucien Carr, meantime, had been awaiting trial and appeared in court on September 15, 1944, where he pleaded guilty to manslaughter. Sentence was passed on October 6, the judge committing him to an "indeterminate term" in the Elmira Reformatory, which he would enter on October 9, and where he would eventually serve two years' incarceration.

Despite the horrific circumstances surrounding David Kammerer's death, which meant the disbanding of the "New Vision" group in the short term, by the end of 1944 Allen Ginsberg, Jack Kerouac, and William Burroughs were reunited.

# the birth of beat

"One belongs to New York instantly, one belongs to it as much in five minutes as in five years."

Thomas Wolfe

Allen Ginsberg, the only one of the group not to be directly involved in the Carr-Kammerer case, was still living in the Warren Hall residence, where Jack Kerouac joined him after leaving Edie Parker and Grosse Pointe in September 1944. Now he was free of Edie, and with Lucien Carr in jail, Jack hoped to start an affair with Céline Young (who he had always found attractive), or at least get her to bed. His other immediate intention was to concentrate on developing his writing.

He was thwarted in the first ambition by the fact that the beautiful Céline was now seeing a bright anthropology student at Columbia—Hal Chase—whose name would frequently figure in the regrouping of the ex-Lucien Carr crowd over the upcoming months. But he threw himself into his second goal at full tilt.

Renting an artist's garret of a room in the same building as Allen, Jack decided he had to perfect a "method" for writing before he could produce any viable work. Writing by candlelight, he would first listen to music while allowing scenes to build up in his mind, and then type furiously in a 100-words-a-minute stream of consciousness; in a nightly purge of his own creativity he would finally consign that day's work to the candle's flame. Kerouac named this process "Self-Ultimacy," a variant of the New Vision, which reached its apogee when he wrote "BLOOD" in his own blood on a business card, which he also labeled "The Blood of the Poet" after the 1930 Jean Cocteau film of the same name. He secured it to the wall as a testament of his own commitment. At the time, in order to concentrate on his work, he saw few people apart from Allen, until Bill Burroughs returned from St. Louis in December 1944.

Although he sympathized with Jack's desire to develop his writing, Burroughs thought the nightly ritual was self-indulgent "nonsense," and, reintroducing him to the real world of New York City, for the next three months they spent a lot of time in each other's company. They even collaborated on a Dashiell Hammett-style crime novel based on the Carr-Kammerer affair, each of them writing alternate chapters. Cryptically titled *And the Hippos Were Boiled in Their Tanks*, Burroughs and Kerouac finished the book by March 1945; it was considered by Simon and Schuster, but never published.

Edie Parker also came back to New York in December, attempting a reconciliation with Jack that was hardly successful, and by the end of that year she was back with her family. They were still good friends, and would go out together to bars and jazz clubs, often in the company of Jack's old chum, Seymour Wyse, or their former flatmate, Joan Vollmer. She was now living in a sprawling five-bedroom apartment on West 115th Street which, over the next 18 months or so, would become the nerve-center of the nascent Beat Generation.

Born in 1924 in Loudonville, a smart suburb of Albany, New York, Vollmer would be the most prominent female member of the early Beat circle. She left her upper middle-class family to attend Barnard College (an affiliate of Columbia University) as a journalism student, soon afterward marrying Paul Adams, who was studying law. After her newlywed husband was drafted into the services at the start of the War, she shared the apartment on 118th Street with Edie Parker.

She had met Edie in the West End bar, which the latter frequented while still rooming at her grandparents on nearby 116th Street. Vollmer's marriage had been largely on impulse, an act of rebellion against her conservative family background, and with Adams now out of the picture, she wasn't inclined to practice a bourgeois celibacy in his absence. Early in 1944 she became pregnant and after her daughter Julie was born in June of that year, she signed a lease under her married name of Mrs. Paul Adams for apartment 35 at 419 West 115th. It cost $150 a month, and she planned to take in flatmates to share the rent. Who paid rent, and who didn't, is open to conjecture, but the pad quickly became a social magnet through the early months of 1945.

Allen Ginsberg moved in during March 1945, after being suspended from Columbia for "entertaining" another man in his bed. The offending guest was Jack, though in actuality no sexual activity took place whatsoever, Jack merely crashing in Allen's dorm after one of their late-night discussions. During her on-off reunion with Kerouac, Edie would also stay at the Vollmer apartment when she was not sleeping at her grandmother's, with Jack becoming a permanent fixture there.

Céline Young's paramour Hal Chase became a regular tenant, while Vollmer herself had a number of boyfriends coming and going through number 35, including John Kingsland, a young Columbia student with whom she had a typically casual affair. With a high-powered sex drive matched by a dynamic personality and lively mind, Joan Vollmer was promiscuous, though, in the view of Edie Parker, not "wild." But she certainly attracted men, and they in turn were deeply attracted to her.

Unaware at this stage of Bill Burroughs' homosexuality, Jack and Allen decided their older friend should meet the intellectually vivacious Joan. By fall 1945 Bill had taken the last

**Previous pages:** Brooklyn Bridge by night, with the spectacular Manhattan skyline in the background, 1948.

**Below:** The Beats weren't the only ones who liked "slumming it" in jazz joints. The heiress Doris Duke is serenaded by the honkin' tenor sax man Big Jay McNeeley at Birdland on West 44th Street.

**Below:** Neon-lit Broadway around Times Square. The heart of New York's theater district, it was also the hub of the sleazy nightlife world that Burroughs introduced to the other early Beats via "low-life" characters like Huncke.

**Opposite:** Hustler, heroin addict, and petty thief Herbert Huncke in 1944. John Clellon Holmes described his aura: "We went to Huncke just because of the kind of life he had lived—he was a source— even more, a model of how to survive."

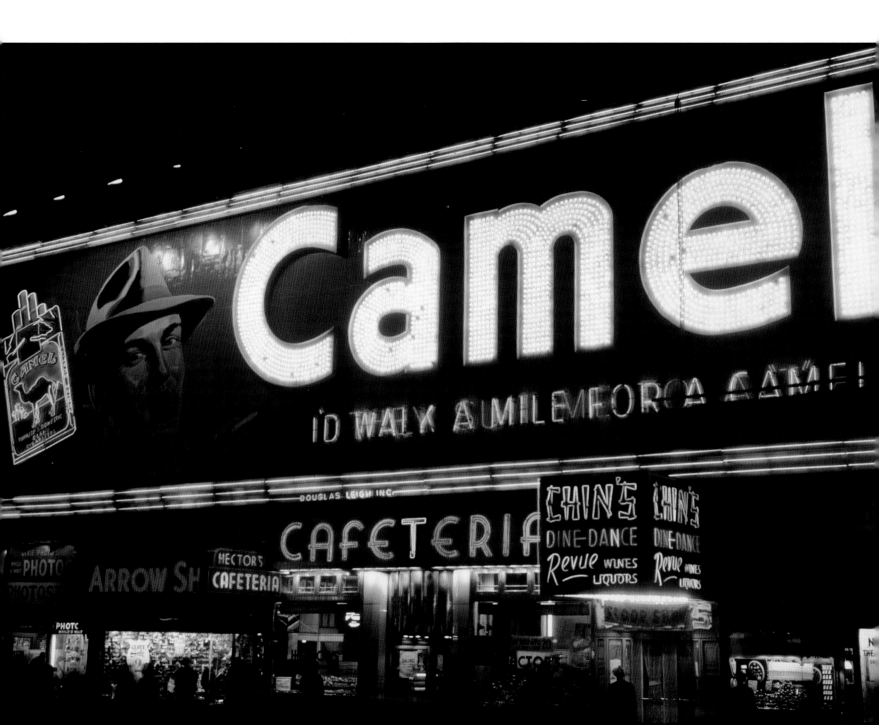

"I think Joan Burroughs was one of the most beautiful women I've known. I don't know how to describe her other than to say that she had an inner beauty that was so warm and so outgoing that it sort of swept one off one's feet."

Herbert Huncke on Joan Vollmer/Burroughs, 1978

vacant room in the apartment, and within a few months he embarked on an unlikely affair with his landlady. His arrival into the 115th Street milieu also heralded a period of genuinely communal living on the part of Ginsberg, Kerouac, Burroughs, and the other habitués with whom they shared their food, their thoughts, sometimes even their beds.

. . .

Ironically, it was also the articulate, smartly attired, and prodigiously well-read Burroughs who introduced elements of "low life" into the fraternity in the person of various "colorful" individuals he came across while slumming it at the seedier end of New York society. Prior to moving into the Vollmer apartment, Bill had rented a cheap room on West 58th and Ninth Avenue, near Columbus Circle, an ideal location for his habitual forays into the sleazy nightlife world of Times Square and 42nd Street. It was his fascination with the underworld of thieves, hookers, pimps, and junkies that was to lead him to his acquaintance with a small-time crook named Bob Brandenburg.

Burroughs' interest in the criminal world was motivated by his long-held belief that only experiencing the downside of life without moral restriction could lead to true fulfillment. To this end he'd taken a job as a bartender, fencing stolen goods for petty criminals as a sideline, and in this last capacity he offered Brandenburg the chance to buy a machine gun and some "hot" morphine syrettes. Brandenburg took Bill to his apartment on the Lower East Side, where he introduced him to his girlfriend, a beautiful, six-foot-tall prostitute by the name of Vickie Russell, and their two flatmates, a gay Turkish-bath attendant called Bozo and a world-weary looking junkie, Herbert Huncke. It was then, along with Huncke and fellow junkie Phil White, that Bill shot drugs into his arm for the first time, beginning a lifetime of (albeit always voluntary) addiction.

On the instigation of Burroughs, the Times Square area soon became a regular stomping ground for Jack and Allen, too,

often with Joan, Edie, Hal Chase, and others in tow. They began to hang out at the Angle Bar (a.k.a. the Angler Bar in some sources) on the corner of 43rd and Eighth, a known meeting-place for hustlers, thieves, dealers, and junkies with plainclothes cops keeping an eye on them all. But for the still-idealistic ex-Columbia students, these motley characters of dubious virtue were the "real" thing.

More dramatic, however, was the impact on life at 115th Street when Herbert Huncke, Phil White, and Bill Burroughs' other low-life "associates" made their presence felt. Huncke, who would later chronicle his life in a modest output of evocative short stories, the first of which were published as *Huncke's Journal* by Diane di Prima's Poets Press in 1965, enthralled the middle-class kids with his tales of the criminal underworld. Real or fabricated, his accounts were peppered with an infectious new usage of words such as "Hip," "Square," and "Beat" that he'd picked up from the jive-talking argot of black American jazz musicians. In truth, he was no proletarian himself, having been disowned by his well-to-do family before entering into a downward spiral of robbery, male prostitution, and drug addiction. Likewise, Harvard-educated Bill Garver, who funded his morphine habit with petty theft, was the son of a well-known banker, while red-haired, $100-a-time hooker Vickie Russell was the daughter of a prominent judge.

It was Vickie who showed them how to use Benzedrine strips taken out of 99¢ inhalers to get an instant, eight-hour high. Jack took to it almost immediately, and wrote much of his work on amphetamines from thereon. Allen, on the other hand, found it made his writing undisciplined and indecipherable, while Joan simply ingested more and more. All the time Huncke and White would rip them off, stealing money and goods from their gullible hosts whenever they got the chance, at the same time using the premises as a depository for all manner of illegal substances and stolen goods. Their hosts reciprocated by turning a blind eye to the often-malign influence. There began to develop what Jack Kerouac would later describe as "a low, evil decadence" around life in the apartment.

" . . . I am completely broke—flat—taped—beat—busted and without."

Letter to Allen Ginsberg from Herbert Huncke in prison, September 23, 1946—one of the first examples of Huncke's use of the word "beat"

Jack's retrospectively moral view suggested a guilt which clearly wasn't apparent at the time, when his life, as much as that of anyone else at 115th Street, was inexorably driven by the concomitant urge for experience, experiment, and excess. He was as sexually prolific as ever. Between intermittent dalliances with Edie, he conducted various casual affairs, including a wild, day-long encounter with Vickie Russell only hours after their first meeting. And he had his first (masturbatory) homosexual experience with Allen, to neither's great physical satisfaction.

Bill's affair with Joan, on the other hand, blossomed on a mental, as much as a physical level. Indeed, the homosexual's shortcomings in the heterosexual bedroom were more than compensated for in the meeting of minds that characterized their relationship, the two holding each other in mutual respect as the intellectual elite of the group. It was a partnership that would last as a common-law marriage until Joan's accidental death by Bill's hand in 1951. But her involvement with the embryonic Beat commune, of which she was the unofficial anchorwoman, was as self-destructive as it was creative as her dependence on Benzedrine reached debilitating proportions.

By summer 1946, the core group at 115th Street had all but fallen apart. Jack had effectively moved out soon after New Year, spending more and more time with his family as his father neared death from cancer of the spleen. Although he continued to visit the apartment through the early months, after Leo's death in April 1946, his main creative activity had moved on from what had been like a two-year preparation for writing to doing it for real. He ensconced himself in front of his typewriter at the family house in Ozone Park as he began writing what would eventually be his first published novel, *The Town and the City*.

Disillusioned by the degeneration of their "community," Hal Chase had gone home to Denver, planning to return to the Columbia Halls of Residence in the fall. Now it was the criminal axis rather than the aspiring artists who dominated life in the apartment, with stolen goods and drug paraphernalia everywhere. Bill had fallen foul of the law when he let Huncke's junk buddy Phil White talk him into forging a signature on blank morphine prescriptions, a misdemeanor for which he would be committed to the care of his parents in St. Louis as part of a four-month suspended sentence. Huncke, meantime, was also arrested for possession of drugs, and began a three-month prison sentence.

In Bill's absence, and taking more Benzedrine than ever, Joan's condition deteriorated rapidly; with sores all over her body and an ashen complexion, she hallucinated and raved to the point where she had to be taken to Bellevue Hospital. Diagnosed as suffering from acute amphetamine psychosis, she remained at Bellevue for ten days, until Bill arrived from St. Louis to take care of her. With her daughter, Julie, they moved to the Rio Grande Valley in Texas, where Bill planned to buy some land (with his parents' assistance) for a citrus farm. They conceived a child, who would be born William Burroughs III in July 1947, and though never legally married, from here on in Joan Vollmer would always formally sign herself "Mrs W. S. Burroughs."

As the era of 115th Street came to a close for all concerned, Allen Ginsberg went to stay with his father in Paterson, New Jersey, until the next term at Columbia started in late September 1946. He rented a room with an Irish family on West 92nd Street, intent on becoming an official student once more, and although he was still suspended, he renewed contact with his professors in the English department. But things could never be the same again, nor would he have wanted them to be. As with Burroughs and Kerouac, over the previous two years Ginsberg's perception of the world around him had changed as irrevocably as the world inside his head had done.

. . .

Crucial to those changes was an event at 115th Street less than a year earlier, in November 1945, which came to be known among the group as "The Night of the Wolfeans." It came about as a result of the regular amateur psychoanalysis sessions conducted by Bill Burroughs, who had studied such things, and it was to be a daily ritual for Jack Kerouac, Allen Ginsberg, or whoever to lie on the couch and free-associate ideas while Bill voiced his observations as resident analyst.

These sessions often led to bizarre charades and therapeutic role-playing, and on the night in question, when they were all high on Benzedrine, their rambling discussion ended up with them dubbing themselves either "Wolfean" or "Non-Wolfean." Thomas Wolfe was a favorite writer of Kerouac's, who famously argued with F. Scott Fitzgerald about the nature of America.

"I said we were a homesick people, and belonged to the earth and land we came from as much or more than any country I knew about—he said we were not, that we were not a country, that he had no feeling for the land he came from."

Thomas Wolfe, quoted in 1930, recalling his argument with F. Scott Fitzgerald at the Ritz Bar in Paris

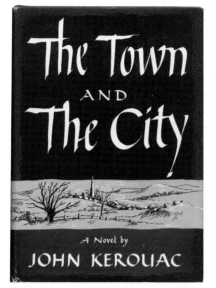

**Top left:** From 1950, the first edition of Jack Kerouac's debut novel *The Town and the City*.

**Top right:** Novelist F. Scott Fitzgerald, who lived in Europe from 1924 to 1931, on a motoring holiday in Italy with his wife Zelda and daughter Scottie.

**Right:** Hal Chase and William Burroughs at Morningside Heights during the winter of 1944–45.

**Above:** The author Thomas Wolfe (1900–38), much admired by Kerouac in particular, and inspiration for the latter's "Wolfean" approach in his early work.

# west coast roots

Nearly 3,000 miles by road from New York City, San Francisco had, from the 30s and earlier, flourished as a quite separate cultural community. By World War II a mix of radical politics, art, literature, and a lively bohemia had produced an avant-garde scene with its own distinct character as vibrant as any on the East Coast. Simultaneous to what was happening around Columbia University and Greenwich Village was the site of a parallel, but independent genesis of the Beat Generation.

The earliest catalyst was in the pages of a radical magazine, *Circle*, which was published from the University of California at Berkeley between 1944 and 1948. Editorially it reflected a strong anarchist and anti-authoritarian tendency mood at Berkeley at the time, alongside writings by the likes of novelist Henry Miller and the poets Robert Duncan and Kenneth Rexroth, the latter a key figure in subsequent developments.

Born in 1905, at age 19 Rexroth had hitchhiked across the US, later working on a steamship that took him to Mexico, South America, and on to Paris. There, he met major names of the artistic avant-garde, including Tristan Tzara and other Surrealists. Moving to San Francisco on his return to America, he was a leading light in the city's left wing and anarchist circles, and was interned during World War II as a Conscientious Objector.

After the War Rexroth and other prisoners of conscience from the internment camp set up the San Francisco Anarchist Circle, meeting at his home every week to discuss libertarian politics, philosophy, and the arts. There were also weekly poetry evenings and dances organized to raise money for the group's activities (which, by 1947, had become the Libertarian Circle); these featured early experiments in reading poetry to jazz. In the long term the most radical development to come out of Rexroth's melding of poetry and politics was the establishment of KPFA, a pioneering commercial-free radio station, peace-oriented and supported by its listeners. The station, which would later trigger similar projects in Los Angeles, Houston, New York, and Washington, spread the influence of artists and writers way beyond traditional parameters.

In 1947 members of the Libertarian Circle set up their own magazine, *Ark*, which was rather more militant than its Berkeley predecessor, and a precursor of a new wave in literary "little magazines" that would sustain much of the output of the Beats throughout the 50s. The magazine, the radio station,

experimental theater and art groups, and an emerging poetry-reading circuit all contributed to a cultural upsurge that became known as the San Francisco Renaissance.

With new young poets from the Bay Area getting involved, including Gary Snyder, Michael McClure, and Philip Whalen, by the early 50s Kenneth Rexroth, largely unwittingly, it has to be said, was presiding over the West Coast birth of the Beat Generation. By the middle of the decade San Francisco, along with New York City, was one of the two undisputed centers of the movement.

"The youngest generation is in a state of revolt so absolute that its elders cannot even recognize it."

Kenneth Rexroth from "Disengagement: The Art of the Beat Generation," first published in *New World Writing*, 1957

**Left:** Kenneth Rexroth (right) looks on as Lawrence Ferlinghetti reads with sax player Bruce Lippincott accompanying, at San Francisco's Cellar club in 1957. The event was recorded live, with the two poets (and Lippincott leading a quintet) featured on either side of an album, *Poetry Reading in the Cellar*, released on the Fantasy jazz label.

**Below left:** Elder statesman of the West Coast poetry scene Kenneth Rexroth, photographed in 1957 wearing a suit given to him by Al Capone in the 20s.

**Below:** Powell Street in the 40s, running through the heart of San Francisco's North Beach district.

Wolfe identified with the mythic pioneers and the idea of America as a land of potential and creative vision, while Fitzgerald took a "modern," cosmopolitan stance, urbane and above what he regarded as insularity and naïve sentimentality.

The dichotomy between the work of the two great writers that so galvanized the Beats had little to do with actual style—both wrote in a conventional, narrative manner—but was about this difference of attitude toward their native land. Kerouac, along with Hal Chase, strongly took the Wolfean corner, while Ginsberg, Burroughs, and Joan Vollmer were of the sophisticated, internationalist "Non-Wolfean" persuasion. Ginsberg and Burroughs professed a more open-minded approach regarding matters political, social, and sexual, though Kerouac would deny—at this point, anyway—being in any way conservative.

This difference of stance helps to explain much about the different direction the key Beats took in the coming years. Kerouac's pro-Americanism was increasingly out of synch with the anti-establishment sympathies of both the 50s Beats and 60s counterculture, though his espousal of back-to-the roots simplicity and Eastern religion did strike a chord with the latter. Burroughs, on the other hand, lived outside the US for many years, and was preoccupied in much of his writing with the destruction of the state and its powers. Ginsberg became a traveling evangelist not just for the Beat ethos as such, but for homosexual law reform, liberalization of drug laws, and antiwar internationalism.

At the time the simplistic polarization of the Wolfean/Non-Wolfean analysis ignored the essential complexity of individual personalities, a factor personified in their circle with the arrival, at the end of 1946, of Neal Cassady.

. . .

Twenty-year-old Cassady hit New York City in December 1946 with his newlywed bride, LuAnne, who was just 16. Their Greyhound bus journey from Nebraska had begun with a safe-cracking theft of $300 and a stolen car. The safe belonged to the girl's aunt, the car to her uncle; when they got to Manhattan, having taken the bus when the car broke down in a blizzard, they had just $35 between them. Cassady had come to the City to hook up with Hal Chase, his friend from Denver, Colorado.

He had spent his childhood in Denver, where he'd arrived with his father in 1932 at age six. His parents separated on account of Neal Senior's alcoholism, and the youngster spent his formative years in a flophouse surrounded by down-and-outs, winos, and junkies. Summers with his father followed a similarly vagrant lifestyle, hitchhiking or hopping freight trains like real hobos, to visit relatives or get casual work in fruit harvesting. Not surprisingly, by the time he was in his teens Neal was a genuine juvenile delinquent, stealing cars for kicks, spending time in a reformatory, and much of the remainder in the bars and pool halls of Denver—or, perhaps more surprisingly, Denver Public Library.

"He [Neal] started at early childhood, and had a photographic memory, he remembered every book he'd ever read. Some of his letters, like from prison, are just like 'Well, I just read all of Mark Twain, and all of Dickens' . . . And he could remember everything, he was much better read than either Kerouac or Ginsberg, because he was also interested in philosophy and such."

Carolyn Cassady, 2006

Cassady also had a voracious sexual appetite. He'd lost his virginity at age eight in a notorious gang-bang involving the sons and daughters of an alcoholic friend of his father's, and as he matured he became an accomplished seducer of almost anyone who caught his eye, male or female. Cars and sex, coming together in what he'd later describe as his "Adventures in Auto-Eroticism," were his main preoccupation in adolescence—along with books.

From childhood, Cassady had found reading to be an escape from the no-hope promise of daily life as he knew it. On the shelves of the local library he discovered philosophy and history, Shakespeare, Schopenhauer, and Proust. By the time he met and quickly married cute-looking LuAnne Henderson in the closing weeks of 1946, he was better read than any 20-year-old raised in charity missions and reform schools could hope to be.

Neal got to know Hal Chase in Denver, when the latter was spending vacations in his hometown between his studies at Columbia University. Hal was as seduced by Neal's unschooled intellect and high-octane conversation as were Cassady's many lovers by his sexual overtures. There was something about his spontaneous verbal outpourings that Hal found compelling, a no-holds-barred use of language that was reflected in his letters when Chase returned to New York. Hearing his tales of this larger-than-life character, Allen Ginsberg, Jack Kerouac, and the rest were intrigued to meet Cassady when they heard he'd arrived in New York City.

When they met at the end of 1946, despite their initial impression that Neal was something of a con man—which of course, in many respects, he was—Jack was soon entranced by this urban cowboy with his athletic, muscular frame, wide grin, and disarming line in what Cassady's Irish ancestors would simply have called "blarney."

**Above:** Neal Cassady's "child bride" LuAnne Henderson in 1946, the year of her high school graduation. When he first saw the 15-year-old he declared "That's the girl I'm going to marry," and within a few weeks he'd done just that.

**Right:** Cassady posing against an automobile while working as a parking lot attendant. He would say of this picture: "I'm a big show-off, but it's a good view of the lot and the cars in the background look good."

"Jack was the observer and Neal was the doer. And that of course was what Jack loved about him, although he envied Neal's ability to enter into everything like he did. They were kind of opposites that attract, because Neal was very quick and nimble, and Jack was clumsy and slow. So, people who say they were so much alike, and looked alike, are totally wrong—they weren't at all. But they both were very compassionate, and non-violent, had those sort of values I like, which attracted them to each other . . . and then of course there was literature—and music."

Carolyn Cassady, 2006

Carolyn Cassady, Neal's wife for 15 years, confirmed how he did indeed manipulate, and charm, those he met: " . . . but on the other hand he was just trying to make everybody happy! He manipulated, but he was different—far from malicious about it, as far as I know. He was just so sharp, and perceptive, about where each person was at. For some reason he had this great gift for knowing exactly where they were coming from, so he kept responding in like manner. That's how it was with me, you see—I thought he was an educated gentleman. He just knew exactly how to approach people.

"And if he wanted something from them, like people say he conned Jack into pretending he wanted to learn how to write when he just wanted a place to sleep, then it was probably a bit of both. But he was certainly sincere about wanting to learn to write as well—if you call that conning, I don't know. As I say, it was never for real personal gain (unless it was a girl!), he never asked for money."

On one level, to Jack, Cassady represented the archetypal American hero, a free-rolling spirit whose exploits (or, more accurately, his accounts of them) were the embodiment of the Wolfean vision. On the other hand, Cassady's language, with its scattergun delivery and his stream-of-consciousness letter writing, would encourage Jack to take a decidedly "Non-Wolfean" approach to his own output. Inspired by Neal's almost anarchic approach he developed his own "spontaneous prose" style, also influenced by the rhythms of jazz, creating a transcendental literary experience which was the opposite to the "Wolfean" narrative style he was pursuing as he still worked on *The Town and the City*.

For him, Neal Cassady represented "A new kind of American saint," a "long lost brother," who reminded him of his own initial urge to write. While for Cassady, Jack Kerouac was the common man, hardly removed from his roots in working-class America, who nevertheless had become the writer that he also aspired to be.

And for Allen Ginsberg, meeting Cassady for the first time on January 10, 1947 was simply a case of love at first sight. Setting eyes on Neal while high on marijuana (which at this stage Cassady had never smoked), he was speechless, though not for long. Over the days that followed, the poet (for the moment ensconced in a grim apartment in Spanish Harlem) and the erstwhile social drifter spent much of their time together. First talking as intently as either had ever spoken with anyone, then consummating their mutual attraction with what for Allen was his first satisfactory homosexual experience. In the realm of his senses Neal Cassady was the muse for his first sexually confessional poetry, though Neal's initial sojourn in New York was not to last for long.

He had taken a job parking cars at a 34th Street hotel while finding LuAnne a job in a bakery shop. But their honeymoon period was short-lived, and LuAnne left for her home in Denver just a few weeks after they'd arrived. Cassady stayed on, basking in the celebrity status he was enjoying among the Columbia crowd, and at the same time genuinely anxious to learn all he could from Jack and Allen, flattery and con-artistry notwithstanding. Then, in early May 1947, he announced he was returning to Denver. Jack and Allen accompanied him to the Greyhound bus station, getting a snap taken in a photo booth before Cassady boarded the bus. Later that month, Allen followed him to Denver. Hal Chase, too, made the journey to his hometown after he had graduated.

Jack, meanwhile, was still living with his mother in Ozone Park, writing his first novel and unable to afford a fare across country. But the pull of the West was too great to keep him stationary for long, and when his old friend from Horace Mann, Henri Cru, suggested he join him on a ship sailing out of San Francisco, he made the break. He planned a trip that would take him to the California port via Denver, where he could catch up on Allen, Neal, and the others, crossing the vastness of America coast-to-coast, through hitchhiking and taking bus rides. It was the start of a saga, with Neal Cassady and Allen Ginsberg playing leading roles, which would form the basis for *On the Road*, a cornerstone of Beat Generation literature when it finally appeared in print a full ten years later.

**Right:** The Carnegie Public Library in Denver (left of picture), where Neal Cassady spent many hours in his youth.

**Below:** Larimer Street in the downtown Denver of the late 40s, which was Cassady's other "patch," with its numerous diners, bars, and pool halls.

# on the road

"Americans should know the universe itself as a road, as many roads, as roads for traveling souls."

Walt Whitman

When *On the Road* was first published by Viking Press in September 1957, it was an overnight success, catapulting Jack Kerouac and his fellow Beats into an arena of celebrity none of them had ever anticipated, and which they were by and large unprepared for. As the book's fame reached epic proportions, so the nature of its creation became central to Beat mythology.

According to legend, Kerouac pounded out the entire work in just three weeks of frantic writing, a nonstop creative outpouring that made "stream of consciousness" almost an understatement. That much is true. Ensconced in an apartment on West 20th Street, in 1951 he furiously typed the entire first draft of the work on one long roll of teletype paper, with no margins, single spacing, and no paragraph breaks.

But what the myth ignores is the fact that much of the book was written over the seven years of his travels on which it was based, in the small notebooks in which he was constantly jotting down his thoughts, and writing at length in his spare time. It also takes no account of his often-painstaking preparation before the famous typewriter blitz, or the fact that he went on to revise the text several times before it was finally published.

Opening with a description of Neal Cassady arriving in New York in 1946, the book follows Jack to Denver in summer 1947, and his subsequent criss-crossing of the US, back and forth in a monumental journey. With the true-life characters renamed and Kerouac's multiple trips condensed into what feels like one long trek, *On the Road* was neither a factual journal nor a pure work of fiction.

Jack himself became the narrator, Sal Paradise, Neal Cassady—the central focus of much of the narrative—Dean Moriarty, Allen Ginsberg was Carlo Marx, Bill Burroughs, Old Bull Lee, and so on. But the real-life odyssey that Kerouac embarked upon in the summer of 1947, involving many of the main players as well as the key places of the Beats' saga, would prove as crucial as the book it was to inspire.

. . .

When Allen Ginsberg left New York to join Neal Cassady in Denver in May 1947, Jack made up his mind he wouldn't be far behind. His plan was to hitchhike across the country to pick up the ship in San Francisco that Henri Cru had signed on to, checking out the Denver scene on the way. Bidding farewell to his mother Gabrielle, he hit the road on July 17, 1947. It was a far from promising start.

Kerouac hitched a few short rides, which took him up the Hudson River, from where he wanted to pick up Route 6, the road out West, and then he waited all day in the pouring rain for a lift, but to no avail. Finally giving up and taking a bus back to Manhattan, the next day he got another bus to Chicago, and another to Joliet, Illinois, where he joined Route 6, and finally began his hitchhiking adventure across the Midwestern plains and prairies. This was the America he had always dreamed of, but never-before experienced—the wide-open spaces of Thomas Wolfe, Jack London, and innumerable Hollywood movies. It was the country of the big sky, where cornfields stretched from horizon to horizon, a vista interrupted by the occasional grain silo or telegraph wires, and the road ran arrow-straight into a heat-haze infinity. He passed through one-horse towns that didn't even have a horse anymore, sparse settlements clustered around roadside diners and gas stations. He talked to people in bars and cheap motels—cowboys in tall Stetsons, short-order waitresses, gum-chewing truck drivers—scribbling what they had to say in the little notebooks he carried everywhere.

Arriving in Denver after his 1,000-mile-plus hitchhike, he first met up with Hal Chase, who it transpired had distanced himself from Cassady and Ginsberg since returning to his respectable Denver family. It took him some days before he tracked down Allen and then Neal, only to find them embroiled in one of Cassady's habitual emotional entanglements. On his return to Denver, Neal had seemingly patched things up with his wife LuAnne, but almost immediately began the simultaneous pursuit of Carolyn Robinson, a beautiful graduate from the University of Denver. Neither woman knew he was seeing the other, a deceit that was further complicated by Allen's continued infatuation, which Neal didn't reject out of hand. Allen and Neal would talk through the night, with Neal eager to learn all he could from his literary friend—though their sexual activity had come to a halt, much to Allen's frustration. There was no way either LuAnne or Carolyn were aware at this stage of the intimacy of Neal's relationship with Allen. Just to add a further twist to his already convoluted love life, Neal was also involved with two waitresses, the Gyllion sisters (one of them had a one-night stand with Jack), who would appear in *On the Road* as the Bettencourt sisters.

Not surprisingly, considering his busy social diary, Neal didn't have a lot of time to spend with Jack in Denver, though he did show him round some of his old childhood haunts. He also introduced him to Al Hinkle, who would become a good friend, and naturally to Carolyn Robinson. Jack was immediately attracted to Neal's girlfriend; he sensed the innocent vulnerability

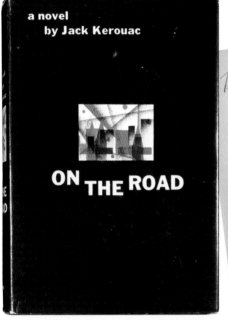

a novel
by Jack Kerouac

ON THE ROAD

*To Joyce*
*with love*
*from amigo*
*beholden Jack*

**Previous pages:** The open highway that inspired Jack Kerouac: a stretch of the now-legendary Route 66 in Arizona, 1947.

**Left:** A copy of the original Viking edition of *On the Road*, with a page signed by Kerouac, dedicated to his girlfriend of the time, Joyce Glassman.

**Below:** Once dubbed "the James Dean of the typewriter," Kerouac at work wearing his trademark checked shirt.

# "We have a System...
## that saves our Car ... our Time and our Money"

### "We use the Family Car...

**in a hundred convenient ways"**

The family automobile is indispensable for many, many trips! It is one of the most important factors in our pleasant American way of life ... but there's a better, more economical way to enjoy *certain kinds of travel.*

**It's smart to have two cars, when one of them's a Greyhound!**

Families who have discovered this new "two-car system" are getting *more miles* of enjoyable travel, and *paying less* for those miles—while avoiding the driving strain and parking problems that go with today's increased motor traffic. Furthermore, they've settled that old family feud of *"Who gets the car today?"*

They do it by *balancing* their travel—taking the shorter, easier trips around home, and on less traveled roads, in the faithful family auto. Most of the longer trips, business and pleasure travel to the big cities, and trips over busy highways are made by Greyhound SuperCoach.

The happy result is *less cost* for travel that is far safer and far more relaxed. No more "traffic nerves" when you go Greyhound!

## A LOT MORE TRAVEL...
## *for* A LOT LESS MONEY!

# GREYHOUND

### "We use **GREYHOUND**

**...to avoid driving strain and 'traffic nerves'"**

Forget all about crowded highways and car troubles when you go Greyhound. One of the world's finest drivers gets you promptly to your destination—refreshed, rested and ready for enjoyment.

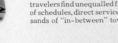

**...on short or long trips, to all America**

No parking problems, no storage bother, whether you travel across the *county* or across the *continent!* SuperCoaches are designed for long-ride comfort ... hundreds of them are fully air-conditioned.

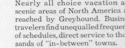

**...for business or for pleasure travel**

Nearly all choice vacation and scenic areas of North America are reached by Greyhound. Business travelers find unequalled frequency of schedules, direct service to thousands of "in-between" towns.

**...on "Amazing America" Expense-Paid Tours**

These popular tours, with hotel reservations and entertainment arranged in advance, give you all the fun with none of the bother! Available at the Greyhound Travel Bureaus in principal American cities.

of this "straight" college girl, who he felt was being conned by Cassady, despite her being three years Neal's senior. The attraction was mutual, the initial frisson of what would later become a full-blooded love affair evident when they danced together while Neal fed the jukebox, as Carolyn recalled in her 1990 autobiography *Off the Road*: " . . . here was the warm physical attraction Neal lacked. This realization disturbed me and was difficult to brush away. Jack's manner was tender without being suggestive, although he did betray some tension. As though he had read my thoughts, he said softly in my ear, 'It's too bad, but that's how it is—Neal saw you first.'"

Jack stayed just ten days in Denver; he'd run out of money and had to telegraph his mother for $50. As planned, he took the bus to San Francisco, moving in with Henri Cru and his girlfriend Dianne in Mill Valley. The ship job had fallen through (Jack was two weeks' late for it in any case), but Henri fixed him up with a job with the company for whom he was now working—as a uniformed (and armed) security guard. So it transpired that Jack Kerouac, in summer 1947, went to work every day, wielding the baton and wearing the badge of a Marin County special police officer.

He was earning the considerable sum of $45 a week, most of which he sent home to his mother, and he had access to the company office and its stationery, which allowed him to write while fulfilling his guard duties. While there, he completed a screenplay, which Henri passed on to a Hollywood connection (to no avail), honed up his on-the-road scribblings, and wrote regularly to Neal Cassady, Allen Ginsberg, and Bill Burroughs. Though for the moment absent friends, Jack was convinced that he and the other three were all linked in a way that would reach artistic fruition in the not-too-distant-future.

"I was so totally unstreetwise for one thing, so sheltered, and even things like divorce were never mentioned. And people don't realize how very conventional they [Jack and Neal] really were. Their background was like mine, as far as social values and things, and they both had a Catholic starting out. It's like they never swore, in public, and never in front of mixed company. I'm sure by themselves they did, and it's in Jack's books . . . but they never did publicly. I mean, we get language wall-to-wall these days, and they didn't do that. People just don't realize they were gentlemen —and women's lib hadn't bothered them— they were very respectful of women really."

Carolyn Cassady, 2006

Jack's own future in San Francisco, for the moment at least, would be abruptly curtailed after an embarrassing incident, when he turned up drunk to a dinner with Henri Cru's father, Albert L. Cru; the eminent academic was less than impressed by his son's friend's inebriated ramblings.

Kerouac headed south toward Los Angeles, hitchhiking to Bakersfield, then caught a bus from there. On the bus he fell into conversation with a striking-looking Mexican girl, a migrant worker named Bea Franco, and by the time they had pulled into the City of Angels they were planning to hitchhike to New York and live together.

They spent the night in a cheap hotel room and then, after an abortive attempt at hitchhiking out of LA, went down to Selma, where Jack tried his hand at joining Bea in cotton-picking. The affair only lasted a couple of weeks, during which time he felt he had experienced the underbelly of America for the first time—seeing what real poverty was like through the hand-to-mouth life of Bea and her relatives, who also looked after her seven-year-old son. But it was all grist to the mill as far as he was concerned, like most of his on-the-road experiences, material to be used later in his writing. The affair with Bea ended up as a short story, "The Mexican Girl," which first appeared in *Paris Review*, and as a section of *On the Road*.

Jack returned to Los Angeles, and with another $50 transfer from his mother, he bought a bus ticket to Pittsburgh, from where he hitched the rest of the way to New York City and his home in Ozone Park. There, he resumed work on *The Town and the City*, the 300,000-word (and counting) chronicle of his early life which he would finish in spring 1948.

"Neal's big ambition in life was to become respectable. And of course that's what my appeal was—I don't know if he was ever that much in love with me, but I represented a respectable home life. And in all his learning, and when he spoke in a cultured way and so forth, there was a desperate desire for that. Then, when he got the railroad job (any job he had, he had to be the best, so he was the best man there), it was a perfect job for him, and he worked for them for ten years. It was great, and he liked it. This was one pillar of his respectable support, and the family was the other."

Carolyn Cassady, 2006

**Above:** An ad for the 1948 Hudson, the car in which Neal embarked on his first cross-country trip "on the road."

**Left:** Cassady surveys possible purchases in a used car lot in the North Beach area of San Francisco.

**Opposite:** Looking older than her 15 years, the exuberant LuAnne Henderson in 1946. At the end of 1948, after they had separated, she rejoined ex-husband Cassady on his automobile odyssey.

"Neal and I both in white gas station coveralls. It was his [Jack's] sister's house, and when the three of us walked in, you can't even begin to imagine the shock. Here I am, with long, blonde stringy hair to my waistline. It looked like a hippie troupe of today. In those days you just didn't go around like that."

LuAnne Henderson, 1978

For Kerouac, 1948 was a year of inactivity as far as traveling was concerned. As such it was only brusquely mentioned in *On the Road*: "I stayed home all that time, finished my book, and began going to school on the G.I. Bill of Rights," referring to the small income he received from the Government for his short spell in the US Navy. But while he spent months within the city limits of New York's boroughs, others were hitting the road.

Neal Cassady, whose marriage to LuAnne had been annulled in early 1948, had moved to San Francisco with Carolyn Robinson, and there they had married in April 1948, their daughter Cathleen being born just five months later. They found themselves an apartment, and with the help of his friend from Denver, Al Hinkle (who'd also moved to California), Neal got himself a job as a guard with the Southern Pacific Railroad. In Carolyn's eyes, Neal—whose waywardness she was by now well aware of—appeared to be putting down some solid roots at last.

But Neal had other plans. In December 1948, when the railroad company had a seasonal lay-off, he announced to a stunned Carolyn that he'd spent most of their savings on a sleek new maroon Hudson car. With Al Hinkle (and Al's new wife, Helen) he planned to drive to the East to bring Jack back to California. The cross-country drive would take them to Rocky Mount, North Carolina, where Jack was going to be spending Christmas with his mother at the home of his sister Caroline ("Nin") and her husband, Paul Blake.

Leaving a distraught Carolyn with money for herself and their daughter, Neal and the Hinkles set off—and, in a typically audacious fashion, he decided their first port of call would be Denver, and the home of his ex-wife. They arrived at three in the morning, and LuAnne (who was about to marry a sailor, who at the time was away on duty) jumped at the chance of joining them when Neal promised he'd take her back "to where we belonged."

It seems Helen Hinkle's presence was mainly to fund the trip—she was the only one with any money—and when that ran out sooner than Al expected, she was more or less dumped in Tucson, Arizona. Her husband was thoughtful enough (this was, after all, their "honeymoon") to give her his railway pass, and suggest she visit Bill and Joan Burroughs in New Orleans, where he promised to join her in a couple weeks. (Burroughs had left Texas after the marijuana-growing business on his "citrus farm" had fallen through.)

After a crazy trip during which they slept in the car and Neal filched fuel by turning back the meters at gas stations, they rolled up at the Blake household on Christmas Eve, just as Jack and the Blake family were sitting down to their turkey dinner.

To his sister's alarm, Jack invited the road-weary travelers to join them, but Nin was soon won over by Neal's charm—especially when he offered to move her and her belongings to Ozone Park, where she and the family were moving in with Gabrielle. The exercise entailed two trips back and forth between Rocky Mount and New York, over 2,000 miles through rain, wind, and snow, which Neal accomplished in just three days.

House-moving over, for the quartet of Neal, LuAnne, Al, and Jack, it was party time. The first three weeks of 1949 were spent raving around Manhattan, usually in the company of Allen Ginsberg and Lucien Carr. During this time there was a definite buzz between Jack and LuAnne, and although Neal hinted more than once that he didn't mind if Kerouac slept with his ex-wife, for the moment Jack erred on the side of caution and played it cool. But the idea of an affair with LuAnne persisted in Jack's mind, especially when Neal decided the four of them should take off in the Hudson once again. It was January 19 when they set off for California, heading first for New Orleans and the Burroughs household. Jack was on the road again.

# the legendary "road" scroll

For literary enthusiasts and Beat fans in particular, the tattered scroll of almost translucent teletype paper on which Jack Kerouac typed his first full version of *On the Road* has become a sacred icon on a par with the Declaration of Independence or the Shroud of Turin.

When he died in 1969, the scroll was bequeathed to his third wife Stella as part of the Kerouac archive, which the author himself had put together between 1968 and 1969. On Stella's death in 1990, the estate passed to her brother John and his son Tony Sampas, who to this day conduct its administration. For some years the scroll was kept in storage, along with other items of memorabilia including manuscripts, letters, notebook scribblings, and suchlike, at the New York City Library. Rarely viewed by the public, one occasion when the manuscript did see the light of day was in an exhibition titled *Beat Culture and the New America: 1950–1965* staged by New York's Whitney Museum in 1995–96, which also toured museums in Minneapolis and San Francisco.

In May 2001 the scroll was put up for auction at Christie's in New York, after Tony Sampas decided to sell it to help pay off various estate debts. Once journalists, photographers, and fans filled the second-floor room for the sale, the scroll (item 9652 in lot 307) was bought after just a few bids by Jim Isray. The owner of the Indianapolis Colts football team bid a record $2.43 million, the highest amount ever paid for a literary manuscript. In 2004, Isray, whose collection of iconic pop culture pieces includes guitars owned by Elvis Presley and Stevie Ray Vaughan, put the manuscript on tour, with a visit to Lowell, Massachusetts, scheduled in 2007 to coincide with the 50th anniversary of the first publication of *On the Road*.

Yellowed over the years, each end of the scroll is tattered—one end was chewed by Lucien Carr's dog not long after Kerouac finished work on it. It contains various passages that were subsequently cut out of the novel on account of the way in which they dealt with sex and drugs, as well as penciled corrections, notes, and numerous crossings-out over the typewritten text. The scroll also includes a number of sections later edited out, and uses the original names of the characters who were modeled on Bill Burroughs, Allen Ginsberg, and so on.

Also, to mark the anniversary of the book's first edition, in 2006 the Kerouac Estate agreed to an edition to be published by Viking Penguin in 2007, which retained the scroll version intact. Like the teletype manuscript, it would have no paragraph breaks and include everything Kerouac and his editors subsequently changed or deleted between the scroll's creation in 1951 and the book's published debut in 1957.

The iconic artifact itself, meanwhile, continues to be a source of veneration for anyone with an interest in the writings and history of Jack Kerouac and the rest of the Beat Generation.

"Other people were also there to view the scroll. We all just sort of stared at it. It was not going to do anything but we watched it very closely just the same. One couple was there from London. They were here visiting family, and read about the viewing and just had to come. Several students of literature were also there, trying to soak up some inspiration by being near the scroll (as if touching the Plexiglas case would make you a better writer)."

James Eimont (literarytraveler.com) on viewing the scroll at the 2001 Christie's sale

**Above:** Poster for the exhibition staged at the Whitney Museum in New York in 1995–96, featuring an iconic shot of Kerouac taken by Allen Ginsberg at his New York apartment c. September 1953.

**Left:** As displayed on tour, a 36-foot section of the original 119 foot, 8 inches of nonstop, unedited writing which was the original *On the Road* manuscript.

**Left:** The Cassady apartment on Liberty Street, San Francisco, where they lived during the early part of 1949.

"Neal seemed to absorb everything he read. He never gets any credit for that, mind, but you'll find most of it in his letters rather than in what's written about him. Or in *The First Third* of course, though it's not too revealing that way, but in his letters; a lot of his letters . . . were what changed Kerouac's style, because of course they were so energetic and spontaneous, and his use of language was good, too."

Carolyn Cassady, 2006

This would be the trip that was to become the centerpiece of *On the Road,* with Jack absorbing everything around as the already beat-up-looking Hudson roared south. There was Neal Cassady (in a white T-shirt despite the weather), driving like a maniac as he beat the dashboard in time with the rhythm and blues and jazz on the radio; LuAnne in hour-after-hour close proximity, Jack fantasizing about her constantly; and the road as an end in itself—"The only thing to do was go."

It was this sense of the trip for its own sake, seen purely as a set of experiences without any other reason or justification that motivated Kerouac and Cassady. Neal in terms of the sheer stimulation of its execution, Jack as raw material for his writing, which he'd been working on furiously since finishing *The Town and the City* a year ago. And it was the apparent "purposelessness" of such journeys that riled Bill Burroughs when they pitched up at his home in Algiers, Louisiana, just across the Mississippi from New Orleans.

Suddenly Jack found himself between two mentors, the sage-like Burroughs, who thought the whole enterprise—including Neal—highly dubious, and Cassady, whose beguiling character was the personification of the "live for the moment" ethic. But there was no doubt on his part where his immediate destiny, and source of inspiration, lay—across the Wolfean expanses of what, for him, was still an unexplored frontier. They stayed with Burroughs (who seemed to spend most of his time either shooting airgun pellets at his wife's empty Benzedrine inhalers, or shooting up) for just a week, until Jack's G.I. pay check arrived.

Al Hinkle stayed on in New Orleans with his wife Helen, while the others forged west through towns with legendary names and a landscape to match in Texas, New Mexico, Arizona. But Jack's money soon ran out, Neal and LuAnne had none, and they resorted to picking up hitchhikers, who they then begged off. They would steal food from diners and gas stations, and even sold the spare tire to pay for fuel. In Arizona, Jack pawned his watch for a dollar's worth of gasoline.

When they finally reached San Francisco, Neal stunned Jack by dropping him and LuAnne off at the corner of O'Farrell Street and Grant Avenue, simply telling them to find a room together—he was off to reunite with his wife and child. They were flat broke and tired out, but LuAnne was less taken aback by her ex-husband's behavior, affirming he'd "leave you out in the cold any time it's in his interest."

Taking charge of the situation, she sweet-talked the manager of a hotel where she'd once lived, the Blackstone, to let them have a room on credit. There, over the next two days and nights, they had passionate sex interrupted only by occasional, but intense, conversation. It left them both physically and mentally exhausted, with Jack ringing Neal to beg him to fix him somewhere else to stay. Leaving LuAnne at the hotel, Neal took Jack to where Carolyn now had an apartment on Liberty Street. Though pleased to see her again, Kerouac only stayed a few days, checking out the local jazz spots with Neal at night. He decided it was time to head back to New York, choosing a different route for his return, and taking in even more of the America he'd never seen before.

"I got the idea for the spontaneous style of *On the Road* from seeing how good old Neal Cassady wrote letters to me, all first-person, fast, mad, confessional . . . "

Jack Kerouac

"Neal was such a good driver—his perception was so sharp, and he'd come so close to things, but never even scratched the paint, never dented a fender ever. But our perception isn't that sharp, and Ginsberg was always terrified to ride with him—although he didn't admit it, but we knew when he climbed in the back seat and complained. But Neal wasn't a wreckless driver."

Carolyn Cassady, 2006

**Opposite left:** Road and rail meet in an otherwise barren Texas landscape in the 40s.

**Opposite right:** The point where the US meets Mexico, on the bridge over the Rio Grande at Laredo.

**Opposite below:** A gas station in Mexico City; Jack and Neal visited the Mexican capital on their 1950 road journey.

Jack journeyed by bus through the Northern states of Washington, Idaho, Montana, and Michigan—where he briefly visited his wife, Edie—and on to New York and Ozone Park. There, he once more threw himself into *On the Road*, drawing on his latest travels with Neal for material but still leaving it open-ended, with more overland treks to inspire him before the final draft. Six weeks after his return home, on March 29, 1949, Harcourt Brace told him they would publish *The Town and the City* (after some editorial changes), offering him an advance of $1,000.

Working with editor Robert Giroux on *The Town and the City* during the day and on *On the Road* by night, Jack decided in May 1949 to move to Denver with his mother, sister, and brother-in-law, using his newfound "wealth" for a deposit on a property. But things didn't work out; most of his friends had left town, and Gabrielle didn't take to the change and soon moved back to New York. Tempted by letters from Neal Cassady, there was nothing left for him but once more to head back to San Francisco.

He arrived at the Cassadys' new address in Russell Street, in the Russian Hill area, at two in the morning, much to Carolyn's consternation. She liked Jack being around in as much as it pleased her husband and distracted him from his habitual womanizing, but inevitably it meant being left at home with their small daughter while the boys went on the town—added to which she was pregnant again. After a week of Neal and Jack carousing the 'Frisco jazz haunts, drinking and smoking pot, and returning home at dawn (if at all), she could take no more and threw them out. Sharing a life with Cassady was becoming more impossible,

family responsibilities (for which he showed no aptitude) loomed even greater with another child on the way, and Jack's visit marked the last straw.

Deciding to head for Denver, where Neal hoped to track down his long-lost father, the two men managed to find a drive-away car that was to be delivered there. Neal didn't even have the good grace to tell Carolyn personally that he was going. Instead he just left a note (written for him by Helen Hinkle) promising: "(I) won't ever bother you again." But Denver was a dead-end as far as finding Cassady Senior was concerned, and so they quickly found another car dealer with a delivery to make, this time a black '47 Cadillac limousine that needed to be driven to Chicago.

The drive to Illinois, with Neal making a steady 110 miles an hour on the straight, would be graphically recalled in *On the Road*, a rollercoaster of a trip of some 1,180 miles before "Great Chicago glowed red before our eyes." There, they caught some more jazz before taking a bus to Grosse Point and for Jack there was another reunion with Edie, who was still living at home.

Edie arranged for Jack and Neal to stay at the home of a friend whose well-to-do parents were away; it was a mansion of a house where the two travelers lived in the lap of luxury for a week. They enjoyed candle-lit dinners, cooked and served by the family maid, and luxuriated in tasting life with the smart set in their genteel country clubs and private bars. It was also a chance for Jack and Edie to talk seriously for the first time in ages, after which they amicably agreed to have divorce papers drawn up by the Parker family lawyer.

**Left:** The second Mrs. Kerouac, Joan Haverty, who Jack married in mid-November 1950. The ceremony, in front of a judge in Greenwich Village, was attended by Allen Ginsberg as best man, Lucien Carr and John Clellon Holmes as witnesses, and "at least 200 people, almost all of them strangers," who were recruited for the ensuing party.

**Opposite:** The four journeys made by Jack Kerouac which formed the basis for *On the Road*:

KEY

1. Starting in New York, between July and December 1947.
2. Starting in New York, between January and March 1949.
3. Starting in San Francisco, through the fall of 1949.
4. Starting in New York, between April and July 1950.

Jack Kerouac also drove from New York to San Francisco (via a short stay in Denver) in May 1949.

Neal Cassady (with LuAnne Henderson, Al and Helen Hinkle) drove from San Francisco to New York via Jack's sister's home in Rocky Mount, North Carolina, in December 1948.

The last lap of Neal and Jack's journey, in late summer 1949, was to New York, this time in a Chrysler drive-away car, in which they were both passengers for a change. Neal stayed briefly at the Kerouac home, which was now in Richmond Hill in Queens, before embarking on a long affair with a model called Diana Hansen. Jack, meanwhile, was committing to type the latest pieces in the saga that would be *On the Road*, while awaiting publication in early March 1950 of his *The Town and the City*. Despite some encouraging reviews, the debut novel didn't do as well as Jack had fancifully hoped and by the end of May 1950, the publishers reacted to poor sales by pulling the plug on the advertising budget. Jack, meanwhile, had taken a bus to Denver, where he did a signing at a local department store arranged by Justin Brierly. (Brierly, a high school teacher, had been responsible for introducing Hal Chase to Columbia University; he also initiated the teenage Neal Cassady in his first homosexual experience.) In Denver, Jack met up with old buddies Ed White and Al Hinkle, and Frank Jeffries, a friend of Neal's. Cassady was also in town. He'd driven from New York in a 1937 Ford Sedan and was planning to drive south to Mexico City to get a quickie divorce from Carolyn (who'd had their second child, Jamie, in January that same year). This was a scheme prompted by the fact that Diana Hansen was now five months' pregnant.

Jack didn't take any persuading when Neal asked him to come along on the Mexico jaunt on which Frank Jeffries also joined them. Speeding down into New Mexico and across the plains of West Texas, they crossed the Mexican border over the Rio Grande at Laredo. They were entranced by what they saw as the exotic simplicity of the Mexican people; neither had been to a non-English speaking country before—indeed, it was Cassady's first time out of the US.

Passing through Ciudad Victoria, they sampled home-grown marijuana from a friendly local, who also took them to the local brothel, where they spent a frantic three hours before continuing their journey. The casual attitude to sex and drugs—with Neal "tipping" a policeman, who was hovering outside the whorehouse—convinced them Mexico was, in many ways, a Beat paradise. Arriving in Mexico City, they rented an apartment next-door to the house where Bill and Joan Burroughs had been living for the previous seven months, the couple having been similarly attracted by the cheap and easily available drugs and relaxed attitude. Bill was also studying Mayan and Mexican archaeology at Mexico City College, where Frank Jeffries would soon enroll in an acting course.

Spending all his money (probably including the money his girlfriend Diana had given him to pay for the Mexican divorce)

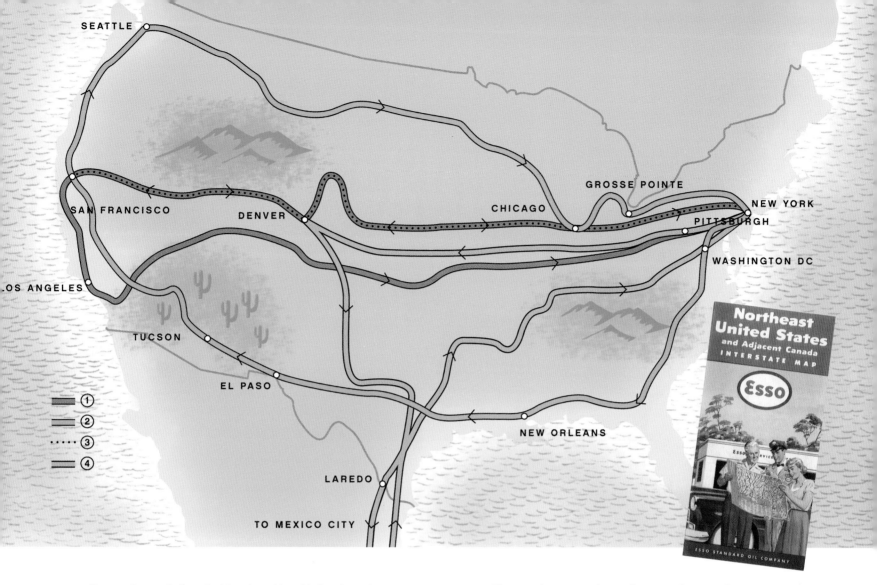

on marijuana, Cassady headed back to New York, where he married Diana Hansen, in all likelihood bigamously, on July 10, 1950. It was seemingly a "marriage" devised merely to legitimize their yet-unborn child, with Neal leaving New York immediately afterward to rejoin his legal wife in California.

Jack stayed on in the Mexican capital, smoking a lot of dope, reading the Bible, and ruminating on where his writing was taking him, or not. "I want to work in revelations, not just spin silly tales for money," he would write to Ed White, early in July, and by the end of the month he'd decided he was ready to hitchhike back to New York to resume work on *On the Road*.

. . .

The next few months would prove crucial for Kerouac, in his personal life as well as the direction his literary output was about to take. On November 3 he met Joan Haverty, a tall, attractive 20-year-old, with whom he fell instantly in love, and married (to everyone's amazement), with Allen Ginsberg as best man, two weeks later. After briefly living at his new wife's loft apartment on 21st Street, they moved in with Gabrielle on Richmond Hill. There, his search for the style he felt was hampering his literary efforts finally began to bear fruit.

The catalyst was a letter from Neal Cassady. It was a long letter (at least 13,000 words, according to others who read it, though Kerouac always claimed it was nearer 40,000), in which Neal recounted his sexual adventures over the years, along with scenes from his childhood. It was written in a highly "natural," non-literary style, which to Jack seemed to have the immediacy of everyday speech, conveying a potency which he compared to that of Dostoevsky or James Joyce.

In January 1951, Gabrielle went to North Carolina to stay with Nin and the family who had moved back there, while Jack and Joan found themselves a place on West 20th Street. It was here that his stream-of-consciousness outpourings really began in earnest, and when he found that changing the pages of typing paper interrupted his creative flow, he had the idea of writing on 20-foot-long sheets of teletype paper, which he scotch-taped together to make one unbroken typesheet.

He wanted his account of his travels to sound like a long letter to Joan, who would be hearing many of his stories for the first time. Beginning in early April 1951, he worked from dawn to the small hours, kept awake by Benzedrine and sheer compulsion. By the third week the work was almost complete, with over 86,000 words on the nearly 120-foot continuous manuscript. Though not published for another six years, *On the Road* was born.

# jazz, jive talk & hipsters

"We felt like blacks caught in a square world that wasn't enough for us."

John Clellon Holmes

Beat wasn't born in a cultural vacuum—far from it. Despite being overshadowed by the images of a devastated Europe and atom-bombed cities in Japan, the immediate postwar years were a time of unprecedented affluence for Americans. Booming wartime industry gave way to a prosperous peacetime economy, at a price. With memories of the Depression still fresh in the collective consciousness, mainstream America closed in on itself. By the time Dwight D. Eisenhower was elected President in 1953 a bland conservatism haunted the Land of the Free, gripped by a paranoia that was fueled by the anti-Communism of Joe McCarthy and the Cold War.

It was against this background that the Beats were seeking a new freedom through the honest baring of the soul, an expression of the subconscious self based on spontaneity and improvisation—and they were not alone. Right across the cultural spectrum the old rules were being broken and established aesthetics challenged, as the instantaneous dynamics of the moment came into play as never before.

On the stage, and even more potently on the movie screen, actors, writers, and directors embraced "the Method," after Marlon Brando rocked Broadway with his performance in Tennessee Williams' *A Streetcar Named Desire*, which opened in December, 1947. The Method, pioneered by Lee Strasberg at the Actors Studio in New York, was based on the teachings of the early 20th-century Russian director Stanislavsky, who encouraged actors to improvise from their own experience. "You must live the part every moment you are playing it," was his dictum, a strategy that could equally be used to describe the Beat writers' impulsive approach to their art.

Likewise, with the painter Jackson Pollock, or "Jack the Dripper," as *Life* magazine was to dub him in 1949. The pioneer of "action painting" took the Surrealists' notion of allowing spontaneity to the actual painting to its ultimate limit, letting the work take over and carry the artist (and subsequently the viewer) wherever it (or his/her subconscious) dictated.

Along with fellow Abstract Expressionists Franz Kline, Willem de Kooning, and others Pollock hung out in Greenwich Village bars such as the Cedar Tavern before his move to Long Island in 1945, where he painted his masterworks. At the Cedar, he got involved in fistfights on a regular basis, and was once banned for ripping the men's-room door from its hinges. Jack Kerouac was similarly barred from the bohemian watering hole, supposedly for urinating in an ashtray.

But it was in the subterranean clubs and cutting-edge records of the jazz world that the free-flowing stream-of-consciousness expressionism of the Beats found its prime inspiration. An all-American art form just a quarter century old in

"When I am in a painting, I'm not aware of what I'm doing. It is only after a sort of 'get acquainted' period that I see what I have been about. I have no fears about making changes, destroying the image, etc., because the painting has a life of its own. I try to let it come through."

Jackson Pollock, 1947

**Previous pages:** 52nd Street in New York, known as "Swing Street" in the 50s.

**Right:** An early RCA bebop album from 1948.

**Far right:** Outside Minton's, jazz stars (left to right) Thelonious Monk, Howard McGhee, Roy Eldridge, and Teddy Hill, in 1947.

**Below:** Charlie Parker with Miles Davis on trumpet, playing 52nd Street, 1947.

**Opposite:** So-called "action painter" Jackson Pollock.

"This tenor/alto/bass/baritone/soprano/moan/cry &
shout-a-phone! sex-oh-phone/tell-it-like-damn-
sho-isa-phone! What tremors ran through Adolphe
Sax the day Bean grabbed his ax?"

Ted Joans, from "The Sax Bit," referencing the 19th-century inventor of the saxophone
Adolphe Sax and its first great jazz exponent, Coleman "Bean" Hawkins

the mid-40s, jazz was undergoing one of its most radical changes yet. Jack had been an avid jazz fan ever since he was first introduced to New York's Dixieland scene by fellow Horace Mann students Peter Gordon and Bob Olsted. But more crucially—via Seymour Wyse, a long-term friend he had met at Horace Mann—he soon became familiar with the groundbreaking sounds of a new breed of players, who were creating what would become universally known as "modern" jazz.

With Wyse, Kerouac would frequent all the hottest venues, including Harlem nightspots such as the Savoy Ballroom, the Apollo Theater, and Minton's Playhouse, the latter on 118th Street, just a couple of blocks from where he lived in the early 40s with Edie Parker and Joan Vollmer.

Minton's was the crucible where the new sound was forged, in wild jam sessions featuring some of the greatest instrumentalists in the music's—or indeed any music's—history. As alto saxophonist Charlie Parker fought pitched musical battles with trumpeter Dizzy Gillespie, trading frantic breaks on complex chord changes at breakneck tempos, the music soon acquired a nickname imitative of its rhythm, which quickly became its official label: "Bebop."

"Bop," as it was often shortened to, famously spread downtown to the 52nd Street area and, in the process, clubs such as the Onyx, the Three Deuces, and the Royal Roost (also known as the Metropolitan Bopera House), attracted more predominantly white audiences. As did Greenwich Village venues such as the Village Vanguard, and the Café Bohemia, all of which were regular Beats' hangouts through the late 40s and 50s.

In its heyday in the early 50s the Bohemia, at 15 Barrow Street, showcased some of the greatest jazz names ever, including Cannonball Adderley, Miles Davis, John Coltrane, and Charles Mingus. Jack Kerouac was a frequent face in the audience, as was Beat writer Diane di Prima, who wrote of watching Miles Davis perform on its tiny stage: " . . . slick and smart as they come, exchanging sets with Charlie Mingus—cool then and cool now."

Another Café Bohemia patron was the poet Ted Joans. The archetypal black hipster of the Village Beat scene, with his "bop" beret and jive-talking jazz poems, Joans had been born in 1928 in Cairo, Illinois. In the early 50s Ted had a tiny one-room apartment down the road on Barrow at number 4, with space for just one single bed and not much else. But that didn't stop him allowing a neighbor who'd lost his own place to move into the cramped space along with the neighbor's "house guest," none other than the founding father of bebop, Charlie "Bird" Parker himself, who was "between homes" at the time. Joans would later describe how they would even share the bed: "Bird said, 'I don't come in till three or four in the morning—you cats should get up and let me sleep.'" Which, of course, they did.

When Parker died in 1955, it was Ted who first instigated the "Bird Lives!" graffiti that began to appear all over New York and elsewhere in the wake of the great saxman's death.

Ted Joans also played trumpet, and was a painter and collagist (his painting *Bird Lives* hangs in San Francisco's De Young Museum); he was also known as a "jazz poet"— a description he would go along with, but with a caveat. Reading regularly at Village poetry venues, including Café Bizarre, Café Wha, and Café Rafio, he was always keen to distance himself from many of the poets performing "poetry-with-jazz" when such collaborations became fashionable.

"I had developed a method of reading my poems that was similar to the way I blew trumpet," he wrote. "Each time I took a solo on my horn, on any of the standard songs, that solo would inevitably be different . . . I would soar off into spontaneous creativity that would sometimes surprise me as well as my fellow musicians. This is my method of creating jazz poetry, which is totally different from most of the so-called self-styled 'jazz poets.'" As individual poems and published collections of Joans' work attest—with titles like "Jazz Is My Religion," "The Sax Bit," *Funky Jazz Poems*—jazz was an integral part of his subject matter, not just appropriated as a background embellishment to give a live reading a "hipper" feel.

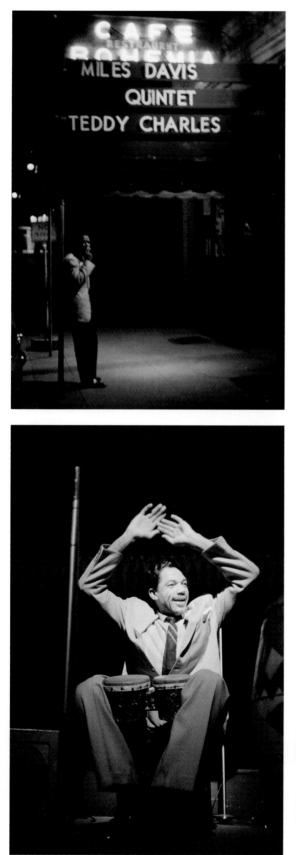

# birth of the cool

The landmark album *Birth of the Cool* represented a synthesis of the two styles of modern jazz that inspired the Beats—New York-based bebop and the emergent West Coast "cool school"—and epitomized the notion of the Hipster in the process.

The bebop conflagration that consumed jazz wasn't restricted to the nightspots of Manhattan, where Charlie Parker and Dizzy Gillespie had first ignited the flame in the early 40s. By the end of the decade players such as trumpeter Shorty Rogers and sax men Gerry Mulligan, Art Pepper, and Lee Konitz—in the main, white musicians—were establishing a West Coast jazz scene based in and around Los Angeles and San Francisco. Taking the innovations of the bebop pioneers, they fashioned their own style around the daunting chord structures and tricky time signatures.

As in New York City, the emerging West Coast Beat scene identified with jazz right from the start. Some of the earliest readings organized in San Francisco by Kenneth Rexroth and his Libertarian Circle even involved the yet-to-be-fashionable collaboration of poets reciting their verses to a live jazz backing.

Eighteen-year old fledgling trumpet star Miles Davis arrived in New York from his native St. Louis in 1944 to study at the Juilliard School of Music. But he was soon drawn into the orbit of Charlie Parker, Dizzy Gillespie, Bud Powell, and the rest, and by 1945, he was part of the regular line-up of the Charlie Parker group at Minton's and elsewhere. In 1947, having contributed an

understated contrast to Bird's lightning-fast runs on some of Parker's legendary recordings on the Savoy label, he was voted top new star in the influential *Esquire* magazine critics' poll.

With the modern jazz world suddenly at his feet, in 1948 Davis put together a nine-piece band, broadcasting from the Royal Roost, and the following year Capitol Records put the outfit in the studio for what would prove to be three legendary sessions. Uncannily in parallel with *On the Road, Birth of the Cool* (as the sessions came to be known) was created in 1949–50, yet wasn't released until 1957. The nine-piece was billed as the Miles Davis Nonet, featuring bebop luminaries Miles Davis, trombonist JJ Johnson, and drummer Max Roach alongside rising West Coast stars, including alto saxist Lee Konitz and baritone player Gerry Mulligan. With the titular leadership of Davis, the band came together under the artistic auspices of arranger Gil Evans, though he didn't actively work on every number.

Between the recording and release of *Birth of the Cool*, jazz—and the Beats—had certainly moved on. The music is considered significant as marking a reaction to bebop. In fact, Charlie Parker participated in the preliminary discussions with Davis and Evans, most of the musicians were from the bebop scene, and continued to play in the bop style for years afterward. But it signaled a fresh approach to modern jazz, then just a decade old, on the part of a body of musicians—particularly in California—thereafter referred to as the "cool school." As potently as early bebop had transfixed the original Beats in the 40s, so the cool jazz of the 50s would become the soundtrack of the Hipster.

"Gil lived in a room in a basement on 55th Street, near 5th Avenue. Actually it was behind a Chinese laundry . . . a sink, a bed, a piano, a hot-plate, and no heat."

Gerry Mulligan, 1971, recalling the frugal pad occupied by arranger Gil Evans, where musicians gathered to work on the *Birth of the Cool* sessions

**Opposite bottom:** Miles Davis playing at the New York club Birdland in 1949, in a picture made by the renowned jazz photographer Herman Leonard.

**Below left:** Recorded in three sessions—in January 1949, April 1949, and March 1950, all in New York City—despite its collaborative nature, *Birth of the Cool* is universally recognized as being the creation of Miles Davis. "He took the initiative and put the theories to work" Gerry Mulligan would later recall, "He called the rehearsals, hired the halls, called the players, and generally cracked the whip."

**Below right:** By the time *Birth of the Cool* was released Miles had moved on. The poster for San Francisco club The Blackhawk—restored by Dennis Loren—billed a Davis quintet featuring sax giant John Coltrane, a partnership which peaked with *Kind of Blue* in 1959, the best-selling jazz album ever. The Blackhawk was also the venue for jazz-and-poetry sessions featuring Kenneth Rexroth, Kenneth Patchen, and others.

Of the original Beat nucleus of Jack Kerouac, Allen Ginsberg, and Bill Burroughs, it was Jack whose enthusiasm for jazz was most evident in his own work. Having broken free of the formal disciplines of writing and having developed what Allen would later call "spontaneous bop prosody," he allowed the untempered flow of ideas to direct the way his words fell on paper much the same way as Pollock "allowed" his paintings to dictate their own direction. Asked to describe his technique, he made a direct analogy with jazz improvisation when he wrote: "Time being of the essence in the purity of speech, sketching language is undisturbed flow from the mind of personal secret idea-words, 'blowing' (as per jazz musician) on the subject of image . . . "

Jazz also featured in much of his subject matter. *On the Road* is replete with jazz imagery, with references to records being listened to during the narrative, and dazzling descriptions of actual performances witnessed by him. He recalls vividly when he and Dean Moriarty (Neal Cassady) caught a show by the British-born pianist George Shearing: "Shearing began to rock . . . slowly at first, then the beat went up, and he began rocking fast, his left foot jumped up with every beat . . . " But of the musicians mentioned in *On the Road*, the one whose style was most apposite to Kerouac and the Beats in general was Slim Gaillard.

Gaillard was a larger-than-life singer, pianist, guitarist, and bongo player, whose scat-singing vocals had much in common with their own often surreal adaptations of the English language. Gaillard made records with Charlie Parker and Dizzy Gillespie, the Gods of bebop, as well as having several hits in his own right, including "Flat Foot Floogie" and "Cement Mixer (Put-ti Put-ti)," singing scat with his self-invented jive language "Vout," which involved the liberal use of the words "vout" and "oreenee," suffixing words with "orooni." Kerouac describes him performing in a San Francisco club: " . . . he slowly gets up and takes the mike and says, very slowly, 'Great-orooni . . . fine-ovauti . . . hello-orooni . . . bourbon-orooni . . . all-orooni . . . how are the boys in the front row making out with the girls-orooni . . . '"

Slim's brand of scat singing was just one, albeit highly individualistic, example of a jazz tradition that went back to the earliest vocalizations of Louis Armstrong. Scat would hit the pop consciousness via Armstong and his sometime duettist Bing Crosby, while it was popularized in the strictly jazz arena by the often acrobatic vocalizations of the likes of Babs Gonzales, Leo Watson, and bop trumpet maestro Dizzy Gillespie. "Salt Peanuts," with some energetic scatting from Gillespie, was one of Kerouac's favorite records.

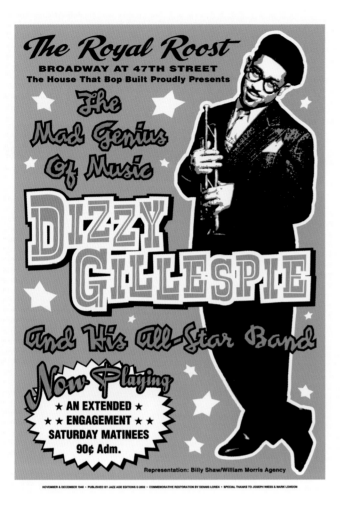

The Royal Roost
BROADWAY AT 47TH STREET
The House That Bop Built Proudly Presents
The Mad Genius Of Music
DIZZY GILLESPIE
And His All-Star Band
Now Playing
★ AN EXTENDED ★
★ ★ ENGAGEMENT ★ ★
SATURDAY MATINEES
90¢ Adm.

Representation: Billy Shaw/William Morris Agency

NOVEMBER & DECEMBER 1948 · PUBLISHED BY JAZZ AGE EDITIONS © 2002 · COMMEMORATIVE RESTORATION BY DENNIS LOREN · SPECIAL THANKS TO JOSEPH WEISS & MARK LONDON

**Left:** With his goatee beard, black horn rim glasses, and often wearing a "bop" beret, jazz extrovert Gillespie (pictured here in a poster from the 40s) was the best-known symbol of the jazzman as hipster.

**Opposite:** Architect of bebop Dizzy Gillespie in 1955. Gillespie is playing his custom-built trumpet with its unique upturned bell—which, he claimed, enabled him to hear himself more clearly.

"Yes, jazz and bop, in the sense of, say, a tenor man drawing a breath and blowing a phrase on the saxophone, till he runs out of breath, and when he does, his sentence, his statement's been made . . . "

Jack Kerouac comparing his art to that of jazz musicians, 1968

Critic Ira Gitler called Leo Watson's jive singing "stream of consciousness," a much-used phrase in descriptions of improvisational art, be it painting, music, poetry, or prose. His line was in the sleeve notes to an album by King Pleasure, architect of the style known as "vocalese," in which the singer interpreted actual instrumental solos as vocal breaks. Vocalese, in the hands of Pleasure, Eddie Jefferson, Annie Ross, and others, was hugely popular among the Beats. King Pleasure described his style simply as "blowing"—the word Kerouac used in drawing a parallel between his own work and jazz performance, though his was a sophisticated, musicianly art, akin to the instrumental prowess of those whose solos he transcribed vocally. Gaillard's "vout," on the other hand, had more in common (as did Leo Watson's) with the everyday "jive talk" of Black America, a phraseology eagerly adopted by the Beats and their followers.

Herbert Huncke first introduced expressions like "man," "hip," "square," (and indeed "beat") to the all-ears audience of middle-class students at West 115th Street, words employed in the same way he'd heard them used by black musicians. For the Beats, using such language represented a rejection of bourgeois academia and its linguistic niceties in favor of the "authenticity" of the finger-snapping jargon of the jazz world. As the Beat

Generation reached its broadest constituency among a new bohemia in the mid-50s, it became the oral badge of credibility for the archetypal Hipster.

One of the earliest (if not *the* earliest) appearances of the term "hipster" was in an article by the black American literary critic Anatole Broyard titled "Portrait of a Hipster" in the June 1948 edition of *Partisan Review*. In it he described the Hipster as the "illegitimate son of the Lost Generation," a cross between the existentialist intellecto-rebels of the Paris Left Bank and a very American breed of hedonistic experience-seekers seemingly fixated with sex, drugs, and jazz. These new bohemians—"Holy Barbarians," as Lawrence Lipton called them in his 1959 book of the same name—were radical without being overtly political, romantic but not idealistic. By the mid-50s "hip" was virtually interchangeable with "beat." Neal Cassady, for instance, called his account of meeting Williams Burroughs, "The History of the Hip Generation."

In his celebrated long essay "The White Negro," Norman Mailer saw the Hipster in terms of white non-conformists identifying with Black Americans, who had themselves been marginalized socially and culturally for two centuries, but who had, as a result, evolved their own social mores and art—the greatest contribution to the latter being jazz.

**Opposite left:** Kerouac reading live on the Steve Allen TV show in 1959.

**Opposite right:** The sleeve of Jack Kerouac's 1959 poetry-and-jazz album, *Blues and Haikus*.

**Right:** Norman Mailer's landmark essay "The White Negro: Superficial Reflections on the Hipster," published in book form by City Lights in 1957, after first appearing as a feature in *Dissent* magazine earlier that same year.

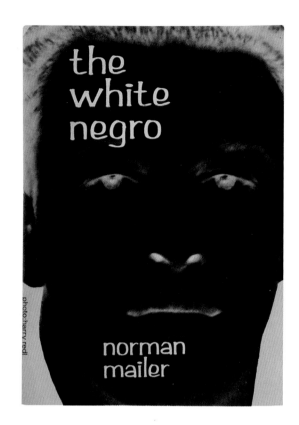

"I do not sing the words; I swing the words, which is different."

Ted Joans

Mailer first found literary fame with *The Naked and the Dead*. Based on his own experiences in World War II, and throwing a harsh light on the realities of combat, the novel was a worldwide best-seller when it appeared in 1948. He wrote a weekly column for the radical Greenwich Village newspaper, the *Village Voice*, from its launch in October 1955, in which he spotlighted the rebellion fermenting under America's bland surface in reaction to the social straitjacket imposed by McCarthyism and the Cold War. In his column in May 1956, he wrote of "the destructive, the liberating, the creative nihilism of the Hip, the frantic search for potent Change . . . "

"The White Negro" was first published in *Dissent* magazine in 1957. In the highly cerebral, 9,000-word discourse Mailer listed, for a largely white, middle-class, academic readership, what he felt was the essence of the Hipster's lingua franca: "I have jotted down perhaps a dozen words, the Hip perhaps most in use and most likely to last with the minimum of variation. The words are man, go, put down, make, beat, cool, swing, with it, crazy, dig, flip, creep, hip, square"—jive talk in a nutshell.

The confluence of the world of the Beats and the jazz scene was most conspicuous in the live performance of poetry-with-jazz, which became something of a fad during the late 50s. The practice of reading verse to a jazz backing went back to the 20s, when Langston Hughes, Maxwell Bodenheim, Kenneth Rexroth, and others first explored the idea. In the early 50s Rexroth, as father figure and standard-bearer for the San Francisco Renaissance, reintroduced it on the West Coast poetry scene, alongside like-minded writers—notably Lawrence Ferlinghetti and Kenneth Patchen.

Very much a disparaging voice as regards many aspects of the Beat Generation that he helped spawn, Rexroth would castigate those who crudely set poems to background music rather than making them an integral part of the music "as another instrument." In a 1958 essay he identified the main culprits as the "sockless hipsters," who were merely out for "a fast buck or a few drinks." His disenchantment, however, didn't stop him from recording an album—*Poetry and Jazz at the Blackhawk*—at the famous San Francisco jazz spot in 1960.

Kenneth Patchen was another voice on the California scene that performed with a jazz ensemble—the Chamber Jazz Sextet—at the Blackhawk. They appeared opposite cool school idols, the Art Pepper Quartet, in October 1957, and their two-week engagement was so well received they were given a return booking, alternating weekdays and weekends with cult West Coast favorites the Dave Brubeck Quartet. An album—*Kenneth Patchen Reads with Allyn Ferguson and the Chamber Jazz Sextet*—was subsequently released in December 1957.

There were famous jazz names involved in some of these collaborations and, conversely, the idea of the spoken word being set in a jazz instrumental context was also explored by experimentally-inclined musicians themselves. One such avant-gardist was the great bass player (and formerly bebop trailblazer) Charles Mingus. In February 1957 Mingus recorded "The Clown" for Atlantic Records, with a story he had "composed" but left to narrator Jean Shepherd to improvise—Shepherd being a well-known radio commentator and story-teller, who also performed a stand-up routine at the Limelight Café in Greenwich Village.

"The Clown" was the only "spoken word" track on the album of the same name, as was "Scenes In The City," which appeared as the opening track on another Mingus album recorded in October of that year, the misleadingly-titled *A Modern Jazz Symposium of Music and Poetry*. Narrated by Melvin Stewart, Mingus' verbal vignettes about New York street life had already been recorded in a different version on his *Tijuana Moods* session in August 1957, though they were not included on the album as released. Called "A Colloquial Dream," that earlier version was narrated, with the Mingus band's backing, by Lonnie Elder.

Mingus also performed with Kenneth Patchen, a collaboration of which, unfortunately, there are no known recordings in existence. It was, however, mentioned in Mingus' autobiography *Beneath The Underdog*, and Diane Dorr-Dorynek's original liner notes to Mingus' 1959 album *Mingus Ah Um*: "Mingus played with poets in 'Frisco ten years or so ago. He feels he hasn't had the proper chance in New York, despite the many efforts to present it, including his own concerts last March with Kenneth Patchen. But music and poetry . . . does seem to have a definite future . . . "

But the best-known words-and-jazz partnerships of the era were undoubtedly those involving Jack Kerouac. The first to be committed to record came after an ill-advised week-long residency at the Village Vanguard just before Christmas, 1957, which ended in chaos most nights because of Kerouac's drinking, which by this stage in his career was becoming something of a problem. However, the Vanguard gig had one silver lining: TV presenter and pianist Steve Allen was in the audience on the first

night—in fact, he accompanied Jack for his second set and decided he wanted to cut an album with Kerouac. This they did in spring 1958, with the sessions being supervised by eminent jazz producer Bob Thiele; the album—*Poetry For The Beat Generation*—appeared in June 1959, on the Hanover label. (The delay in release was caused by the president of the original releasing company, Dot, who decided they wouldn't distribute the disc after all, on account of its "bad taste" and "off-color" material.)

When Thiele mooted the idea of recording a follow-up, Kerouac agreed, but he decided that this time, rather than using Allen on piano he'd prefer two of his favorite tenor sax players, West Coast giants of the instrument, Al Cohn and Zoot Sims. The resulting album—*Blues And Haikus*—was an artistic success, though Thiele would later report that Jack was bitterly disappointed when his heroes packed up and left immediately after the date, treating it as just another studio session.

*Blues and Haikus* appeared in October 1959, and was followed by *Readings By Jack Kerouac On The Beat Generation*, a voice-only collection of poems and prose pieces released on Verve in January 1960. But the biggest media exposure of Kerouac reading, with jazz accompaniment, was in November 1959, when he appeared once again with Steve Allen at the piano on the latter's NBC TV show *The Steve Allen Plymouth Show*. Reading selections from *On the Road* and *Visions of Cody*, the $2,000 appearance put Kerouac-with-jazz into the homes of 35 million Americans. It personified in the popular consciousness the inextricable link between the uniquely American art form of jazz music and the Beat Generation.

# publish & be damned

"Poetry . . . is the outlet for people to say in public what is known in private."

Allen Ginsberg

During the late 40s and early 50s, the San Remo bar, on the northwest corner of Bleecker and MacDougal streets, was the most popular meeting place in Greenwich Village for the bohemian community. In his 1987 book *Down & In: Life in the Underground*, Ron Sukenick described the San Remo as "an actual Village-Bohemian-literary-artistic-underground-mafioso-pinko-revolutionary-subversive-intellectual-existentialist-anti-bourgeois café."

Starting business as a neighborhood working-class bar in 1925, in the postwar years its regular clientele included painters Jackson Pollock and Larry Rivers, avant-garde musician John Cage, Julian Beck and the embryo of his Living Theater group, the novelist James Agee, choreographer Merce Cunningham, writer Frank O'Hara, trumpet star Miles Davis, playwright Tennessee Williams, and the ex-Columbia set of Allen Ginsberg, Lucien Carr, and Jack Kerouac, when he was in town. Ginsberg dubbed the San Remo crowd "subterraneans," a term subsequently used by Kerouac for the title of his 1953 novel (published in 1958), loosely based on the bar's boho patrons, though "hipsters" was the more generally used label at the time.

"It's time we thought about our material. Call them hipsters, the 'beat generation,' 'postwar kids,' or our own displaced persons, whatever you will."

John Clellon Holmes to Jack Kerouac, 1950

Allen Ginsberg—who once encountered the great Welsh poet Dylan Thomas at the San Remo and, embarrassingly, tried to impress him with his work—first visited the bar with Carl Solomon, who took him there to meet the San Francisco poet Philip Lamantia. He had met Solomon, to whom he would dedicate his epic poem "Howl" a few years later, after being admitted as an inpatient to the Columbia Psychiatric Institute (CPI) in June 1949. Ginsberg had been committed to the asylum after being arrested—in the company of hooker Vickie Russell and her fellow-thief and boyfriend Little Jack Melody—in a car filled with stolen goods. The option of the "mad house," as he called it in letters to Jack Kerouac, rather than jail, came about after pressure was brought to bear on the court by his Columbia tutor, Lionel Trilling, and his father, Louis. His eight months in the asylum proved therapeutic, if only because of meeting Carl Solomon.

The two "disturbed" young men struck up an instant friendship. Allen was impressed by Carl's first-hand knowledge of French writers such as Antonin Artaud and Jean Genet (Solomon had lived in Paris for some time) and the fact that he was incarcerated at the CPI for throwing potato salad at the speaker at a Brooklyn College lecture on Dadaism. Similarly, Carl was intrigued by Allen's accounts of his own inspirations and literary ambitions, and those of his hedonistic comrades: Jack Kerouac, Bill Burroughs, and Neal Cassady.

Another San Remo regular was John Clellon Holmes, who would have the distinction of being the first writer to have a book relating to the Beat scene as such published. Certainly, Jack Kerouac was the first of the Beat writers to have a novel published per se, but 1950's *The Town and the City* was an account of his early life in a "Wolfean" narrative genre and not of the free-flowing style he would pioneer with *On the Road*.

**Previous pages:** Lawrence Ferlinghetti at his City Lights bookstore in 1957, prior to his trial for publishing Ginsberg's *Howl*.

**Opposite:** Carl Solomon in his SoHo, New York, apartment in 1953.

**Below:** William Burroughs (left) with the poet, author, and playwright Alan Ansen, outside the San Remo Café c. 1953.

"Only the most bitter among them would call their reality a nightmare and protest that they have indeed lost something, the future. But ever since they were old enough to imagine one, that has been in jeopardy anyway."

John Clellon Holmes, "This is the Beat Generation," *New York Times Magazine*, November 16, 1952

Born in Holyoke, Massachusetts, in 1926, Holmes first came across the Beats-to-be at a 1948 July 4th party thrown by Allen Ginsberg in a meager Spanish Harlem apartment he was subletting. Alan Harrington, a critic for the *New Yorker* magazine, was one of the guests and he brought Holmes along. It was there that he met Allen Ginsberg, Lucien Carr, and, crucially, Jack Kerouac, with whom he had an instant rapport.

The two writers became good friends, even though Holmes was essentially a more "square" individual. But, as a shrewd observer, and with a sympathetic understanding of what the embryo Beat scene was about, he soon became a part of it himself. In fact, a conversation between Kerouac and Holmes at the latter's Lexington Avenue apartment in fall, 1949, is credited with the first use of the term "Beat Generation," for it was there that they discussed what they would call this movement as opposed to the "Lost Generation" associated with Hemingway, F. Scott Fitzgerald, and company. Back then, before any of them had had any writing published, they were of course referring to the scene generally rather than to a group of writers. Though Holmes credited Kerouac with actually coining the term, both

Kerouac and Ginsberg later acknowledged they'd first heard "beat" used as an adjective by Herbert Huncke.

Immersing himself in the scene, Holmes began chronicling it in much the same way as Kerouac had done on the road, but with more immediate results. In March 1951, he showed Jack the manuscript of his recently completed novel, titled *The Beat Generation*, closely based on the characters and lives of Jack Kerouac, Allen Ginsberg, Neal Cassady, and Herbert Huncke. Jack was dismayed that Holmes could appropriate what he felt was "his" term as a title and cover territory with which he had been persevering for literally years. His response was to declare that he was going to finish his own novel, "as fast as I can, exactly like it happened, all in a rush," and he proceeded with his typewriter marathon that produced *On the Road*. He also claimed some kind of ownership of the term "Beat Generation," suggesting Holmes call his book *The Beat Ones*. In the event Holmes named his novel *Go*, and it became a best-seller when it was published by Scribner (with Holmes receiving an impressive $20,000 advance) in fall 1952. It was the first Beat novel to go into print.

Holmes was also responsible for raising the profile of the Beats when he followed up the publication of *Go* with an article in the *New York Times Magazine* titled "This is the Beat Generation." The piece brought the notion of "Beat" into the popular arena for the first time: "It involves a sort of nakedness of mind and, ultimately, of soul; a feeling of being reduced to the bedrock of consciousness." The term was coined once and for all as far as the public consciousness was concerned.

Allen Ginsberg, in the meantime, had been developing his writing to the point where he too would soon see his work in print. A month after his discharge from Columbia Psychiatric Institute, in late March 1950, he'd attended a reading by the eminent poet William Carlos Williams at the Guggenheim Museum in New York. Williams lived and worked near Ginsberg's hometown of Paterson, New Jersey, and had been publishing an epic poem called *Paterson* since 1946. In it, he intermingled his own poetry and prose with quotes, letters, excerpts from newspapers, and so on, and by 1949 he had published Book Three of the ongoing work.

Following the reading, Allen wrote a long letter to Williams expressing his literary ambition and also enclosing nine poems. The 66-year-old was delighted with the communication and impressed enough by the letter to include it—and a later one—in its entirety in Book Four of *Paterson*, published in 1951. Although he wasn't as enthusiastic about Allen's poetry at that juncture, it was the beginning of a long literary relationship that Allen would later claim to have helped free his poetic voice. Over the next couple of years, under Williams' influence, his writing went through radical changes to the point early in 1952 where Williams declared it merited publication. The open form Williams inspired in Allen's poetry—framed by the page, the lines defined by syllable count or breath length—would subsequently result in his first major publishing triumph, *Howl* in 1956, for which Williams would write the Introduction.

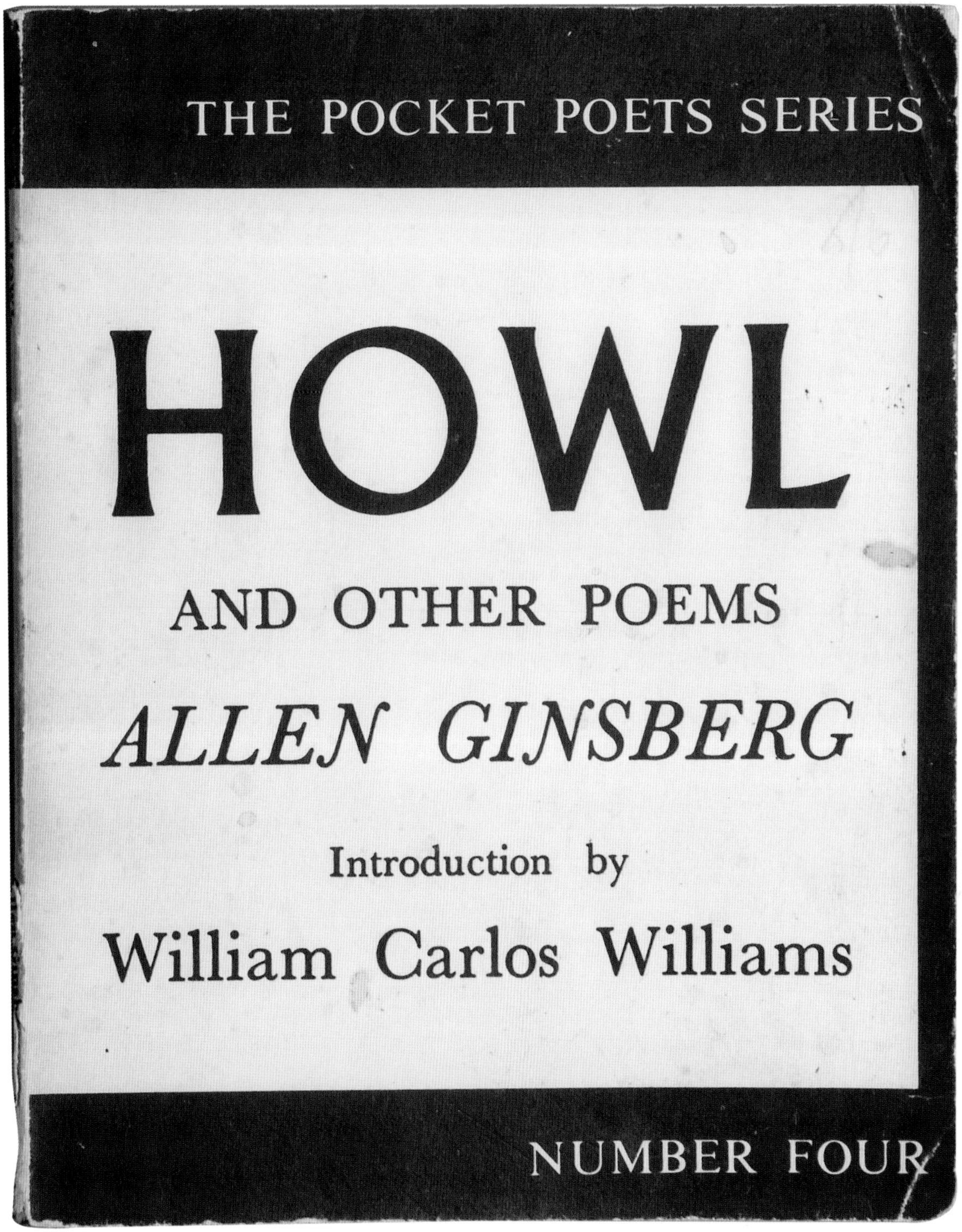

THE POCKET POETS SERIES

# HOWL
## AND OTHER POEMS
### ALLEN GINSBERG

Introduction by

William Carlos Williams

NUMBER FOUR

**Opposite:** John Clellon Holmes (left) with Jack Kerouac in 1960, by which time both were literary celebrities.

**Above:** The original edition of Ginsberg's *Howl*, as published in 1956 as part of City Lights Books' Pocket Poets series.

# the killing of Joan Burroughs

Bill Burroughs' first trip in search of the little-known drug yage, which it was claimed increased telepathic sensitivity in its jungle Indian users, as well as inducing vivid hours-long "visions" while awake, began early in July 1951. Accompanied by Lewis Marker, a 21-year-old American studying at Mexico City College, he set off for the high Andes in Ecuador.

Burroughs' quest turned out to be fruitless, as did his hopes of consummating a relationship with the heterosexual Marker, but he would return in search of the "ultimate high" a year and a half later in very different circumstances.

Joan Burroughs, whose amphetamine habit had given way to alcoholism, was in an even more debilitated state than when she was on Benzedrine. When Lucien Carr and Allen Ginsberg visited in August 1951, while Bill was still on his South American quest, they were shocked by her bloated face, thinning hair, and rough skin pockmarked with open sores. She told Hal Chase, also now living in Mexico City, that she was suffering from an incurable blood disease.

Burroughs arrived home at the beginning of September, just missing his friends. A few days later, on the 6th, he went over to the apartment of another friend, John Healy, carrying in a bag a cheap .38 Star automatic handgun he wanted to sell because it was shooting low. Since childhood Bill had been fascinated with firearms and had spent most of his days living in Texas doing "target practice" with an array of weapons. He continued to think of himself as a marksman, something Joan would tease him about when she wanted to annoy him.

There was a party developing at Healy's place above the American-owned Bounty bar, where he worked at 122 Calle Monterrey, with people coming and going around the time Bill—and soon after him, Joan—arrived. He and his wife had already had a lot to drink during the day, and now it was early evening. Lewis Marker and a friend (Eddie Wood) were there, as were Healy and one of Burroughs' oldest friends, Kells Elvins, and several others. What happened next has become the stuff of legend—even though the details have always been open to conjecture.

Apparently in response to Joan goading him about his shooting ability as he drunkenly waved the automatic in the air, Bill suggested they play their "William Tell act," though it seems they had never done anything like that before. Joan put an empty

water tumbler on her head, turning sideways as she giggled, "I can't watch this—you know I can't stand the sight of blood." Bill fired from about six feet away, and missed, the bullet entering his wife's brain through her upper left forehead. She died soon afterward at a nearby Red Cross station, while he waited outside.

The shooting took place in an alcove off the main room of the apartment where the party was getting into full swing, and the only actual witnesses to her death were Marker and Wood. Initially, when questioned by police, Bill stuck to the "William Tell" version of events and the Mexican newspapers had a field day, the headline in the next morning's La Prensa screaming in Spanish, "HE WANTED TO DEMONSTRATE HIS MARKSMANSHIP, AND HE KILLED HIS WIFE." He was held in custody for two weeks on murder charges, during which time he changed his story, claiming the gun had accidentally misfired while he was trying to sell it to one of his friends.

The new testimony was probably at the instigation of his Mexican attorney, Bernabé Jurado—who one newspaper later referred to as "the underworld lawyer"—who coached the witnesses in getting the same story right (of how Burroughs accidentally fired the gun while pulling back its slide). It's also since been claimed that the attorney bribed four ballistics experts to support the story. Whatever, via the generally corrupt legal system in Mexico at the time, Burroughs was released just 13 days later on bail of $2,312, which sum was donated by his brother Mortimer, who had hotfooted it from St. Louis.

His bail was a form of probation, with Burroughs having to check in at the prison every Monday. The restriction of Burroughs' liberty probably spurred his decision to abscond from Mexico City in December 1952. Unable to return to the capital without risk of arrest, Burroughs resumed his search for the elusive yage in the jungles of Peru, finally sampling "the most powerful drug I have ever experienced . . . the most complete derangement of the senses."

**Opposite:** Joan Vollmer Burroughs, one of the few known pictures of her after she began living as the common-law wife of William Burroughs.

**Below:** A disheveled-looking Burroughs giving his side of the story, while being interrogated by the Mexican police authorities after the fatal shooting.

'I wish to put on record my gratitude to the Mexican authorities, who have treated me with every kind of consideration and in the most correct way."

Bill Burroughs, *Excelsior* newspaper, September 8, 1951

7

NEUROTICA

50f

THE *NEWEST* SCIENCE OF MENTAL HEALING

# Epizootics

"If you believe you're a poet, then you're saved."

Gregory Corso, 1987

Among the movers and shakers who frequented the San Remo was Jay Landesman, who edited an influential arts/culture magazine called *Neurotica*. In the spring 1950 edition a powerful piece by Carl Solomon (who'd been discharged from CPI in December 1959) appeared, titled "Report from the Asylum— Afterthoughts of a Shock Patient," published under the pseudonym Carl Goy, plus four verses by Allen Ginsberg. The Ginsberg poetry, "Song: Fie My Fum," was an excerpt from a longer poem, "Pull My Daisy." It was the first time his work had appeared in a commercial publication.

In late 1950 Allen Ginsberg was having a drink in a Greenwich Village lesbian bar called the Pony Stable, when he noticed a young man sitting nearby, accompanied by a stack of typed poems. They fell into conversation, and he was struck both by the 20-year-old's fervor, and by the quality of his writing. From then on, he and Gregory Corso would be friends.

Corso had been born in 1930, just across the street from the San Remo bar. Coming from a broken home, he had passed through the care of several foster families. His teenage years had been spent living on the street, where petty theft was one of the few options for survival. When he wasn't on the street,

he was in and out of various penal institutions, culminating in a three-year sentence at a prison near the Canadian border in 1947 for an audacious robbery at a branch of the Household Finance credit company. Like Neal Cassady, in prison Corso had educated himself by reading voraciously—*The Brothers Karamazov*, ancient Greek and Roman history, and European classics—finding in poetry (his particular favorite was the English romantic poet Shelley) intellectual stimulus and emotional escape.

Ginsberg introduced Corso to Jack Kerouac, John Clellon Holmes, and the others, and though he quickly became accepted on the scene, he would later admit it was harder for him to feel one of them because of the time he'd spent in jail. "To me, friends were very hard to make, especially in prison . . . you're a poet and the other guy's a poet, automatically you were friends . . . I didn't see it that way. It took a little while before I became friends with these guys."

Gregory Corso would, however, become a central figure and major voice among the Beat Generation writers, initially aided in no small way by Allen Ginsberg's support—which was characteristic of the active enthusiasm Ginsberg frequently displayed for the work of those around him.

During the closing months of 1951, Allen Ginsberg found himself acting as unofficial literary agent for Jack Kerouac's first draft of *On the Road*, hawking it round publisher after publisher with little success. His options narrowing, he spotted a chance when Carl Solomon started work as an editor on an occasional basis for his uncle AA Wyn, founder and owner of Ace Books. Though Ace was a "pulp fiction" publisher specializing in cheap mass-market paperbacks dominated by hard-boiled crime novels, westerns, and science fiction, it was worth a shot. After intense lobbying on his behalf by both Ginsberg and Solomon, Ace eventually offered Jack an advance of $1,000 for *On the Road*, a sum he felt was somewhat derisory in light of John Clellon Holmes receiving 20 times that amount for *Go*. (In fact, it would be another five years and many re-writes later before *On the Road* was finally published, and not by Ace but instead the Viking Press.)

It was during this time, in early 1952, that Jack embarked on his affair with Carolyn Cassady, after moving into the Cassady home on Russell Street, San Francisco. He was working on revisions to *On the Road* and Carolyn made him living quarters in the attic, complete with a mattress on the floor, a desk, radio, and lots of books. Neal's railroad job was about to take him south for a couple of weeks, to San Luis Obispo, leaving his best friend alone with his wife and the three Cassady children: Cathleen, Jamie, and John. As he bid farewell, he made a cryptic remark that was to re-awaken the sexual frisson Jack and Carolyn had sensed back in Denver in 1947: "I don't know about leaving you two—you know what they say, 'My best pal and my best gal' . . . " Adding, "Just don't do anything I wouldn't do—okay, kids?"

But they were shocked and embarrassed. Carolyn, despite being aware of her husband's womanizing, held strictly conventional views regarding marital fidelity. Jack's attitude was similarly puritanical regarding sleeping with the wife of his best friend—you didn't even think about it. But when Carolyn confronted her husband about the remark on his return, his reply was to say that he wouldn't have been upset if something *had* happened between them—" . . . why not? I thought it would be fine." She was so taken aback and angry at his indifference that she seduced their house guest one night while Neal was working. It was the start of a bizarre three-way relationship that was, nevertheless, no conventional *ménage à trois*. Neither party mentioned it to the other, though Neal was probably aware of it almost from the start, as Carolyn told Kerouac biographer Steve Turner: "I think Neal must have known right away, but he never said anything . . . We wouldn't have dreamed about discussing it. We didn't even admit it to ourselves." Uncharacteristically, Jack never referred to the affair, even obliquely, in his writings: "People don't realize the times we were living in. We were still ruled by Victorian ideals. That's why Jack never wrote about the affair—it just wasn't done."

In July 1952, Allen Ginsberg secured another $1,000 advance from Ace, this time for what would be Bill Burroughs' debut novel and the next published book to come out of the Beat Generation. While he was still living with Joan in Mexico City, Burroughs began writing the autobiographical narrative in spring 1950 under the working title *Junk*. By the end of that year he had completed the first draft under the pseudonym of William Lee, who was also the first-person central character.

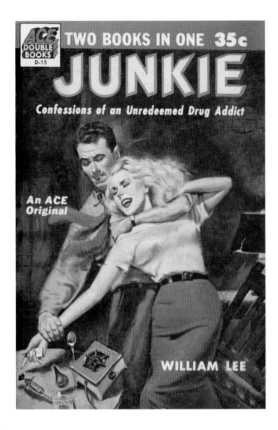

"I think all writers write for an audience.

There is no such thing as writing for yourself."

William Burroughs, to Allen Ginsberg

Initially unenthusiastic about writing the novel, Burroughs had been cajoled into it by an insistent Allen, who was impressed by his letter-writing and verbal accounts of life as a small-time heroin pusher. It turned out to be a harrowing document of his 14-year-old heroin addiction and it is still considered by many as the definitive statement on the subject. The text proved memorable in subject matter and style, the laconic and deliberately distant tone of the narrator contrasting with the brutal frankness of the actual narrative. Burroughs talks directly to the reader as an observer, reporting the feelings and motives of the various characters he encounters on the streets of New York, at a narcotics hospital/prison in Kentucky, and in New Orleans and Mexico City. When the novel finally appeared, Ace felt obliged to accompany the text with various disclaimers stating: "For the protection of the reader, we have inserted occasional parenthetical notes to indicate where the author clearly departs from accepted medical fact or makes unsubstantiated statements in an effort to justify his actions."

The Burroughs' "marital" life was under pressure most of the time the couple lived in the Mexican capital. Both were nursing their addictions—his predominantly with heroin, while Joan had turned to alcohol in the absence of a ready supply of Benzedrine inhalers. Their sexual relationship was similarly unsatisfactory—Bill was impotent when he was high on heroin, and when he wasn't he preferred to indulge himself with local rent boys (at 40 cents a time). But, as Lucien Carr observed when he visited the pair in August 1950, intellectually they still enjoyed an almost telepathic understanding, playing weird brain games

where one "mind read" what the other was drawing on a sheet of paper.

Perhaps, therefore, it was an element of mental trust (along with inebriation on both parts) that led to the bizarre "William Tell" shooting game in which Burroughs fatally shot his wife through the head on September 6, 1951. After the trial and his release on bail, Burroughs left Mexico in December 1952, headed not for the US but instead for South America, where he would make his second trip in search of the native Indians' hallucinogenic drug yage.

*Junkie* was published in May 1953 as a 35-cent back-to-back double with *Narcotics Agent* by Maurice Helbrant. At the time such two-for-the-price-of-one editions were a trademark of Ace Books (though the publisher didn't originate the concept) and the lurid cover for *Junkie*, along with the sensationalist sub-title "Confessions of an Unredeemed Drug Addict," likewise reflected the newsstand readership on which the publisher relied for the bulk of its sales. But the downmarket strategy worked. Although the book received no reviews, it nevertheless sold more than 113,000 copies in its first year. Burroughs wasn't around to witness its publication, which went unnoticed by the literary world, and it would be six years before his next book would be published. By that time, the Beat Generation had become recognized as a potent force in modern American culture.

# the west coast scene

"We had gone beyond a point of no return—

and we were ready for it, for a point of no return . . .

We wanted voice and we wanted vision."

Michael McClure

With its roots in the artistic community that had flourished there since the immediate postwar years, by the mid-50s San Francisco and the West Coast scene generally were key in the emergence of the Beat movement. 'Frisco had become as vibrant a nucleus for the Beats as Greenwich Village, with dozens of jazz clubs, coffeehouses, art galleries, and bookstores—the most famous being City Lights, opened in 1953 by Lawrence Ferlinghetti.

Ferlinghetti was born into an Italian-Portuguese-Sephardic immigrant family in Yonkers, New York, in March 1919. After attending the University of North Carolina he served in the US Navy during World War II as a Lieutenant Commander, going on to Columbia University after the war, where he received a Masters degree. Ferlinghetti moved to Paris to continue his academic work in 1947, enrolling for a doctorate at the Sorbonne. While living in the French capital he met up with Kenneth Rexroth, a prime architect of the West Coast poetry scene, and of what became known as the San Francisco Renaissance.

Rexroth persuaded Ferlinghetti to move to San Francisco, which he did in 1951 (at this time he was still using his family's anglicized name of Ferling). Ferlinghetti spent the next couple of years painting and teaching French in an adult education program. He also began covering local exhibitions for *Art Digest*, and writing poetry reviews for the *San Francisco Chronicle*. Through Rexroth's literary get-togethers he got to know the local writing community, and in 1953 he met Peter D. Martin, who told him he wanted to open a bookstore promoting what he was sure represented an imminent revolution in "literary" reading—the coming-of-age of the paperback.

In June 1953, after they became business partners with a $500 investment by Ferlinghetti, the two opened America's first bookstore to be devoted exclusively to paperbacks, located at

"Paperbacks weren't considered real books in the book trade. Up till then it was just murder mysteries, potboilers, 25-cent pocket books sold in newsstands. When the New York publishers started publishing quality paperbacks, there was no place to buy them."

Lawrence Ferlinghetti

261 Columbus Avenue. They called it City Lights, the same title as a magazine Martin had started up in July 1952, which published work by San Francisco writers including Robert Duncan, Philip Lamantia, and Ferlinghetti (as Ferling). Martin named the magazine—which only ran to five issues—for the Charlie Chaplin movie *City Lights*.

From the start Ferlinghetti thought his partner's idea of a paperback bookstore was brilliant. "Pocket books," as Martin called them, were still not taken seriously in the book trade, their main point of sale being drugstores, newsstands, and displays on revolving racks in bus and railroad stations. The format was generally associated with down-market books, and although a few brave companies such as Dell, Avon, and Signet published some "serious" literature in paperback, their titles didn't receive much exposure in the local drugstore. Traditional bookstores carried few paperbacks—except for Penguin books, which in any case had to be imported from England as the company had yet to establish a North American operation.

The "flatiron"-shaped shop (on the junction of Columbus and what is now Jack Kerouac Alley) was an immediate success, selling new quality paperbacks along with radical newspapers and avant-garde magazines, with stock moving faster than they were able to replace it. Within a few months City Lights, with its letter rack for customers of no fixed address, and lost-and-found, pads-to-let, and even lonely hearts ads pinned to the notice board, became a magnet and focal point for the San Francisco Beat scene and its growing number of followers.

When the *City Lights* magazine folded, Martin decided to move back to his native New York, and Ferlinghetti, now using his family's original name, bought him out for $1,000 in early 1955. From his days as a student in Paris, Ferlinghetti was familiar with the idea of independent booksellers also publishing books, and he set up City Lights Books to publish small editions of poetry in paperback. On August 10, 1955 he launched the "Pocket Poets" series with a collection of his own work, *Pictures of the Gone World*; this was quickly followed by titles by Kenneth Rexroth and Kenneth Patchen. Then, in October 1956, City Lights made literary history when it published number four in the Pocket Poets series, *Howl and Other Poems*, by Allen Ginsberg.

**Previous pages:** Allen Ginsberg's apartment at 1010 Montgomery Street, San Francisco, where, in spring–summer 1955 he wrote the first draft of *Howl*.

**Right:** Three key titles from City Lights' ground-breaking Pocket Poets series.

**Below:** Outside the City Lights bookstore in 1956 (left to right): Bob Donlin, Neal Cassady, Allen Ginsberg, Robert LaVinge, and Lawrence Ferlinghetti.

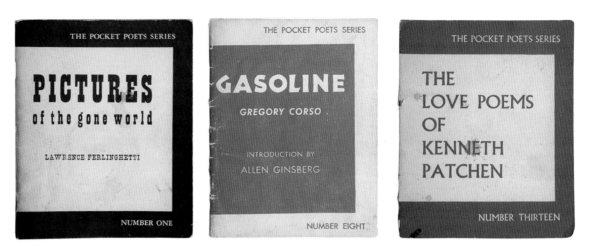

# the "howl" trial

The first print run of *Howl and Other Poems* was only 1,000 copies. But in a letter to Lawrence Ferlinghetti, Allen Ginsberg wondered whether they would ever sell even that many.

*Howl* appeared on the shelves of City Lights in October 1956. Because of the extreme sexual language contained between its simple black-and-white covers, Ferlinghetti had taken the precaution of consulting the American Civil Liberties Union (ACLU), who were on hand to defend the volume in the event of prosecution. The feared legions of the law failed to descend on the Columbus Avenue bookstore, however, and *Howl* remained on display, selling in sufficient numbers to warrant a second printing within a few weeks.

It was when that second delivery was made from the British printers, Villiers, that legal problems first appeared on the horizon, in the shape of US Customs officer Chester McPhee. McPhee declared the material to be obscene and seized 520 copies of the book on March 25, 1957.

Ferlinghetti quickly arranged for a new edition to be printed in the US, thus avoiding any Customs action or embargo. But local police had been alerted to the ploy, and when the US Attorney decided not to prosecute City Lights and the Customs department had to release the books, officers of the law quickly stepped in and raided the bookstore. They arrested City Lights shop manager Shigeyoshi Murao for selling literature likely to corrupt juveniles, and his boss Lawrence Ferlinghetti for publishing it in the first place.

The *San Francisco Chronicle* ran a headline based on the sing-along tune "Mama Don't Allow," which read: "The Cops Don't Allow No Renaissance Here" as they reported the raid, while Ferlinghetti wrote a piece for the same newspaper, thanking the Collector of Customs and now the police for the great publicity job they'd done on behalf of the Pocket Poets series.

The "Howl" obscenity trial eventually came to court in early summer 1957, by which time the book was selling in thousands, in front of Judge Clayton Horn. Chief council for the defense was J.W. "Jake" Ehrlich, while the prosecution was represented by the elderly D.A. Ralph McIntock. Through the following months the defense presented an array of written and verbal statements in support of the poem (only "Howl" was on trial, not any of the other poems). Local poets, including Kenneth Rexroth, Robert Duncan, and Kenneth Patchen were arraigned on its behalf, as well as respected literary critics such as Mark

# "Probably the most remarkable single poem published by a young man since the Second World War."

Kenneth Rexroth in his court statement in support of "Howl"

**Above:** Ferlinghetti in court (left) next to his co-defendent, bookstore manager Shigeyoshi Murao, on August 1, 1957.

**Opposite:** Ferlinghetti proudly displays the offending title in the City Lights store while the City of San Francisco prepares its case against him. He would be charged with violating section 311 of the Penal Code, which prohibits a person from writing, composing, printing, publishing or selling "any obscene pictures or print."

Schorer. Judge Horn directed these experts to testify whether they thought the language was "relevant" to the intent and theme of the poem rather than if they themselves saw it as obscene.

Summing up, the prosecution asked Judge Horn to consider the effect it would have on American society if such "Filthy, vulgar, obscene and disgusting language" was permitted. The judge took two weeks to make up his mind and on October 3, 1957, he declared "Howl" could not be obscene if it had "redeeming social significance," ruling that the poem could not be suppressed by the local authorities. Over the coming years the legal precedent was to be used by the Grove Press and numerous others to publish such classic works as D.H. Lawrence's *Lady Chatterley's Lover* and Henry Miller's *Tropic of Capricorn*

"I can remember driving down to North Beach with my folks and seeing Bob Kaufman out there on the street. I didn't know he was Bob Kaufman at the time. He had little pieces of Band-Aid tape all over his face, about two inches wide, and little smaller ones like two inches long—and all of them made into crosses. He came up to the cars, and he was babbling poetry into these cars. He came up to the car I was riding in, and my folks, and started jabbering this stuff into the car. I knew that this was exceptional use of the human voice and the human mind."

Ken Kesey, describing how he saw Bob Kaufman on the streets of San Francisco's North Beach during a visit to the city with his family in the 50s

Others were drawn to California in the early years of the 50s. While Ferlinghetti was still in Paris in 1950, nearly 600 miles north of San Francisco, in Portland, Oregon, three undergraduates at Reed College moved into the basement (previously the coal cellar) of a rooming house on Southeast Lambert Street. All three residents of the gloomy pad—Gary Snyder, Philip Whalen, and Lew Welch—were budding poets, who subsequently became embroiled in the San Francisco scene. Snyder, their most prominent voice, published poems in the college's literary magazine, and by the time he'd moved to the Bay Area of San Francisco in 1952, sharing an apartment with Philip Whalen, he was already immersing himself in oriental art, Chinese poetry, and Zen meditation. He would subsequently exert considerable influence on the Beats—particularly Jack Kerouac, who saw in Snyder's rigorously simple lifestyle and oneness with nature, the *dharma* to which he could only aspire.

While early versions of *On the Road* were rejected by successive publishers, Jack was spending longer periods in San Francisco, staying with Neal and Carolyn Cassady on Russian Hill. It was there in 1952 that he completed his greatest work of "bop prosody" spontaneous writing, an alternative version of *On the Road*, eventually published in 1973 as *Visions of Cody*. In August 1952 the Cassadys moved to a much bigger house, 50 miles south of San Francisco in San José, Neal having resumed his job as a guard with the Southern Pacific railroad. Jack arrived there in February 1954, as did Allen Ginsberg later in June, having spent the first six months of the year in Mexico. The Beats were still on the road, but the West Coast was increasingly as much an anchor between their wanderings as New York City.

After spending a couple of months with Neal and Carolyn, Allen moved up to San Francisco in August 1954, where he would meet movers and shakers of the local scene, including Kenneth Rexroth (through an introductory letter from William Carlos Williams) and Robert Duncan. He would also renew his friendship with Philip Lamantia and, in December 1954, meet and fall in love with Peter Orlovsky. Ginsberg was entranced by a portrait of the 21-year-old poet painted by Robert LaVigne and even more so by LaVigne's companion at the time, Orlovsky himself, when they met at the artist's apartment. Soon they became lovers, and remained so for the rest of Ginsberg's life. He also met the three Zen Buddhist acolytes from Portland—Snyder, Whalen, and Welch—and introduced them to Jack when he arrived back in California after a spell in Mexico, in September 1955.

Other influential new faces in San Francisco between 1954–55 included New Orleans-born Black American poet Bob Kaufman, who had met Bill Burroughs and Allen Ginsberg in the 40s when he was studying literature at the New School university in Greenwich Village. Kaufman wrote surrealist poetry variously influenced by Walt Whitman, jazz, and the French existentialists. A committed anarchist—police once confiscated from the window of the Co-Existence Bagel Shop one of his poems, which described the day Hitler "moved to San Francisco, became an ordinary/policeman, devoted himself to stamping out Beatniks"— he remained in San Francisco until his death in 1986.

Another key name was Michael McClure, who would be responsible for initiating a seminal milestone in Beat history, and in Ginsberg's career in particular. They met at a reading given by the eminent British poet W.H. Auden, and McClure told the *New Yorker* about a reading he was planning that was to be held at the Six Gallery on October 7, 1955. He confessed he didn't have the time to put into the organization of it all, and Allen agreed to take over the reins. Advertised as "Six Poets at the Six Gallery," the event was emceed by Kenneth Rexroth, and featured Rexroth, McClure, Philip Lamantia, Gary Snyder, Philip Whalen, and Allen Ginsberg. In the audience were Jack Kerouac—who was invited to read, but declined—Neal Cassady, Lawrence Ferlinghetti, and Peter Orlovsky.

What marked the occasion as historic was when Allen read for the first time his epic—and yet to be completed—"Howl for Carl Solomon," the first and final sections of which he'd written in a marathon session the previous August. The audience was shell-shocked from the moment he launched into what would become the most famous opening lines in Beat literature: "I saw the best minds of my generation destroyed by madness, starving hysterical naked / dragging themselves through the negro streets at dawn looking for an angry fix . . . ," delivering his verses more in the manner of a revival meeting preacher than a poet. Often described as the catalyst that launched the so-called San Francisco Renaissance, as well as establishing Allen Ginsberg as a literary voice to be reckoned with, the event would come to symbolize the bringing together of the East and West Coast wings of the Beat Generation.

The Six Gallery reading made all who took part local literary heroes, especially Ginsberg, who had only read the first part of "Howl" at the event. He now set about writing the middle section, and finalizing the incomplete third, as well as adding "Footnote to Howl," which would form a fourth section. Immediately after the reading he had decided that "Howl" would form the basis of a Pocket Poets edition, and set himself a deadline of April 1956 to get the poem finished and to select the others for inclusion.

The entire poem was premièred before a live audience on March 18, 1956, when a repeat of the Six Gallery event was staged at the University of California, Berkeley. The audience reaction, as Allen read (performed would be a better word) the complete "Howl" for the first time in public, was ecstatic, the crowd hissing and booing when he invoked the name of the Biblical idol Moloch in his tirade against the worship of money in the capitalist metropolis:

"Moloch whose mind is pure machinery! / Moloch whose blood is running money! / Moloch whose fingers are ten armies! / Moloch whose breast is a cannibal dynamo! / Moloch whose ear is a smoking tomb!"

The other poems chosen by Ginsberg to be featured in the slim, 75-cents City Lights volume included classics-to-be "A Supermarket In California," "America," and "Sunflower Sutra," but when *Howl and Other Poems* finally appeared in October 1956, it was the title poem which attracted most attention. Notoriety, too, when it was brought to court on charges of obscenity, with the judge eventually ruling in its favor, having widespread implications for the whole issue of freedom of expression and censorship in the literary arena.

Opposite left: Michael McClure reading in San Francsico, February 1957.

Opposite right: Lawrence Ferlinghetti performing at a reading, March 1957.

Below: Ginsberg working on "Howl" in the kitchen of his San Francisco apartment.

"We had all those people, they came to the house before all that happened. (Like Phil Lamantia came round, I think, when they discovered the [magic] mushrooms, and had a mushroom session.) But there was no big thing, that was made up by the media, and then Ginsberg pushed it along. None of it was in a 'movement,' they were just funky individuals, artists, and poets, just doing their own thing, but they got blocked together by journalists."

Carolyn Cassady on the San Francisco scene, 2006

# zen and the beats

Though famously practiced by Jack Kerouac and Allen Ginsberg, the earliest figure on the Beat scene to take up Zen Buddhism was West Coast poet Gary Snyder. Fascinated by Chinese painting from age nine—and subsequently with Chinese poetry as a teenager—when he moved to the Bay Area in 1952, the 22-year-old created for himself an austere lifestyle based on the teachings of the great Zen masters and the writings of Japanese philosopher D.T. Suzuki, in particular. Suzuki, who died in 1966 at age 96, was the author of several key books and essays which were highly influential in spreading interest in Zen to the West.

Suzuki had also been a major influence on the Englishman Alan Watts, who first heard him lecture in London in 1936. Watts had moved to the US in 1938, and would become the leading popularizer of Zen in America in the 50s and 60s. Along with another important Zen teacher, Saburo Hasegawa, he taught at the American Academy of Asian Studies in San Francisco, attended by Snyder in the mid-50s, and which Suzuki visited while teaching at Columbia University in the same period. In 1957 Watts published one of the most widely read Zen primers, *The Way of Zen*.

Along with the basic tenets of Zen—of the importance of moment-by-moment awareness and understanding the nature of things by direct experience—Suzuki stressed Zen wasn't just a state of consciousness but a way of life. It was a life of humility, labor, service, prayer, gratitude, and meditation, that Gary Snyder embraced wholeheartedly.

Snyder lived in a primitive, 12-foot-square retreat in Marin County, to the north of San Francisco. There were no chairs, and Snyder sat cross-legged on a straw mat when he was meditating or eating his specialty horsemeat sukiyaki, cooked on a portable Japanese hibachi grill. When they met him in fall 1955, he had a profound influence on Allen Ginsberg and Jack Kerouac, particularly Kerouac.

Early the previous year Jack had begun studying Buddhism and meditating after reading and being deeply moved by *Life of the Buddha* by 1st-century Indian poet Ashvagosha. In Buddhism he found a humanitarian ethic based in personal humility, the antithesis of the guilt-and-redemption postulated by the Catholicism with which he'd grown up. For him, the basic Zen emphasis on the importance of "the moment" confirmed his belief in the role of sponaneity in his writing, encapsulated in his own personal motto: "first thought, best thought."

Snyder's spartan existence and devotion to Zen impressed Jack profoundly. At the end of October 1955, the two climbed the 12,000-foot Matterhorn mountain in the Yosemite National Park, the expedition becoming the inspiration for *The Dharma Bums*, published in 1959. The novel, with Snyder represented as "Japhy Ryder," described the influence of Zen on aspects of the West Coast Beat scene at a time when Snyder himself was preparing to leave for Japan to pursue a more formal study of Zen in 1956. When he returned, 12 years later, he had become a seminal figure in post-Beat hippie counterculture.

Like Jack, Allen Ginsberg had already been aware of Zen before meeting Snyder, as far back as his undergraduate days at Columbia. But it was after meeting him that he really immersed himself in Zen-inspired meditation, distinguished by the repetitious "Om" that he carried with him as a personal mantra for the rest of his life.

Jack, on the other hand, never actually practiced a meditation posture he could sustain for any length of time due to a problem with his knees. But he did write a summary of Buddhism in 1953, initially meant as "guide notes" for Ginsberg, which by 1956 became a vast collection of poems, haikus, meditations, pieces from letters, even blues lyrics, under the title *Some of the Dharma*, eventually published by Viking in 1997.

By the end of the 50s, Zen had become something of a cult interest among the Beat-inspired bohemian young, especially on the West Coast. In 1959, a Zen priest called Shunryu Suzuki arrived in San Francisco from Japan. He had been sent over to

**Right:** The 1997 first Viking edition of Jack Kerouac's enormous Zen treatise, *Some of the Dharma*, written between 1953 and 1956.

**Far right:** Zen teacher and author D.T. (Daisetz Teitaro) Suzuki.

**Below:** Gary Snyder after his move to Kyoto, Japan, in 1956, where he studied at Zen monasteries until 1968.

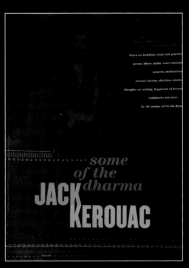

serve as high priest at a small Japanese-American temple, Sokoji, in the city's Japantown. His presence became an immediate talking point among the would-be Zen disciples; some even mistakenly thought he was the guru D.T. Suzuki, to which he would reply, "No, he's the big Suzuki, I'm the little Suzuki."

Attracting far more western followers than those from the Californian Japanese community, Suzuki went on to establish the San Francisco Zen Center and later, in 1966, a hot springs resort in Los Padres National Forest—the Tassajara Zen Mountain Center. By then Zen could have been thought of as just another of the numerous Eastern religious cults springing up in California in the mid-to-late 60s, but in the 50s, it represented a genuine and radical manifestation of the spiritual side of the Beat attitude.

"Absolute faith is placed in a man's inner being. For whatever authority there is in Zen, all comes from within."

D.T. Suzuki, Zen teacher, philosopher, and writer

By the end of 1956 the media spotlight turned on the Beat Generation in a big way, its focus very much on the West Coast, where most of the action now seemed to be. The North Beach area of San Francisco became ultra-trendy among the young bohemian crowd and their would-be-boho followers, with bars and coffeeshops such as the Co-Existence Bagel Shop, the Place, and the Vesuvio Café all competing for the custom of Beats and tourists alike, while experiments in poetry-and-jazz attracted a lot of attention at venues such as The Cellar and the Coffee Gallery. In late October 1956 Allen Ginsberg hit the headlines when he challenged a heckler to strip at a Los Angeles reading and then proceeded to take off his own clothes, too. It was in the *San Francisco Chronicle* that the word "beatnik" first appeared in April 1958, reporting on a North Beach party thrown by *Look* magazine for a picture spread on the West Coast Beat Generation. Southern California was the location for a Beat-inspired "colony," which sprang up in Venice, a Pacific Coast suburb of LA, and became the subject of *The Holy Barbarians*, a famous—some would say infamous—study of the Beat lifestyle by Lawrence Lipton, published in 1959.

In a less sensationalist vein, in September 1956 the *New York Times Book Review* reported enthusiastically about the "Pacific Coast upstarts" in a piece titled "West Coast Rhythms" by Richard Eberhart, which was the first East Coast recognition of the San Francisco Renaissance by the mainstream press. The San Francisco Renaissance was also the subject of a piece in the unlikely context of the influential women's magazine *Mademoiselle*, in February 1957. Also, in spring 1957 *Evergreen Review* first appeared. This was a seminal literary journal publishing a broad range of writers including Albert Camus, Samuel Beckett, Bertolt Brecht, and Jean-Paul Sartre, as well as all the leading Beats. Published bi-monthly by the Grove Press in New York, its second issue was significantly devoted to "The San Francisco Scene."

A short-lived, but important magazine concentrating on Beat was the San Francisco-based *Beatitude*, launched in May 1959 under the auspices of Allen Ginsberg, Bob Kaufman, John Kelly, and William Margolis. Its demise the following year, in July 1960, was seen by many to mark the end of the San Francisco Renaissance. But the West Coast scene had made its mark, confirmed that same year with the publication of Donald M. Allen's anthology *The New American Poetry: 1945–1960*, which brought together for the first time in a mainstream collection the work of the Beat Generation, the San Francisco poets, and writers associated with Black Mountain College. Though it closed in 1957, Black Mountain was a name that loomed large in the culture of the New America, of which the Beats were, by 1960, considered an essential part.

# distant shores

"There is no line between the 'real world'
and [the] 'world of myth and symbol.'"

William Burroughs

## 8

Bill Burroughs' ill-fated residence in Mexico and his subsequent "escape" from probation into the Peruvian jungles was indicative of a general restlessness on the part of all the nascent Beats that took them far beyond the borders of the US. Throughout the 50s they seemed to be constantly on the move, seeking new insights and experiences, physically and spiritually.

Once Burroughs had succeeded in locating the mythic yage (he was violently sick and delirious when he overdosed on his first sample of the drug), he arrived back in New York City in August 1953 with two suitcases filled with the rare plant. Almost immediately he embarked on a sexual relationship with Allen Ginsberg. This would prove far from satisfactory, at least so far as Ginsberg was concerned. When the older man asked him to move in with him, Allen declined perfunctorily—"But I don't want your ugly old cock"—and ended their affair. In December 1953, Ginsberg took off for Mexico.

After hitchhiking to Florida he flew from Key West to Havana, the first time he'd ever traveled by air. Disappointed with the Cuban capital—as far as he could see it was just a decaying shadow of its past glory, now run by the Mafia—he sped on to Yucatan in Mexico, and the ancient ruins of Chichén Itzá. From a professor of archaeology in New York, he'd acquired a pass to stay free of charge in the various archaeological sites of the area, and on his very first night there he pitched his hammock at the top of the 11th-century El Castillo pyramid.

It was the start of a spiritual odyssey among the temples and cities of the Toltec/Maya civilizations that he felt were the Americas' equivalent of the Roman and Greek ruins of the Old World. He was further inspired meeting Karena Shields in the monuments of Palenque. A 50-year-old American, who had inherited her parents' vast cocoa plantation in the area, Shields had made a life study of the Maya, their history, and mysticism, via their descendents, the local Indians. Ginsberg stayed at the Shields plantation for several months, making adventurous forays into remoter areas, where he experienced life with the Indians. In the meantime he wrote to Bill Burroughs, Neal Cassady, and Jack Kerouac describing his various exotic adventures, including an experience of a volcanic earthquake, and a visit to a legendary cave "as big as St. Patrick's Cathedral."

Many of Ginsberg's letters, however, failed to get through, and Burroughs—now ensconced in Tangiers—despaired at the fate that may have befallen his recent paramour. Allen, meanwhile, was writing with a new passion: his Central American sojourn was providing social breathing space, and a multitude of inspirations. To Neal Cassady he wrote that he felt rejuvenated, "back on the ball," and in June 1954 he headed back to the US to stay with Neal and Carolyn at their home in San José.

"It was very cheap then. Yeah, man, I lived like a king for $200 a month."

Bill Buroughs, on living in Morocco in the 50s, interviewed in 1977

After splitting with Allen Ginsberg at the end of 1953 Bill Burroughs traveled to Tangiers via a short stay in Rome. He only knew the city from the novels of Paul Bowles, who'd lived in the Moroccan port with his wife Jane since the late 40s, but was lured by its timelessly degenerate aura. At the end of World War II Tangiers had been declared an "International Zone" (in *The Naked Lunch* Burroughs called the city "Interzone") and it had become a sanctuary for a motley community of smugglers, drug runners, the tax-dodging rich, and cop-dodging low-lifes. In short, it was just the sort of place Burroughs felt he could occupy comfortably, with few moral restraints, and as much anonymity as he might wish.

Soon realizing that the "exotic" side of the local culture was just "oriental shit" promoted by writers such as Bowles, Burroughs settled for a seemingly bland routine in his 50-cents-a-day room next-door to a male brothel. He spent his days poised between withdrawals and fixes, visiting the pharmacy, and spending the unbearably hot afternoons with an 18-year-old Spanish boyfriend, Kiki—and he wrote. In the self-imposed solitariness he, too, felt a new liberation of the spirit: words were being committed to paper, bit-by-bit, note-by-note. Out of the fractured, broken mirror-maze of images that began to coalesce—in his mind, if not as yet on the page—would come the embryo of his first great work, unhindered by the conventional style of *Junkie*, *The Naked Lunch*.

In late evening Burroughs would meet up with various other expatriates and talk the night away in the Mar Chica bar, but they were uninspiring company. He wrote incessantly to Allen Ginsberg, of whose exact whereabouts he had no idea, and became increasingly concerned when his letters to a Mexico collecting address remained unanswered—especially when he heard from Cassady that some money Neal had forwarded at Allen's urgent request had been unclaimed. That was in April 1954. In May, Burroughs at last received a letter from Ginsberg, who conversely was beginning to worry about his friend's state of mind, fearing his concern for him was becoming obsessional.

**Previous pages:** The rue Git-le-Coeur in Paris, site of the fabled Beat Hotel.

**Right:** On a visit to Mexico City in November 1956, standing (left to right) Jack Kerouac, Allen Ginsberg and Peter Orlovsky, and kneeling, Gregory Corso and Peter Orlovsky's brother Lafcadio.

**Far right:** Allen Ginsberg during his trip to Mexico in early 1954. Years later he described himself in the picture "tanned and bearded satisfying Whitman."

**Below:** Allen (left) while staying at Karena Shield's cocoa plantation, Finca Tacalapan de San Leandro, in 1954. The mock sword fight is with the local state agricultural advisor, watched by the family retainer Antonio and his grandson, and an American girl "passing through."

" . . . the most beautifully executed, the clearest, and the most important utterance yet made by the generation Kerouac himself named years ago as 'beat,' and whose principal avatar he is."

Gilbert Millstein, reviewing *On the Road* in the *New York Times*, September 5, 1957

Burroughs had become addicted to a drug called Eukodol, a synthetic form of codeine. He was getting a more stimulating high than from heroin (initially at least, as with any addictive opiate), and was soon shooting up every couple of hours. He was hallucinating badly, sometimes staggering around the streets of Tangiers in a paranoid haze, all the time recalling his ecstasies and nightmares in frantic writing.

Like Jack Kerouac at his typewriter, driven by Benzedrine, Burroughs was disgorging a stream of images and ideas, weird characters, and apocalyptic scenarios, but with no sequential rhyme or reason. As his addiction got worse and his appearance and manner became more disquieting, those who would otherwise have been interested in his writing (Paul Bowles, for example) simply steered clear. His only audience was Allen Ginsberg, on the other side of the ocean, the letters to him being the only conduit for his creative outpourings.

Like junkies before him, and since, Burroughs swore he'd kick the habit, tried a few times, and failed. He'd undergone hospital treatment, attempted graduated morphine reductions, and even got Kiki to lock him in his room without his clothes—

"I am getting so far out one day

I won't come back at all."

Bill Burroughs in a letter to Allen Ginsberg, October 13, 1956

the old "cold turkey" technique. But it was when he booked into a London clinic in March 1956, for an anomorphine treatment he'd heard about—funded by $500 reluctantly donated by his parents—that it looked like this time he might succeed. After four days without sleep, and another week of painful withdrawals, his intake of morphine had gone down from 30 grains a day to zero. Returning to Tangiers, he felt renewed.

He rented a simple single room in the Villa Mouneria and, after a daily morning routine of modest food and exercise, he simply wrote, and wrote. With his only working stimulant marijuana, as he finished pages he'd throw them on the floor, never bothering to sort them out. Unlike Kerouac's seamless narrative (literally so, on its continuous teletype roll), there was no order or logic to his particular stream of consciousness.

Now visibly back in the "land of the living," he struck up the friendship with Paul Bowles that the novelist had seemingly been avoiding up till then, and soon there was a genuine rapport between the two of them. Then, in early 1957, Burroughs was joined in Tangiers by long-term confidants Jack Kerouac and Allen Ginsberg.

For Jack, the last quarter of 1956 had buzzed with anticipation. *Howl* hit the streets in October, amid considerable publicity; the *New York Times Book Review* ran a feature on the West Coast poetry scene, and *Life* magazine planned features on Allen Ginsberg, Gregory Corso, and Jack himself. The flurry of publicity undoubtedly helped tip the scales in favor of Viking Press finally making their long-delayed decision to publish *On the*

"I have a strange feeling here of being
outside any social context."

William Burroughs in Tangiers

*Road*, after numerous rewrites and painstaking lobbying by editor
Malcolm Cowley.

Looking back, had the book been picked up by a
publisher earlier in its long gestation, it might never have taken
off at all. But by the mid-50s, the cult of youth—as heralded by
such movies as *The Wild One* in 1953 and *Rebel Without A Cause*
(1955), and celebrated to the brash new sound of rock 'n' roll—
had changed the cultural landscape of the US forever. Though
never intended as a primer for disaffected teenagers (Jack was
in his mid-30s by this time), *On the Road's* time seemed to
have come.

As well as the continuing revisions to *On the Road*,
of course, Jack had been writing furiously on other projects in
the years since he had penned the first draft. Although yet to
be published, by the middle of 1956 he had written *The
Subterraneans*, *Doctor Sax*, *Maggie Cassidy*, *Mexico City Blues*,
*Tristessa*, *Visions of Gerard*, his "Buddhist notebook" *Some of
the Dharma*, and a portion of *Desolation Angels*.

The final weeks before he signed his contract with
Viking were fraught. Cowley insisted on further last-minute
revisions that annoyed Kerouac, but he nevertheless agreed to
them. While the ink was barely dry on the contract (it was
eventually signed in February 1957), he booked himself a berth on
a Yugoslavian freighter that was bound for Tangiers, Burroughs
having assured him that sex and drugs were easily available and
very cheap in the city. His plan was to spend the spring in
Morocco, then travel across Europe through the summer, and
finally return to the US in time for the September publication of
*On the Road*.

In the event, Kerouac soon found Tangiers less of a
paradise than Burroughs had led him to expect. He hated the
food, found the hashish and opium below par, couldn't stand the
general dirt and squalor, and considered the prostitutes to be too
expensive. By the time Allen Ginsberg and Peter Orlovsky arrived
a couple of weeks later, Jack knew he wouldn't be sticking round
much longer.

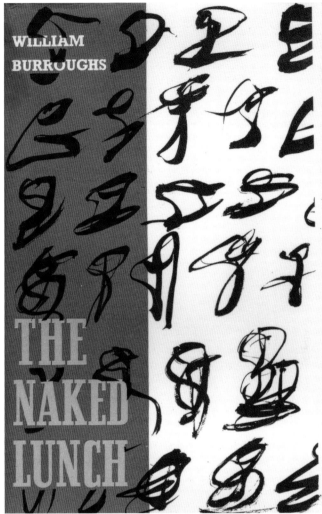

All three visitors made the trip at the express invitation of Burroughs, who realized that he would need considerable assistance if he were ever to sort out the growing mountain of typescript, notebooks, and scribbled jottings he had accumulated. Jack began the process by putting the shambles of a "manuscript" into some sort of preparatory order, working in a room one floor above Burroughs at the Villa Mouneria (dubbed "Villa Delirium" by its permanent residents). Speed-typing day and night, it was Jack who came up with the title for the book-to-be, *The Naked Lunch*.

Allen Ginsberg arrived in early March 1957, deliberately bringing his boyfriend Orlovsky with him to confirm to Burroughs that any sexual relationship they might have previously shared was definitely a thing of the past. He set about editing Bill's work in a highly organized fashion, working in alternating shifts at the typewriter with Alan Ansen, who had arrived from Venice. With meticulous attention to detail, Ansen indexed everything, and worked six hours a day for two months with Allen to produce a fresh-looking, straight-from-the-typewriter, 200-page manuscript.

Although it underwent subsequent revisions before finally being published, the manuscript represented what is still considered to be Burroughs' masterwork, and a landmark in American literature. In fact, this early version was essentially the one that appeared as the first American edition of the book (published by Grove Press in 1962, simply titled *Naked Lunch*). It was a later version that constituted the very first publication of the novel, via the Olympia Press in Paris, in 1959.

Controversial in the extreme, the novel broke virtually every literary taboo, and was banned in many parts of the world. It was also one of the last American books to be put on trial for obscenity. Written as a series of only loosely connected episodes, featuring a cast of bizarre characters centered on Burroughs' alter ego, police agent Bill Lee, it explores the seedy underbelly of mid-20th century America through a nightmarish prism. As a piece of modern-day satire it was unprecedented in its shock value, and it heralded the challenge to social hypocrisy that would characterize the "culture clash" of the 60s.

"The rats were on the ground floor, not on the top floor, and it's only when the Seine would come up that the rats would come up out of their holes. And when there's junkies around there's rats. It was a ghastly thing, an atmosphere a bit like *The Naked Lunch*."

Artist Jean-Jacques Lebe, who lived nearby on the rue de l'Hotel Colbert, interviewed by Barry Miles in *The Beat Hotel*, 2000

On April 5, 1957, Kerouac left Tangiers, making his way to Paris via the French port of Marseilles, and then taking what was known as the "boat train" to London, England. Among other delights, he listened to a riveting performance of Bach's choral "St Matthew Passion" in St. Paul's Cathedral, and saw Shakespeare's *Antony and Cleopatra* performed at the Old Vic theater.

Ginsberg and Orlovsky stayed with Burroughs until June, before traveling to the exotically Moorish cities of Seville and Cordoba in southern Spain, the Spanish capital Madrid, and the Catalonian city of Barcelona. They then made their way to Venice (where they spent a month, and again met up with Alan Ansen), before journeying on to Florence and Rome, finally arriving in Paris at the end of the summer.

. . .

Ginsberg immediately fell in love with the city, taking in the sights—the Eiffel Tower, the Louvre, and so on—like a bona fide tourist, while the romantic in him also sensed the ghosts of Lautrec and Renoir in its sunlit boulevards, winding streets, and narrow alleyways. "Paris is beautiful," he wrote to his father Louis, "The only city I've seen so far that would tempt me to expatriate and settle down . . . "

When Allen and Peter arrived in Paris they met up with Gregory Corso, who seemed to be sharing his time between the French capital and Amsterdam. They also caught up with Guy Harloff, a Dutch painter they had met through Alan Ansen in Venice, who lived in a 42-room hotel at 9 rue Git-le-Coeur, on the Left Bank. Harloff introduced them to Madame Rachou, the hotel's formidable landlady, who told them all the rooms were full, but that there would be a vacancy available for them from October

15th. The nameless hostelry would become a nerve center of the Beat Generation over the next six years, in due course becoming known internationally as "the Beat Hotel."

The hotel was a "class 13" establishment, the lowest grade tolerated under France's then-minimal health and safety standards. The building was over three centuries old, and the sloping floors and noisy, inefficient plumbing testified to its antiquity. There was little natural light in the rooms—most of the windows faced the interior stairwell—and the 40-watt light bulbs did little to compensate. Hot water was only available on certain days of the week and there was only one bathroom, so if a guest wanted to have a bath, it had to be booked well in advance, and a surcharge paid for the privilege. The uncarpeted rooms were basic, with no phones or other amenities, and there was only one primitive toilet on each landing. The drapes and bedspreads were changed and washed every spring, the bed linen—in theory at least—once a month.

The hotel had been managed by Madame Rachou and her husband (who died in a traffic accident in 1957) since 1933, and from when the Beats moved in she looked after it by herself. Previously having worked at a country inn at Giverny frequented by the painters Monet and Pissarro, she always encouraged artists and writers to stay at the hotel, even accepting paintings or manuscripts in lieu of rent. The $30-a-month rooms were home to a diverse community of jazz musicians, prostitutes, artists' models, writers, and painters. The bohemian clientèle was particularly attracted by the fact that they could paint and decorate their rooms in whatever fashion they wanted. Also Madame Rachou wasn't concerned about what went in the rooms in the way of sex, drugs, or whatever, as long as any "overnight" visitors remembered to sign the guest register.

# capital of cool

As well as being historically one of the artistic capitals of Europe, in the late 40s and 50s and more than any other European city, Paris was at the cutting edge of contemporary culture. In more ways than one, August 1944—the end of the Nazi occupation—had been a liberation. Once again the Paris that shone earlier in the century, of the Impressionists, the Surrealists, of Pablo Picasso and Jean Cocteau, asserted itself as an intellectual and creative hotbed on a par with New York City or San Francisco.

It was the age of existentialism, when Albert Camus, Jean-Paul Sartre, and Simone de Beauvoir held court in Les Deux Magots and other boulevard cafés of Saint Germain, just yards away from the Beat Hotel itself. At the same time the French—always passionate about *le cinéma*—were leading the way with young "new wave" *Nouvelle Vague* filmmakers such as Francois Truffaut, Claude Chabrol, and Jean-Luc Goddard, who sipped coffee and cognacs in those same Left-Bank bistros.

Throughout the 50s, Eugene Ionesco pioneered his Theater of the Absurd in the city, while expatriate Irishman Samuel Beckett was a permanent resident. His best-known work, *Waiting For Godot*, premièred in the original French at the Théâtre de Babylone in 1953. A year later, at age 18 and having failed her entrance examinations to the Sorbonne mainly because of her nightlife in the Paris clubs, the playwright and novelist Françoise Sagan became a local celebrity with her best-selling first novel, *Bonjour Tristesse*.

For the Beats who spent time there—and indeed, other American writers before them, including Ernest Hemingway, Henry Miller, and James Baldwin—Paris was undoubtedly something of a cultural home-from-home, not least because the French had embraced jazz, which, like movies and good food, was almost a national institution.

During the 20s the Black American singer and dancer Josephine Baker had become a French superstar with her exotic performance in the spectacular jazz-influenced *La Revue Nègre*. In 1929, Jean Cocteau and fellow Parisian intellectuals even demanded that jazz should be recognized as an art form on a par with cinema and modern painting. As well as producing Europe's first jazz legend in the 30s—the Belgian guitarist Django Reinhardt with the Quintette du Hot Club de France—the French capital became a magnet for a colony of Black American musicians after World War II, the most famous being saxophone star Sidney Bechet. There were also such luminaries as pianist Bud Powell, blues man Memphis Slim, drummer Kenny Clarke, and saxophone players Don Byas and Johnny Griffin.

Mostly they came not just for the work, but because of the more relaxed racial attitude found in Paris, at least in the bohemian atmosphere of the Latin Quarter and Saint Germain. Miles Davis famously spent some time there in 1957, playing the Left-Bank clubs and it was there that he struck up a relationship with the iconic French film actress/singer Juliette Greco, recording his celebrated soundtrack to Louis Malle's film *Ascenseur pour l'Echafaud (Lift to the Scaffold)*.

Among the tenants of 9 Git-le-Coeur were some jazz musicians, including the tenor saxophonist Allen Eager, while others, such as the great drummer Kenny Clarke, would call on Ginsberg and the other Beats, scoring dope or simply hanging out.

With its cheap wine and inexpensive accommodation, Paris in the 50s was a place where one was able to buy books banned elsewhere, where young men affected the casually louche manner of Jean-Paul Belmondo, and all the girls looked like Brigitte Bardot, where Ray Charles was worshipped almost as a god. Capital of cool: it was irresistible to would-be hipsters from around the world.

It was a special place and time where Existentialists, Beats, and beboppers once mingled. Jean-Paul Sartre and Simone de Beauvoir were drinking tea in the Café Flore. The writer Boris Vian blew his pocket trumpet in the Tabou. The Chameleon presented Allen Eager. Allen Ginsberg, Gregory Corso, and William Burroughs were guests in the so-called 'Beat Hotel'."

Jazz writer Mike Zwerin, Paris, 2001

Before moving in, Ginsberg and Orlovsky went to Amsterdam to visit Corso, who returned with them and also checked into the hotel. Initially, Allen and Peter were given a temporary room with a leaky roof and paper-thin walls, but they were soon assigned to the better-appointed Chambre 25, which was equipped with a double-burner gas stove, and where Madame Rachou assured them they could make as much noise as they wished. Corso, meanwhile, was given the tiny attic garret (Chambre 41) in the roof of the building.

It was during his first few weeks at the hotel that Ginsberg began working on the elegy for his mother that was to be published by City Lights as "Kaddish" in 1960. Naomi Ginsberg had died in June 1956, in the Pilgrim State mental hospital. Allen had not been able to attend her burial, which his brother Eugene described as "the smallest funeral on record"—with just seven attending, there were not even the ten men required to read the Jewish *Kaddish* prayer for the dead.

Ginsberg decided then that it was up to him to write the *Kaddish*, but it would be over a year before he addressed the issue again. Now, settled in Paris after his frantic criss-crossing of Europe, the time had come. On November 13, 1957, sitting in the Café Select, a legendary Paris bistro since the 20s, he wept as he wrote the first lines of what was to become one of his greatest works. Over the coming months his Paris journals, often written in the confines of the room in Git-le-Coeur, would include pages headed "Elegy for mamma," although the finished work was not to materialize until a year later.

Back in the US through that fall, meanwhile, things had been happening fast. The "Howl" trial had attracted much publicity, and the book was about to be reprinted for the fourth time. *On the Road* made the best-seller list soon after it appeared, and albums of poets reading their work were being released. Beat was becoming big. Ginsberg, Orlovsky, and Corso were treated as ambassadors of the Beat Generation by like-minded souls in Paris, with number 9 Git-le-Coeur standing in as their embassy. Corso decided to dub the place "the Beat Hotel," and although Allen never liked the name, it stuck.

Soon after settling in his Left-Bank residence, one port of call Ginsberg knew he had to make was to the office of the Olympia Press, in nearby rue Saint-Séverin. Olympia had been founded by Maurice Girodias in 1953, carrying on the tradition of his father Jack Kahane, who had pioneered the Obelisk Press in the early 30s, publishing a mix of erotic novels and avant-garde literary works including first editions of Henry Miller's *Tropic of Cancer* and *Tropic of Capricorn*. The Olympia list included many books banned in their country of origin, ranging from the potboiler "DBs" (dirty books) to landmark first printings of modern classics, including Vladimir Nabokov's *Lolita*, J.P. Donleavy's *The Ginger Man*, and the first English translation of the erotic masterpiece *The Story of O* by Pauline Réage.

Ginsberg confronted Girodias with "the masterpiece of the century," the manuscript of *The Naked Lunch* that he, Kerouac, Ansen, and Burroughs had toiled over in Tangiers, which was now looking somewhat tattered after being carried across Europe stuffed in his backpack. Though initially put off by the appearance of the manuscript (and, possibly, its emissary), Girodias went on to publish Bill Burroughs' seminal novel in 1959.

In a frequent exchange of letters, Ginsberg had urged Burroughs to make the trip from Tangiers to Paris, not to rekindle their sexual relationship but because he thought it would be a good move for him. Nevertheless, when Bill announced he was arriving in a few days' time, things became a little tense between Allen and Peter, not least because Orlovsky was due to leave for the US one day after Burroughs' arrival on January 16, 1958.

It transpired that Burroughs had become a different man to the one they had left in north Africa. He'd given up drinking, and writing, and planned to visit a psychoanalyst in Paris. He now viewed his life, including his feelings for Allen, in a more dispassionate, distanced way; he'd come to Paris simply to visit Allen. In the first few nights after Burroughs' arrival at the Beat Hotel the two reached a mutual, and tranquil, understanding about their relationship in which sexual considerations were transcended.

Burroughs' tenure at the hotel—he had moved into Room 15, and was still there a year after Allen's eventual departure

"You are the artist when you approach a Dreamachine with your eyes closed. What the Dreamachine incites you to see is yours . . . your own. The brilliant interior visions you so suddenly see whirling around inside your head are produced by your own brain activity. These may not be your first glimpse of these dazzling lights and celestial colored images. Dreamachines provide them only just as long as you choose to look into them."

Brion Gysin

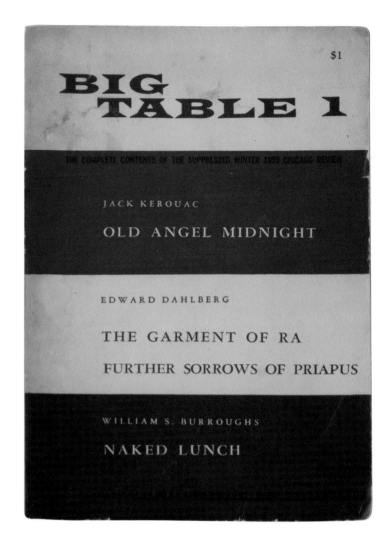

in July 1958—was marked creatively by his friendship and collaboration with a neighboring resident who took over Ginsberg's Room 25, the writer and painter Brion Gysin. The two had known each other in Tangiers, where Gysin had run a café called the 1001 Nights.

It was in Room 25 that Gysin discovered—allegedly by accident, when slicing through copies of the *New York Herald Tribune* and other papers while trimming a picture mount—a "cut-up" technique that involved randomly assembling different sections of newspaper. Burroughs was visiting London at the time, but on his return (in the presence of two *Life* magazine reporters interviewing him), Gysin showed him what he'd been doing: matching up unrelated portions of text to humorous or bizarre effect. Bill was immediately intrigued, and although they initially toyed with the idea purely for amusement, they soon realized the technique could be developed into a literary form in its own right. Burroughs exploited the juxtaposition of lines that the technique produced to introduce a genuine element of randomness into his writing, viewing the results as being on a par with the collages of the Dadaist Tristan Tzara and other avant-garde artists from earlier in the century.

Unlike the Dada experiments, which left the juxtapositions to the laws of chance, here there was a deliberate choice in selecting the words and passages of text used, and the order in which they were arranged, to achieve a new end product. Burroughs and Gysin, with the help of Gregory Corso and another resident, South African poet Sinclair Beiles, began to cut up pages of Burroughs' text (and other material), putting them in four baskets. The text would then be rearranged arbitrarily to see what might result, as Burroughs explained to biographer Barry Miles in *William Burroughs: El Hombre Invisible*, 1997: "The page is actually cut with scissors, usually into four sections, and the order is rearranged . . . The composite text is then read across, half one text and half the other. Perhaps one in ten works out and I use it."

Beiles and the others were also involved in Burroughs' continuing edits of *The Naked Lunch*, which after being the subject of legal action when the US magazine *Big Table* published excerpts in March 1959, was finally published by Olympia Press in July 1959. Though Corso distanced himself from the final "selection" of texts, the four were responsible for the first-ever cut-up book, *Minutes to Go*, published in 1960 by the Paris-based Two Cities Editions. Contrary to popular misconception, *The*

**Opposite:** The #1 edition of *Big Table* from March 1959, which featured an excerpt from *The Naked Lunch*. It was taken to court after its predecessor, *Chicago Review*, had already been censored for running the same piece.

**Below:** The first UK edition of Burroughs' *The Ticket That Exploded*. Published in 1968, it included several alterations to the original Olympia Press edition from 1962.

**Right:** Its words arranged in the shape of a nuclear mushroom cloud, Gregory Corso wrote *Bomb* at the Beat Hotel. Reading about the huge Ban-the-Bomb protests attracting young people in England, he wrote the poem about "loving" the Bomb, arguing that to hate the Bomb "is to make yourself vulnerable to it." City Lights published it as a single 25-cent broadsheet in 1958—and many UK nuclear protesters were not amused.

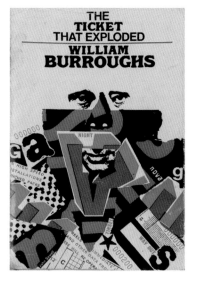

*Naked Lunch* was never conceived or developed as a cut-up work as such, though an element of "randomness" certainly featured in the editorial process.

Burroughs continued to live at the Beat Hotel until 1962, and during this period he formed a strong professional and personal attachment to Brion Gysin. The two worked on Bill's subsequent projects, including his novels *The Soft Machine*, *The Ticket That Exploded*, and *Nova Express*, which would be published in 1961, 1962, and 1964 respectively. While at 9 Git-le-Coeur, Gysin and Burroughs also became involved with Ian Sommerville, a young Englishman who also had a room in the hotel.

The Cambridge-educated mathematician, with whom Burroughs would have an on-and-off love affair for the next ten years or so, was instrumental in developing two of Gysin's breakthrough innovations at the Beat Hotel: tape-recorded cut-up "sound poems" and the Dreamachine. With his technical expertise, Burroughs and Gysin produced hour after hour of sound collages, Bill reading his own and other people's texts. These would be spliced and reassembled in much in the same way as the cut-ups, and sometimes played back with music (or more often, weird sound effects) added.

# BOMB

Budger of history   Brake of time   You   Bomb
Toy of universe   Grandest of all snatched-sky   I cannot hate you
Do I hate the mischievous thunderbolt   the jawbone of an ass
The bumpy club of One Million B.C.   the mace   the flail   the axe
Catapult Da Vinci   tomahawk Cochise   flintlock Kidd   dagger Rathbone
Ah and the sad desperate gun of Verlaine   Pushkin   Dillinger   Bogart
And lath not St. Michael a burning sword   St. George a lance   David a sling
Bomb   you are as cruel as man makes you   and you're no crueller than cancer
All man hates you   they'd rather die by ear-crash   lightning   drowning
Falling off a roof   electric-chair   heart-attack   old age   old age   O Bomb
They'd rather die by anything but you   Death's finger is free-lance
Not up to man whether you boom or not   Death has long since distributed its
categorical blue   I sing thee Bomb   Death's extravagance   Death's jubilee
Gem of Death's supremest blue   The flyer will crash   his death will differ
with the climber who'll fall   To die by cobra is not to die by bad pork
Some die by swamp   some by sea   and some by the bushy-haired man in the night
O there are deaths like witches of Arc   Scarey deaths like Boris Karloff
No-feeling deaths like birth-death   sadless deaths like old pain Bowery
Abandoned deaths   like Capital Punishment   stately deaths like senators
And unthinkable deaths like Harpo Marx   girls on Vogue covers   my own
I do not know just how horrible Bombdeath is   I can only imagine
Yet no other death I know has so laughable a preview   I scope
a city   New York City   streaming   starkeyed   subway shelter
Scores and scores   A fumble of humanity   High heels bend
Hats whelming away   Youth forgetting their combs
Ladies not knowing what to do   with their shopping bags
Unperturbed gum machines   Yet dangerous 3rd rail
Ritz Brothers   from the Bronx   caught in the A train
The smiling Schenley poster will always smile
Impish Death   Satyr Bomb   Bombdeath
Turtles exploding over Istanbul
The jaguar's flying foot
soon to sink in arctic snow
Penguins plunged against the Sphinx
The top of the Empire State
arrowed in a broccoli field in Sicily
Eiffel shaped like a C in Magnolia Gardens
St. Sophia peeling over Sudan
O athletic Death   Sportive Bomb
The temples of ancient times
their grand ruin ceased
Electrons   Protons   Neutrons
gathering Hesperean hair
walking the dolorous golf of Arcady
joining marble helmsmen
entering the final amphitheater
with a hymnody feeling of all Troys
heralding cypressean torches
racing plumes and banners
and yet knowing Homer with a step of grace
Lo the visiting team of Present
the home team of Past
Lyre and tuba together joined
Hark the hotdog soda olive grape
gala galaxy robed and uniformed
commissary   O the happy stands
Ethereal root and cheer and boo
The billioned all-time attendance
The Zeusian pandemonium
Hermes racing Owens
the Spitball of Buddha
Christ striking out
Luther stealing third
Planetarium Death   Hosannah Bomb
Gush the final rose   O Spring Bomb
Come with thy gown of dynamite green
unmenace Nature's inviolate eye
Before you the wimpled Past
behind you the hallooing Future   O Bomb
Bound in the grassy clarion air
like the fox of the tally-ho
thy field the universe thy hedge the geo
Leap Bomb   bound Bomb   frolic zig and zag
The stars a swarm of bees in thy binging bag
Stick angels on your jubilee feet
wheels of rainlight on your bunky seat
You are due and behold you are due
and the heavens are with you
hosannah incalescent glorious liaison
BOMB O havoc antiphony molten cleft BOOM
Bomb mark infinity a sudden furnace
spread thy multitudinous encompassed Sweep
set forth awful agenda
Carrion stars   charnel planets   carcass elements
Corpse the universe   tee-hee finger-in-the-mouth hop
over its long long dead Nor
From thy nimbled matted spastic eye
exhaust deluges of celestial ghouls
From thy appellational womb
spew birth-gusts of great worms
Rip open your belly Bomb
from your belly outflock vulturic salutations
Battle forth your spangled hyena finger stumps
along the brink of Paradise
O Bomb   O final Pied Piper
both sun and firefly behind your shock waltz
God abandoned mock-nude
beneath His thin false-tale'd apocalypse
He cannot hear thy flute's
happy-day profanations
He is spilled deaf into the Silencer's warty ear
His Kingdom an eternity of crude wax
Clogged clarions untrumpet Him
Sealed angels unsing Him
A thunderless God   A dead God
O Bomb   thy BOOM His tomb
That I lean forward on a desk of science
an astrologer dabbling in dragon prose
half-smart about wars   bombs   especially bombs
That I am unable to hate what is necessary to love
That I can't exist in a world that consents
a child in a park   a man dying in an electric-chair
That I am able to laugh at all things
all that I know and do not know   thus to conceal my pain
That I say I am a poet and therefore love all man
knowing my words to be the acquainted prophecy of all men
and my unwords no less an acquaintanceship
That I am manifold
a man pursuing the big lies of gold
or a poet roaming in bright ashes
or that which I imagine myself to be
a shark-toothed sleep   a man-eater of dreams
I need not then be all-smart about bombs
Happily so   for if I felt bombs were caterpillars

*(continued—over)*

127

Gysin's idea for the Dreamachine was inspired by the work of a British neuroscientist, W. Gray Walter, who discovered that flashing lights quickly altered brain activity and not only the visual cortex, but the whole mind. There, in the Beat hotel, he and Sommerville constructed their first machine in 1959.

In its original form, the Dreamachine was made from a cylinder with slits cut in the sides, which was placed on a record-player turntable and rotated at 78 or 45 revolutions per minute. A light bulb was suspended in the center of the cylinder, the light coming out of the holes at a constant frequency. The Dreamachine was hailed by Gysin, Sommerville, and Burroughs—who was closely involved in the experiments—as the first artwork to be "viewed" with the eyes closed. The pulsating light stimulates the optic nerve, and the "viewer" experiences increasingly bright, complex patterns of color behind their closed eyelids. The patterns become shapes and symbols, swirling around, until the viewer feels surrounded by unfamiliar colors, swirling patterns, and dream like images. In short, it was psychedelia without the drugs (though, inevitably, Burroughs and co. tried it with chemical enhancement as well), and way before its time.

As the 60s dawned, with interest in the Beats at an all-time high, the Beat Hotel, which was described in the November 1962 issue of *Time* magazine as a "fleabag shrine," became a place of pilgrimage. The list of those who passed though its doors was long and varied; some were *bona fide* residents or overnight "guests" of residents, while others just came to hang out in the small bar. In addition to the well-known Beat writers, paying tenants included photographers Harold Chapman and Bill Cheney, a beautiful Finnish model named Mirja, the publisher Thomas Neurath, poet and painter Harold Norse, Scottish folk singer Alex Campbell, London fashion designer Peter Golding, the Canadian painter Robin Page, and Kay "Kaja" Johnson—a writer, painter, and poet from New Orleans.

Kaja, along with Harold Norse and Brion Gysin, would be some of the last to leave the hotel when it closed in early 1963, Madame Rachou having announced a few weeks earlier that she'd sold the place, and that they would all have to move out. The building was to be renovated and the new hotel at last given an official name: the Relais Hôtel du Vieux Paris. The hotel still operates under this name, describing itself as a "four-star boutique hotel." With its double "executive" room costing $350 a night, it's a far cry from the anonymous rooming-house, where a painting or some poems would often suffice for rent, and the bedspreads were washed once a year—whether they needed it or not!

**Opposite:** Brion Gysin "looking," eyes closed, into his Dreamachine.

**Above:** Ian Sommerville during his time at the Beat Hotel.

"I view life as a fortuitous collaboration ascribable to the fact that one finds oneself in the right place at the right time. For us, the 'right place' was the famous 'Beat Hotel' in Paris, roughly from 1958 to 1963."

Brion Gysin, *The Third Mind*, 1978

# beat & the new culture

"As far as consistency of thought goes,

I prefer inconsistency."

John Cage

9

As its place in American culture developed through the 50s, the Beat movement became closely aligned with various other radical developments taking place in the arts. From the start, as their New York base moved downtown to Greenwich Village, the ex-Columbia students and their friends rubbed shoulders with artists of various kinds who made up the thriving bohemian community. Jack Kerouac and the others hung out at the same bars as the "New York School" painters, including Jackson Pollock, Willem de Kooning, and Franz Kline, but there was more to it than that.

Much of the live poetry reading which the Beats pioneered—on the West as well as the East Coast—took place in independent art galleries. The myriad magazines that sprang up in the 50s also provided an early platform and likewise carried artwork and articles about the new painters, as well as discussing experimental film and avant-garde theater. Perhaps most significantly, there was the genuine crossover between live poetry, theater, and visual art, represented by experimental "performance art," environments, and so-called "Happenings."

The new generation of painters who emerged in the late 40s and early 50s, later known as Abstract Expressionists, lived and worked in the then-cheap studio lofts in the East Village. Their search for a total abstraction with a spiritual effect on a par with that achieved by music—and the degree of spontaneity involved, especially in Pollock's "action painting"—had much in common with the Beats' belief in a "pure" art brought about by the breaking of "literary" rules and conventions.

The term "New York School" was first applied by the painter Robert Motherwell in the catalog for an exhibition of that name at the Frank Peris Gallery in 1951, and later the same year gallery owner Leo Castelli staged a similar collection, billed as "Today's Self-Styled School of New York." The Castelli show included work by many members of the Artists' Club, also frequented by the Beats through the 50s.

But it was with a move by painters such as Robert Rauschenberg—away from total abstraction to "assemblages," whose dynamic lay in the disparate materials used—that ostensibly abstract painting nevertheless took on a figurative, representational quality. One of the earliest exhibitions to spotlight the new assemblage art was on the West Coast in 1951, held at The Place, the North Beach bar which was much favored by the San Francisco poets.

Rauschenberg studied in Kansas City and Paris before enrolling at the Black Mountain College in North Carolina, in 1948. There, he studied under the renowned Bauhaus sculptor Josef Albers, but by 1951 was more taken by the minimalism espoused by another member of the faculty, the composer John Cage. He produced totally blank "white paintings," which contained no images whatsoever, before starting to create his so-called "Combine Paintings," featuring large areas of color combined with collage and found objects attached to the canvas. By the mid-50s they were his stock-in-trade, with birds, a stuffed goat, even his own bed quilt among the objects in his often-disturbing works, eroding the boundaries between painting and sculpture.

From there it was but a small step to the free-standing assemblages and installations of artists like Ed Kienholz and Claes Oldenburg, both of whom came onto the scene at the end of the 50s. Often including figures cast from life, Kienholz's large-scale tableaux made up of found objects presented the viewer with stark visions of the grimmer and sometimes brutal side of 20th-century society.

Oldenburg, whose first one-man exhibition was in 1960, adopted a more humorous approach with his giant sculptures of everyday objects, and his "soft" renditions of normally solid items. Like Kienholz's work, it "involved" its audience beyond being mere gallery spectators—a "soft" tube of lipstick that had to be inflated from time to time, a floppy drum kit that was impossible to play, or the gigantic 45-foot stainless steel clothespin standing on a busy corner in Philadelphia.

In 1960 Oldenburg was also responsible for organizing "Ray Gun Spex," a series of artistic events involving, among others, Allan Kaprow and Jim Dine. Kaprow was a painter, assemblage artist, and pioneer of performance art and the multi-media "Happening." His first such presentation was an environment with sound, light, and odors at the Hansa Gallery in New York in 1958. Although not actually called a "Happening," it was the first event of its kind to be staged in New York City.

"The line between art and life should be kept as fluid, and perhaps indistinct, as possible."

Allan Kaprow

**Previous pages:** The Merce Cunningham Dance Company in rehearsal, 1957.

**Right:** Assemblage artist Robert Rauschenberg, pictured here working with dancers in 1966, was involved with mixed media events from the very first Happening staged at Black Mountain College in 1952.

**Below left:** Jackson Pollock working on a painting at his Springs, NY, studio in 1949.

**Below right:** Claes Oldenburg (right) with model Pat Muschinski in a Happening entitled "Snapshots from the City" at New York's Judson House Gallery, 1960.

**Top left:** Robert Creeley photographed at Black Mountain, 1955.

**Above left:** Merce Cunningham (left).

**Above:** John Cage changing the tuning of a piano with coins between the strings.

**Opposite:** The 1960 Blue Note album of music from *The Connection*, with a cover photo by Hern Snitzer from the New York stage play.

Kaprow first used the word "happening" in *Something to take place: a happening*, which became the script for a live performance environment. Other Kaprow happenings included *Words*, staged in 1962. With its sound playbacks and hanging scrolls of paper covered in graffiti-like painted words, it certainly had resonance with the Beats and their "spontaneous" prose.

Jim Dine, too, was a pioneer of the Happening, which was in stark contrast to the rather more serious tone of the Abstract Expressionists, who still dominated the New York art world—and more in line with the instant impact of art also aspired to by the Beats. Dine's first presentation of this kind was a 30-second performance in 1959 called *The Smiling Worker*, but he became better known after *Car Crash*, which he staged at New York's Judson Gallery in November 1960. In an all-white environment, performers dressed in white groaned like victims of an automobile accident, while an "8-foot" girl (on a ladder concealed under her white garments) recited a series of words relating to cars to the accompaniment of sound effects of car horns, police sirens, and suchlike.

Happenings and live performance environments were a crucial link in the growing interaction of artistic disciplines that characterized the 60s, involving painting, film, theater, poetry, and music—often simultaneously. They anticipated a number of later developments, from mixed-media rock shows heralded by Andy Warhol's Exploding Plastic Inevitable (featuring the Velvet Underground with dancers, lights shows, and so forth) to performance art, conceptual art, and street theater.

But to identify what was subsequently recognized as the first-ever Happening, we have to look back to 1952, and the avant-garde hotbed that was Black Mountain College. It was an event called *Theater Piece No. 1*, involving among its participants the composers John Cage and David Tudor, choreographer Merce Cunningham, painter Robert Rauschenberg, and poet Charles Olson. After Black Mountain was forced to close down in 1956, Cage began teaching at the New School for Social Research in New York. His class there was highly influential on developments in the American avant-garde and among his students was Allan Kaprow and future members of the Fluxus network of mixed-media artists and performers.

Closely related, in fact sometimes inter-related to performance art and Happenings, were developments in experimental theater. One of the earliest groups to emerge was the Living Theater, whose initial participants—including founders Julian Beck and Judith Malina—claimed they came up with the idea in the Beat hangout, the San Remo bar. In 1951 they staged their first program of plays, including works by Gertrude Stein, Federico Garcia Lorca, and Bertholt Brecht.

On the West Coast, a performance art group called the Instant Theater was started up in Hollywood by Lee Mullican and Rachel Rosenthal in 1954, while at the same time, upstate, Anna Halprin founded the equally influential San Francisco Dancers' Workshop. The Workshop directly influenced the move toward "free form" dance, which developed in the 60s.

In 1959 the Living Theater in New York was to tackle a subject closely identified with the Beats when they produced *The Connection*, a controversial play by Jack Gelber. Set in a tenement room where junkies, jazz musicians, and other assorted hipsters await the arrival of "Cowboy"—the "Connection," who will supply them with their heroin fix—this was real Beat territory. The play was to cause even more of a stir when it was released as a film in 1961. Taking on board the stylistic innovations of hand-held *cinéma vérité* and the French *nouvelle vague* with largely improvised dialog, and with music performed by pianist Freddie Redd and alto saxist Jackie McClean, the film won its director Shirley Clarke the Critics' Prize at the 1961 Cannes Film Festival, despite being banned in the US for obscenity.

# black mountain

Founded in 1933 near Asheville, North Carolina, Black Mountain College was one of the most influential experimental education institutions in the US. During the 50s it became a fertile creative breeding ground for interdisciplinary works; combining art, poetry, music, and performance, these works spearheaded the avant-garde movement.

Among the leading names who taught at Black Mountain after World War II were visual artists Josef Albers, Willem de Kooning, Robert Rauschenberg, and Robert Motherwell; also the architects Buckminster Fuller and Walter Gropius, musicians John Cage and David Tudor, choreographer Merce Cunningham, and poet Charles Olson. Guest lecturers included Albert Einstein, William Carlos Williams, and the eminent art critic Clement Greenberg.

The college was the catalyst for a number of milestones in modern art and postwar culture generally. Buckminster Fuller constructed his first geodesic dome at Black Mountain and it was where Merce Cunningham formed his ground-breaking dance company, while John Cage—along with David Tudor, Rauschenberg, Cunningham, and Olson—staged the first Happening there. But it was the group of writers who became known as the Black Mountain Poets who would interact most directly with the Beat Generation.

In 1950, Charles Olson published his essay *Projective Verse*, in which he proposed replacing traditional closed poetic structures with an "open" approach, improvised forms driven by the content of the poem. The basis of a poem would be the line, each of which was determined as a single utterance and breath length: the same "freeing" of the poetic voice that Allen Ginsberg acknowledged as the influence of William Carlos Williams. Again, we can see this in "Howl"; the poem consisted of "one perception immediately and directly [leading] to a further perception."

This narrowing down of the structure to what could fit in an "utterance" led to what became a familiar style among the Black Mountain poets, with words such as "the" or "your" being written in colloquial style as "th" or "yr"—a device which was also much used by the Beats. The essay itself became something of a mission statement on behalf of the Black Mountain writers, who also included Ed Dorn, Jonathan Williams, and, from 1954, Massachusetts-born Robert Creeley.

Creeley taught at the college and edited the influential *Black Mountain Review* for two years, from its first 64-page edition in 1954. A crucial link with the San Francisco Renaissance was forged when West Coast poet Robert Duncan enrolled at Black Mountain in 1955 and the College was forced to close down due to lack of funds the following year. With his students, Duncan moved back to San Francisco. Similarly, Creeley made the move to northern California, staying for a few months with Jack Kerouac in Gary Snyder's "country shack" retreat just north of 'Frisco in Mill Valley, Marin County.

Along with Allen Ginsberg, Creeley co-edited what would be the last (Number 7) issue of *Black Mountain Review*, in a landmark edition focussing on the San Francisco Rennaissance and the Beat Generation. Appearing in 1957, with Allen Ginsberg, Bill Burroughs, Jack Kerouac, Gregory Corso, Gary Snyder, Robert Duncan, Philip Lamantia, and Philip Whalen, the magazine's final edition cemented the relationship between the Beat Generation and the Black Mountain Poets.

"In general, the effort of Black Mountain College is to produce individuals rather than individualists . . . The first step in the process is to make the student aware of himself and his capacities; in other words, 'to know himself.'"

Louis Adamic, Visiting Academic, Black Mountain College

Other, mainly experimental, films were also connected with the Beats in various ways. If only because of its gritty subject matter, Lionel Rogosin's ultra-realistic, fly-on-the wall movie of New York down-and-outs *On The Bowery* struck a chord; and the 1956 documentary went on to be nominated for an Oscar, as well as winning prizes from both the British Film Academy and the Venice Film Festival.

Also in 1956, John Cassavetes was teaching method acting in various New York workshops when an improvisation session inspired him to write and direct his first movie, *Shadows*, in 1959. This was another film that fared better in Europe, both at the box office and with the critics, winning the prestigious Critics' Award at Venice in 1960. Indeed, Cassavetes was unable to find an American distributor willing to take on the movie.

Eventually, the movie was released by the European distributors as an import in the US. But the largely improvisational film—both in acting and direction—which explored interracial relationships among New York hipsters, and with a soundtrack by the pioneering jazz musician Charles Mingus, immediately became an icon in the Beat cultural milieu.

But *the* Beat film of the era was undoubtedly *Pull My Daisy*, directed by Robert Frank and Alfred Leslie, and featuring "acting" roles by Allen Ginsberg, Peter Orlovsky, and Gregory Corso, and narration by Jack Kerouac, who was also credited as writer. Made in six weeks and shot mainly in Alfred Leslie's New York City loft, the loose storyline featured Milo, a railroad brakeman played by painter Larry Rivers, and his artist wife. The 30-minute short, made in black-and-white, looks in on the couple when they are visited by their bishop, but have to contend with the bizarre behavior of the various poets who hang out in their pad.

Despite being regarded as an improvisatory work on its release in June 1959, an article by Alfred Leslie in a 1968 edition of *Village Voice* claimed it was as meticulously scripted and directed as a Hollywood feature film. There were as many takes for each shot as it took to get it right. Even Jack Kerouac's seemingly rambling narration was written out in advance and then mixed from the best of three takes. *Pull My Daisy* has since been hailed as a classic of American independent cinema and remains a unique artifact of key Beat figures when they represented a focal point of the new American culture.

**Opposite:** Made by the avant-garde director Kenneth Anger, *Scorpio Rising* was a highly regarded experimental movie from 1964 starring Bruce Byron as the biker Scorpio. Featuring themes of homosexual erotica, the occult, and leather-clad bikers, the surreal work was one of the first post-modern movies, and influenced later directors including Martin Scorsese and David Lynch.

**Below left:** Director John Cassavetes on the set of *Shadows*.

**Below right:** Allen Ginsberg relaxes across the knees of Peter Orlovsky and Gregory Corso on the set of the 1959 "Beat" movie *Pull My Daisy*.

# village voices

"There was . . . never a time when we had such a flowering of literature, theater, music and painting."

Dan Wakefield

## 10

Since the end of the 19th century Greenwich Village had been a focal point for new movements and avant-garde developments in the arts. By the early 1900s small presses, art galleries, and experimental theaters all thrived to support a burgeoning bohemia, with artists and writers making it their base for decades to come.

The Village became famous for such eccentrics as the street-dwelling writer Joe Gould, who claimed to have written an "oral history" consisting of 20,000 conversations and 9,000,000 words although, in fact, he was simply scribbling revisions of the same few chapters about his own life. There was also the exhibitionist poet Maxwell Bodenheim, known in the 20s as "the King of the Greenwich Village Bohemians." Likewise the Village nurtured many writers, poets, and artists who would one day become famous, such as the Dada artist Marcel Duchamp—who launched balloons from the arch in Washington Square as he announced the formation of the "Independent Republic of Greenwich Village." Writers ranged from F. Scott Fitzgerald and John Steinbeck to the Beats themselves.

When Allen Ginsberg, Jack Kerouac, and company began to make the Village their stomping ground in the late 40s, there was an already thriving scene in the bars and cafés, with a liberal attitude to matters of race, sexuality, drink, and drugs, as well as to social mores in general. Unlike today, most attractively, the rents for accommodation in Greenwich Village were also affordably cheap.

Bill Burroughs was the first of the key Beat triumvirate actually to live in the Village, soon after he moved to New York City in 1943. He rented an apartment on 69 Bedford Street, not far from Chumley's, a favorite literary watering hole since the 20s. During the Prohibition years, Chumley's operated as a speakeasy and the deliberately anonymous doorway just a block or so across the street from Burroughs' apartment was (and remains) evidence of its shady past. Over the years its clientele included artists such as John Steinbeck, Eugene O'Neill, J.D. Salinger, Upton Sinclair, and Orson Welles. When Burroughs dined there—usually in the early evening—another regular whose name and face would have meant nothing to him at the time was Lawrence Ferlinghetti.

Chumley's is the second oldest literary bar in Greenwich Village, the honor for being the oldest going to the White Horse Tavern on Hudson Street. Built in the 1880s, it is renowned as the site where the great Welsh poet Dylan Thomas drank himself to death. His drinking bouts in the White Horse were the stuff of legend—people visited the pub simply to watch Thomas carousing. Famously, on a November night in 1953, he downed one last shot of whiskey, staggered outside, and collapsed, dying at the nearby St. Vincent's Hospital shortly afterward.

Though association with Dylan Thomas made the "Horse" world-famous, its status as a literary landmark was already assured before the poet's death. As well as Lawrence Ferlinghetti, Norman Mailer and James Baldwin also frequented the bar, and Anaïs Nin was one of the few female writers to be a regular visitor. Including Mailer, the staff writers of the pioneering *Village Voice* newspaper also came over from their original office location above a bakery on Greenwich Avenue.

Jack Kerouac had been a frequent White Horse customer when he lived with Joan Haverty on West 20th Street in the early 50s and later in the decade, when his girlfriend Helen Weaver lived on West 11th, conveniently just across the road from the Tavern. His heavy drinking resulted in him being forcibly ejected on more than one occasion, and he even found "Kerouac, go home" scrawled on the wall of the men's room, an episode he would later refer to in *Desolation Angels*.

Another drinking establishment that was a catalyst in the days when bar culture was central to the artistic life of Greenwich Village was the Cedar Street Tavern on University Place—*the* artists' bar in 50s New York City. This was the gathering place of the Abstract Expressionist painters: Jackson Pollock, Willem de Kooning, Franz Kline, and Mark Rothko all

"I suppose what is fondly called by literary historians a 'ferment' was occurring in the arts at this time . . . A number of very diverse things all happened at the same time, all of them linked together, however tenuously, and all of them serving to create what I might call, with some misgivings, an avant-garde community in New York that had cultural and artistic ties to other communities in other parts of the country."

Gilbert Sorrentino, publisher of *Neon* underground magazine in the late 50s, 1978

**Previous pages:** Greenwich Village sidewalk, 1961.

**Below left:** Looking south on a busy MacDougal Street in 1961. The Gaslight was one of the major Village folk and poetry venues.

**Below top:** A beat-looking girl at the entrance to the Gaslight Café.

**Below center:** Poet Dick Woods sits nursing a cup of coffee in the Gaslight.

**Bottom:** The San Remo in the mid-50s.

"There wasn't a tradition of coffeehouse poetry readings in the mid-West, although there is now. I travel all over America now and there's coffee-shop poetry and magazines in every city and college. It was quite different to come to New York because it had a lot of theaters. One of the first things I did was to see Anton Chekov's *Ivanov* and *Playboy of the Western World* and Beckett's *Waiting For Godot*, all in a short time. There were also a lot more bookstores in New York in those days. The rents were cheaper. Then there was the whole wonderful Beat culture, which was combative and controversial at the time."

Poet/musician Ed Sanders, recalling in 1997 his arrival in Greenwich Village in 1958

**Below:** Featuring a cartoon beatnik on its cover, this *Where To Go In Greenwich Village* tour guide, by Rosetta Reitz & Joan Geisler, appeared in 1961.

**Opposite left:** The final issue of *Yugen* magazine, launched by Hettic and LeRoi Jones in March 1958. It ran for eight issues until December 1962.

**Opposite right:** A major Village voice, LeRoi Jones edited *The Moderns*, "an anthology of new American writing" in 1963; this UK paperback edition was published in 1967.

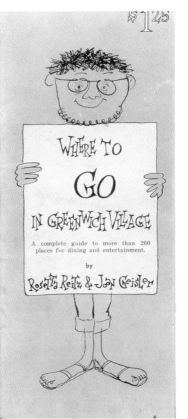

drank there and the early pop artist Larry Rivers painted the Cedar's menu on the wall. The Beat fraternity was similarly well represented, with Jack Kerouac, Allen Ginsberg, Gregory Corso, LeRoi Jones, and John Clellon Holmes all regular visitors. The Cedar was spartan in the extreme. There was no TV, no jukebox, only basic tables with stools and booths—which was just as well, considering the frequent fights that broke out as passions ran high among the painters and writers.

Equally important on the Beats' social circuit was the San Remo on Bleecker Street, which Ginsberg once described as a "center of Kerouac's N.Y. social life."

In *The Subterraneans*, in which he transposed the San Remo to San Francisco and called it "The Masque," Kerouac's "Ginsberg" character (Adam Moorad) referred to the bar's customers as being "Hip without being slick, intelligent without being corny, they are intellectual as hell and know all about Pound without being pretentious or saying too much about it." In other words, they were cool.

With its relaxed atmosphere and liberated social outlook, the Greenwich Village bohemian community was a comfortable environment for independent-minded women, and its members included some of the key female voices of the Beat scene. During the 50s the place of women in mainstream America was clearly defined: with few exceptions, their role was to be housewives and homemakers. Even those in typically "female" professions such as teaching or nursing were expected to give up their careers when they married. Sex (not to mention pregnancy) outside marriage was generally frowned upon—not only this, the idea of unmarried couples living together was considered scandalous, and completely taboo.

Although the predominant male Beats challenged just about every conventional attitude regarding sexual behavior, their female partners often appeared to be little more than passive followers of the (male) leaders of this rebellion. They were girlfriends, mothers of their children, and they provided financial safety nets by working, and also acted as their muses. But that

was not quite always the case, and in Greenwich Village some of the women of the Beat Generation were able to find their voice.

Born Hettie Cohen, Hettie Jones was raised in a regular Brooklyn Jewish family. After earning a drama degree at the University of Virginia, in the early 50s she moved back to New York City to pursue a post-graduate course at Columbia, and then began working for a jazz magazine called *Record Changer*. It was there, in 1957, that she would meet LeRoi Jones, when he applied for a job on the paper; the two soon fell in love and got married in a Buddhist temple in October 1958. Hettie's family disowned her for marrying a black man, and in those days even in the broad-minded Village community, mixed marriages still raised a few eyebrows. But the Jones' union, and their creative work together, was to prove an important force in the Beat movement.

LeRoi, who would become an established poetic voice over the next few years, was transfixed when he first read Allen Ginsberg's "Howl," and he and Hettie decided to launch a little magazine to publish the new poetry. He wrote to Ginsberg (on

toilet paper), asking if he could suggest contributors, which he did with enthusiasm. Hettie looked after the publishing side, drawing on contacts made at the literary journal *Partisan Review*, where she'd worked as business manager after *Record Changer* closed.

They called their magazine *Yugen* and put it together in the large apartment they had been sharing from before they were married on 402 West 20th Street—an address which became something of an informal salon for the New York Beats. The Jones soirées were legendary, and *Yugen* instantly became an influential launch pad for new names on the Beat scene, as did their Totem Press book imprint.

Despite these various literary ventures, Hettie never published any of her own creative writing—she assumed no one would be interested in it. She didn't even share her poetry with LeRoi, although in 1980, long after they had separated in the early 60s, she wrote *How I Became Hettie Jones*. The book was a frank but affectionate memoir of her times at the center of the Greenwich Village Beat scene.

# folk heroes to folkniks

Just as Greenwich Village had long been a center for the literary and artistic bohemia of the US, so it was natural that the 50s boom in folk music would begin there, more often than not in the same venues frequented by the Beats.

After his own "on the road" life during the Depression-hit 30s, America's greatest folk-song hero, Woody Guthrie, settled in the Village in 1941. He would sing in the White Horse, and in McSorley's, the oldest bar in New York, on 7th Street in the East Village. With "This machine kills fascists" inscribed on his guitar, Guthrie was a staunch socialist, forming the Almanac singers with Pete Seeger to play at Union rallies and such. They recorded for the seminal Folkways label, itself based in Greenwich Village.

Radical politics came naturally in the Village, partly because of the proximity of New York University around Washington Square, so the left-oriented folk song movement led by Seeger and Guthrie found a natural home in the cafés and bars around Bleecker Street. From the mid-40s, Washington Square Park had been the scene for impromptu folk sessions every weekend. This in itself was a catalyst for the district's importance to folk fans, confirmed when numerous coffeehouses sprang up catering to the burgeoning folk trade.

Notable establishments, some of which remain open today, included the Café Wha?, the Hip Bagel, the Figaro, and the Why Not? Most offered a mixture of folk, poetry, jazz, and blues. In addition, the Folklore Center that opened on MacDougal Street in 1957 became a focal point for the scene, with a performance space, and books, records, and instruments for sale.

Without doubt the biggest success story of the folk scene was Gerde's, a bar on West 4th Street. After experimenting with jazz, poetry readings, and such, in 1960 the owners decided to adopt a strictly folk music-only policy and to offer it in a "nightclub" environment. Changing its name (via "Gerde's Fifth Peg") to Gerde's Folk City, the Monday night "hootenannies" were key to the bar's success. Perhaps best described as a folk-music version of the amateur nights that were a regular feature of the Harlem Apollo, within a few weeks of opening the Monday "hoots" were highly popular. Amateur and professional singers "jammed" in front of the inevitable capacity crowd of no less than a couple of hundred "folkniks," with as many again waiting in line outside.

And it was in the Village—in Washington Square, in the coffeehouses, at the Folklore Center, and in new clubs such as Gerde's—that a new breed of young singers and songwriters began to appear in the late 50s and early 60s. Among them were Tom Paxton, Richard Fariña, Joan Baez, Dave Von Ronk, Carolyn Hester, Phil Ochs—and a young baby-faced Jewish kid from Minnesota calling himself Bob Dylan.

Dylan arrived in Manhattan in 1961, and right away became a fixture on the Village folk club scene, playing at the Café Wha?, the Gaslight, the Mills Tavern—anywhere that would let him do a set. He had much in common with the Beats, sharing the Guthrie/Wolfe/Kerouac vision of the old, mythic America that lay down the highway. His rapidly-developing song-writing skills revealed the spirit of Walt Whitman and William Blake, who also inspired Allen Ginsberg, with whom Dylan was to become a lifelong friend.

Certainly, as he walked the streets of Greenwich Village, Dylan *looked* Beat. Before the release of his first album, in September 1961, the *New York Times* folk critic Robert Shelton wrote that "A bright new face in folk music is appearing at Gerde's Folk City," describing the 20-year-old Dylan as "Resembling a cross between a choirboy and a beatnik."

"There was a hide-out room above the Gaslight where we could hang out. Once Dylan was banging out this long poem on Wavy Gravy's typewriter. He showed me the poem and I asked, 'Is this a song?' He said, 'No, it's a poem.' I said, 'All this work and you're not going to add a melody?' He did. It was 'A Hard Rain's Gonna Fall.'"

Tom Paxton, talking to writer Robbie Woliver, 1986

**Top left:** Bob Dylan's first New York concert, promoted by the Folklore Center.

**Bottom left:** Woody Guthrie singing in McSorley's Old Ale House, 1943.

**Below:** Singers and spectators gather at one of the weekend folk sessions in Washington Square Park, c. 1961.

THE FOLKLORE CENTER
*Presents*

# BOB DYLAN

IN HIS FIRST NEW YORK CONCERT

SAT. NOV. 4, 1961                    8:40pm

CARNEGIE CHAPTER HALL

154 WEST 57th STREET • NEW YORK CITY

*All seats* $2.00

Tickets available at:    The Folklore Center
                         110 MacDougal Street
GR 7 - 5987              New York City 12, New York

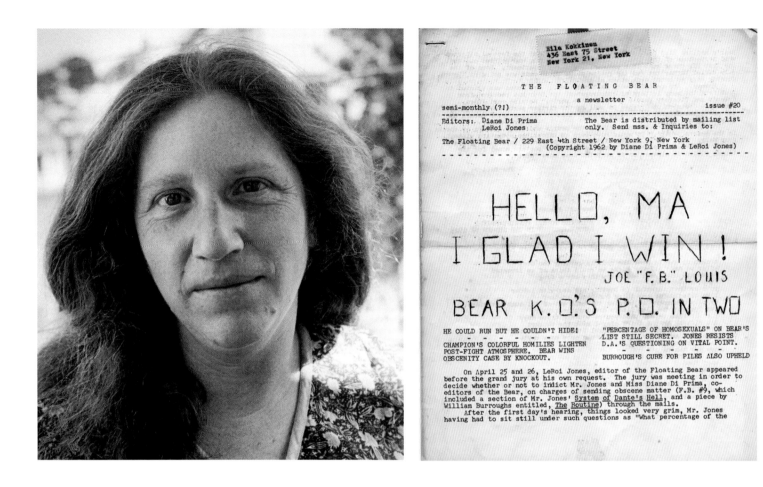

One of the key Village figures who debuted via the Jones' enterprise was Diane di Prima. Born in Brooklyn in 1934, during a formal education that began in the local Catholic school and continued in an exclusive all-girls high school, di Prima decided at age 14 that she was going to be a poet. At the equally exclusive liberal arts college Swarthmore she hooked up with like-minded women, who encouraged her to concentrate on her

"We mailed [the first issue] to 117 people . . . by the end of the first year we were up to 500 copies, and by the time of the last few issues we were printing 1,500 and mailing out 1,250: about 250 abroad and 1,000 all over the United States."

Diane di Prima talking about the increase in the size of
*Floating Bear*'s mailing list, 1973

burgeoning writing, and during her second year there she dropped out to take her place in the bohemian community of Greenwich Village.

It was in the mid-50s and the Beats had yet to be discovered. The 19-year-old fell in with a crowd who styled themselves as "new bohemians." They had much in common with the later Beat archetype, both in the way they dressed— sweatshirts, Levis, and sandals—and in their taste for jazz, modern art, poetry, and marijuana. Di Prima neatly summed up the essence of this growing hipster scene of artists, actors, musicians, writers, gays, and straights based in the Village: "As far as we knew, there was only a small handful of us—perhaps 40 or 50 in the city—who knew what we knew; who raced about in Levis and work shirts, made art, smoked dope, dug the new jazz, and spoke a bastardization of the black argot."

After reading Allen Ginsberg's "Howl," di Prima realized her instinct to make poetry her life was not as pie-in-the-sky as many thought—"he had broken the ground for all of us"—and started a literary correspondence with Ginsberg and several other poets, including Kenneth Patchen and Lawrence Ferlinghetti. Since 1953 she had also been corresponding with Ezra Pound.

In 1958, Hettie and LeRoi Jones' Totem Press published her first book of poetry, *This Kind of Bird Flies Backward*, and as

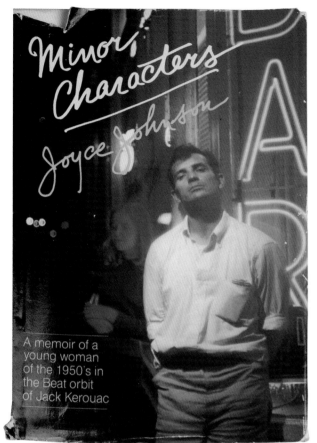

well as helping the couple with their fledgling magazine *Yugen*, in 1961 Diane and LeRoi launched a monthly newsletter for experimental poetry, *The Floating Bear*. *Floating Bear* featured work by newer, unknown poets who'd submitted to *Yugen*, and was distributed free to anyone who put their name on the mailing list. Jones and di Prima also had a brief affair, as a result of which Diane gave birth to a daughter.

The small presses and "little magazine" network represented by enterprises such as Totem and *Floating Bear*, alongside equally important ventures from outside New York such as the Chicago-based *Big Table* and San Francisco's short-lived *Beatitude*, played an essential role in getting new poets published. Usually run on a shoestring budget, and without the reputation of established literary magazines to guarantee sales, they were very much a labor of love for those who published them.

Toward the end of the 60s, di Prima—by then at the hub of the hippie revolution in San Francisco—was invited to write her story by Maurice Girodias of Olympia Press. The Paris-based publisher, who had first put into print *The Naked Lunch* and other banned classics, made most of his money from erotic works, and that was how he wanted Diane to pitch her book, with plenty of emphasis on sex. She needed the money, and her one-and-only "potboiler," *Memoirs of a Beatnik*, became her best-selling work.

Sensationalism apart, like Hettie Jones' book, di Prima's memoir provided a unique insider's view of the Greenwich Village Beat community in the latter half of the 50s. But the most celebrated account of the Greenwich Village of the Beats from a woman's perspective was Joyce Johnson's *Minor Characters*, which was published in 1983.

The Village had long been a magnet for young rebels and Joyce Johnson (then Joyce Glassman) was younger than most when she started making surreptitious Sunday afternoon trips from her parents' smart Upper West Side home to where the bohemian crowd hung out in Washington Square Park. It was 1948, and she was just 13. The Square was the venue for impromptu musical sessions that were the embryo of the Greenwich Village folk music scene and, as she strummed her guitar in her teenage bedroom, Joyce dreamed of being as free as the musicians and singers who played there.

Her trips became more frequent and the Village more familiar as she and her friend Maria discovered places like the Waldorf Caféteria. This was the greasy spoon diner on 8th Street and Sixth where more boho characters, including the Beats-to-be, would gather in the daytime before going on to bars such as the San Remo. Of course by the time they did Joyce would be back home to meet the 7 pm curfew her parents insisted on.

"Jack kept saying, 'I don't want anything to do with all that.' Of course he had to, but didn't want to, in fact, when he was 'King of the Beats' and all that. And that's maybe when he said, 'I'm gonnna drink myself to death.'"

Carolyn Cassady, 2006

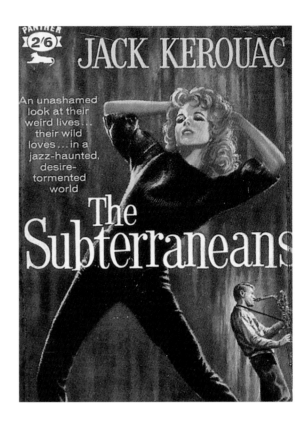

When she entered Barnard College, an affiliate of Columbia University, at age 15, Joyce met Elise Cowan, who seemed a lot more familiar than she with New York's bohemian scene. It transpired Elise was acquainted with a group of aspiring writers, one of whom—Allen Ginsberg—she'd fallen for, though it was not wholeheartedly reciprocated. Eventually she introduced Joyce to Ginsberg in December 1956, and a few months later, on Ginsberg's suggestion, she went on a blind date with his friend Jack Kerouac.

The 21-year-old student and Kerouac met at the 8th Street Howard Johnson's—Joyce paying for the meal as Kerouac was broke—and embarked on a two-year love affair that began just before Jack won fame with the publication of *On the Road*. During those two years Joyce Johnson saw the effects of celebrity on Kerouac and the other Beats too, witnessing at first hand the emergence of the foibles and insecurities in his character that fame exposed, and which she later chronicled in her memoir, *Minor Characters*.

By the end of Johnson's affair with Kerouac in 1959 the Beat phenomenon was in full swing. Hot on the heels of *On the Road*, the Grove Press published *The Subterraneans* in February 1958, and Viking followed with *The Dharma Bums* in mid-October. The film *Pull My Daisy*, including Jack Kerouac, Allen Ginsberg, and Gregory Corso, began production in January 1959.

An excerpt from *The Naked Lunch* appeared in the *Chicago Review* at the end of 1958, only to be subsequently censored. As a consequence, *Big Table* magazine was published in March 1959 carrying the same piece; it was promptly impounded by the US Post Office. The ban was eventually lifted in July 1960.

Bill Burroughs, meanwhile, made himself a virtual exile, moving between Paris, London, and Tangiers between 1958 and 1964. Then, on June 14, 1958, Neal Cassady was sentenced on two counts of five years to life in San Quentin prison for possession of three marijuana "reefers," being released two years later to the day.

Now all the Beats were big news, though the accompanying stardom was easier to handle for some than it was for others. Kerouac, in particular, was finding it increasingly difficult to deal with the burden of what biographer David Sandison (in *Jack Kerouac*, 1995) called "unwanted celebrity and rent-a-quote punditry."

Just a couple of months after *On the Road* hit the best-seller lists Jack had thrown himself into a week-long season at the prestigious Village Vanguard jazz club, which most nights ended up a drunken shambles—a harbinger of his growing problem with alcohol. He made an even more embarrassing appearance in November 1958, when he appeared as a panelist in a debate at New York's Hunter College discussing "Is there a Beat Generation?" He drunkenly turned on fellow panelists, who included the British novelist Kingsley Amis and the *New York Times* editor James Weschler, calling them "a bunch of Communist shits," who were encouraging "the Sovietization of America."

The tirade was indicative of the increasingly right-wing stance Kerouac was adopting, together with a pronounced contempt for the Beat lifestyle that he himself had purportedly pioneered. Pictures made at various Greenwich Village gatherings at the time show Kerouac looking sullen, usually with bottle in hand, and attest to his dischantment with the whole scene. But the success and acclaim continued, whether he wanted it or not.

**Opposite:** Taking its imagery from the 1960 Hollywood movie, a British paperback edition of Kerouac's *The Subterraneans*, which he based on characters he knew in the San Remo Café in Greenwich Village.

**Right:** Jack Kerouac looking dead beat in Allen Ginsberg's New York apartment.

**Below:** Kerouac, here uncharacteristically with a cup of tea in his hand, at a New York Chinese restaurant in 1959.

The huge media attention that followed the publication of *On the Road* and the "Howl" trial, catapulting Jack Kerouac and Allen Ginsberg into celebrity status, heralded the introduction of a new social stereotype in American popular culture: the "beatnik."

The arts have always been represented by caricatures in the popular imagination—the painter in his garret, the struggling novelist burning the midnight oil hunched over the typewriter—but none had such resonance with a mainly youthful mainstream public. As well as members of their own age group who'd seen the War and its aftermath, and didn't like what they saw, the Beats also appealed to an element of that next generation who grew up through the 40s and early 50s. In *The Birth of the Beat Generation* (1995), Steven Watson described the Beats as being greeted as "something akin to American literature's first rock stars." Inevitably, their youthful followers soon found themselves under the spotlight, too.

The (usually derogatory) term "beatnik" was coined in 1958 after the Russian "sputnik," the world's first satellite which, to America's embarrassment, had been launched the previous year. The "nik" suffix became instantly derisory, and as such has remained part of the language, from "draftnik" Vietnam draft-dodgers to "peaceniks" of various kinds. The term first appeared in print on April 2, 1958, in a column in the *San Francisco Chronicle* by the journalist Herb Caen. He wrote: "*Look* magazine, preparing a picture spread on San Francisco's Beat Generation (oh no, not AGAIN!), hosted a party in a North Beach house for 50 Beatniks, and by the time word got round the sour grapevine, over 250 bearded cats and kits were on hand."

It didn't take long for the national—and international—media to catch on, and before you could say "like far out, man," the archetypal beatnik had arrived. The male of the species was characterized as a pot-smoking, goatee-bearded, bongo-playing layabout, wearing a black beret, black jeans, and black sweater. Footwear was usually sandals (or none at all), dark glasses—"shades"—were much favored (especially in dimly-lit jazz cellars), and the hair was outrageously long for the time, hung over the collar. Beatnik "chicks" supposedly dressed in a similar fashion, with long straight hair and pale make-up; black leotards sometimes replaced the jeans.

By mid-1959 it was hard to find a magazine that didn't mention beatniks, real or satirized, somewhere within its pages. *Playboy* had run an excerpt from an address Jack Kerouac had given to students on "The Origins of the Beat Generation" in its December 1958 edition, along with other beat-oriented features. In the piece, Kerouac clearly distanced himself from the "beatnik" tag: "People began to call themselves beatniks, beats, jazzniks, bopniks, bugniks, and finally I was called the 'avatar' of all this."

In July 1959 the magazine ran a pictorial essay by Jim Morod on the Greenwich Village and West Coast coffeehouse scenes with poems by Jack Kerouac, Allen Ginsberg, and Gregory Corso. The issue also included a "Beat Playmate," Yvette Vickers—this was, after all, *Playboy*. Vickers was described as "a beatnik found in a coffeehouse." The pretty, short-haired blonde, readers were told, was interested in acting, the ballet, and the poetry of Dylan Thomas; she also liked classical music—"Prokoviev drives me out of my skull"—and, in the true spirit of the magazine, "driving her Jag through the desert for kicks."

In September 1959 *Life* magazine—which took the anti-American implications of the Russian-sounding "nik" in "Beatnik" more seriously than many—ran a piece titled "Squaresville USA vs Beatsville." The feature contrasted the lifestyle of a typical all-American family in Kansas, pictured cozily gathered in front of the TV, with that of a "beat" family of Venice, California. This family lived in a "cool pad," sprawled on mattresses on the floor and was surrounded by empty beer cans. The *Life* feature was prompted by the news story that three teenage girls in Hutchinson, Kansas, had invited Lawrence Lipton (author of the 1959 book about beat life in Venice, *The Holy Barbarians*) to visit their small town. When word got round that a beatnik invasion was about to take place, concerned parents called in the law, and Lipton's invitation was canceled. A police spokesman told *Life* that a beatnik was someone who "doesn't like work, any man who doesn't like work is a vagrant, and a vagrant goes to jail around here." As they were whisked away from the eyes of the media, one of the penitent girls told a *Life* journalist: "We know beatniks aren't good, but we thought they just dressed sloppy and talked funny. Now we know that they get married without licenses and things like that."

As well as their dubious marital arrangements, the suspect political leanings of the beatniks were confirmed by that scourge of liberal-thinking Americans everywhere, J. Edgar Hoover, when he identified "America's Three Menaces" at the 1960 Republican Party Convention as being "Communists, Beatniks, and Eggheads."

"When you take dehydrated Hipster and add watery words to make Instant Beatnik, the flavor is gone but the lack of taste lingers on."

Critic Herbert Gold, 1960

**Previous page:** A still from the Hollywood adaptation of Kerouac's *Subterraneans*, with West Coast saxophone star Gerry Mulligan.

**Above:** The work of illustrator George Woodbridge with a caricature of "beat" stand-up comic Mort Sahl, the frontpiece of the "Beatnik" special featured in the September 1960 edition of *Mad* magazine.

**Right:** The cover of a 2004 "Dictionary of Hipster Slang," which perpetuated the beatnik stereotype more than 40 years after it first emerged.

**Below left:** Henri Lenoir, owner of the Vesuvio bar in San Francisco, his front window advertising a "beatnik kit" at the height of the Beat craze.

**Below right:** TV's own Maynard G. Krebs played by a goofy-looking Bob Denver.

**Opposite left and right:** The *Beat Generation Cookbook* and its recipe for "Ginsburgers."

**GINSBURGERS**

Like several other recipes in this book, this one comes from neither the west nor east coast Beat hives. This recipe originated with the Salina, Kansas Beat Colony. You may not believe Salina, Kansas has a Beat Generation. We didn't either until we went there and met him.

The Goods:
1 lb USDA inspected ground horsemeat
3 tablespoons finely chopped onion
3 tablespoons finely chopped dill pickle
1/2 cup chopped Pickled Beats (see recipe)
1 cup cooked Square potatoes (see Garret Carrot Squares and fake it)
1/2 cup milk
1/2 teaspoon salt

Method:
Mix all ingredients together well. Shape into patties. Fry until they whinny (about 15 minutes). Serve with horseradish and On The Road Apples.

**EVERGREENS**

Next time you split for Gowhere, make sure you take a Macy's plastic knapsack with you. As you gather your goodies, throw 'em in it.

Make for a lettuce field and pick up a head. Glomb two or three scallions from an onion factory; half-dozen or so radishes here and there. Chop 'em coarsely, and proceed. Probably you'll pass water, so add a bunch of watercress, and four or five fresh tomatoes. Iowa should contribute two or three bell peppers, and you can get vinegar from the first vinyard you hit. Like a little anise? Supply at your own risk.

Turn left at Arkansas. You'll need a third-cup of corn oil (Texas is lousy with it). Need a little seasoning? A salt mine should lick that. Movement in new directions will toss it. Keep moving until time to eat. Pick out the closest grove, and have Evergreens. (NOTE: Never eat at a random house.)

But the ultimate beatnik (perhaps the *only* beatnik) as far as millions of Americans were concerned arrived on their TV screens on September 29, 1959, with the first episode of the teen-oriented sitcom *The Many Loves of Dobie Gillis*. Dobie himself was a straight-looking high school romantic looking for romance (which he never found), while his sidekick, bongo-playing Maynard G. Krebs, was "beatnik" personified. Played by Bob Denver, the laid-back Maynard sported unkempt hair brushed forward, the obligatory goatee, and a torn sweatshirt. He preceded every utterance with "like," and shuddered at the mention of work.

Not surprisingly, the Beats themselves detested the whole beatnik ballyhoo, and its distortion of what "beat" was about. "The foul word is used several times," Allen Ginsberg was to write to the *New York Times Book Review* after an unsympathetic piece about Jack Kerouac, pointing out that the term was the invention of the critics themselves, and not of the writers they might criticize. Referring to the magazine empire of Henry Luce, publishers of both *Life* and *Time* magazines, Kenneth Rexroth commented: "The Beat Generation may once have been human beings—today they are simply comical bogies conjured up by Luce publications."

As with the Greenwich Village habitués who cashed in on the beatnik craze via Rent-a Beatnik, on the West Coast there were those who similarly took advantage of all the media attention. Even San Francisco's Café Vesuvio, right next to the City Lights bookstore and a well-established meeting place for the genuine article, hired a local "beatnik" called "Hube the Cube" to sit in their window looking "beat" for passing tourists.

"Hey man, don't knock my clothes. I'm a symptom." "A symptom of what?" "Of the Beat Generation."

Maynard G. Krebs [Bob Denver] in *The Many Loves of Dobie Gillis*, 1959

In 1961, satirizing the media-generated image of the Beats, the 7 Poets Press in New York produced a tongue-in-cheek *Beat Generation Cookbook*, which included recipes for "Subterranean Spudniks" ("supplied by a young Beat doll, who is also the mother of three Beatlets"), "Ginsburgers," "Haiku Hash," and a "Kerouac Kocktail." The publishers also had *A Pocket Guide to Beat Watching* planned for publication the following spring, though there's no record of it ever appearing.

Notwithstanding spoofs such as the *Beat Generation Cookbook*, for some paperback publishers Beat meant a bonanza. The era saw a plethora of sensationalist titles on the bookstands—cheap exploitation novels with titles ranging from the lurid (including *Beat Girl*, *Beatnik Wanton*, *Lust Pad*, *Pads Are For Passion*, and *Sintime Beatniks*) to the laughable (*Bang A Beatnik*, *Bongo Gum*, *Epitaph for a Dead Beat*, and *Jesus Was A Beatnik*). Pulp author Richard E. Geis had two such potboilers out in 1960: *Like Crazy, Man* featured a buxom, bongo-playing blonde on the cover alongside the blurb "Erotic and exotic . . . the lost world of the beatniks," while *The Beatniks* had a similar girl dancing wildly with a more detailed hint of what lay inside (presumably by the same copywriter)—"The erotic and exotic—a lost world where naked sex flaunts its message to the sensuous beat of a drum."

# rent-a-beatnik

Photographer Fred McDarrah made thousands of pictures of folk on the Village Beat scene, from its leading writers and artists, to oddball characters such as the college student who was nominated "Miss Beatnik 1959." As well as contributing photographs, he also had a job selling ads for the Greenwich Village newspaper *The Village Voice*, and at the end of 1959—initially as a joke, perhaps—he was the prime instigator of the first advertisement in the *'Voice* for "Rent-a-Beatnik."

Seemingly aimed at posh suburban party-hosts, the first ad ran: "Add zest to your Tuxedo Park Party . . . Rent a Beatnik! Completely equipped: Beards, eye shades, old Army jackets, Levi's, frayed shirt, sneakers, or sandals (optional). Deductions allowed for no beard, baths, shoes or haircut. Lady Beatniks also available, usual garb: all black (Chaperone required)."

A later ad in the paper listed services rendered as including "Model for Photographs / Entertain or Read Poetry / Play Bongo Drums."

Joke or not, the ads were taken seriously. Renting a Beatnik cost $40 a night, with props such as bongos and guitars charged extra, and various Village characters indeed rented themselves to square soirées. One such was the poet Jack Micheline, who bemoaned the fact in the *New York Herald Tribune* when it ran a story on Rent-a-Beatnik: "It's sad that a poet of my reputation has to do a whole lot of gigs just to make a buck."

Jazz poet and painter Ted Joans was another who was for hire. As the *Trib'* reported, when he was rented out to a smart party in Scarsdale to read his poetry, by the time of his performance the guests were too drunk to notice. But the host was happy with the sheer presence of a genuine beatnik: "He was there resplendent in his beret and his slightly torn black sweater. It worked out wonderfully. People in Westchester are still talking about it."

Rent-a-Beatnik was neatly satirized in *Mad* magazine when it ran a "Rent A Square" ad "for your next Beatnik Party"—"complete with white-on-white shirt, polka dot bow tie, blue serge suit," etc. It was part of a *Mad* special titled *Beatnik: The Magazine for Hipsters*, with other mock advertisements like "Oversize Sweaters for Beatnik chicks—one size only (too big)." The lampoon, published in September 1960, also included a glossary of "Square Terms," and articles such as "How To Get High On Espresso" and "What To Do If The Landlord Shows Up." The

same year also saw a compilation book of reprints from *Mad*; in true beat parlance it was titled *Like, Mad*, with the magazine's goofy mascot character Alfred E. Neuman on the cover sporting "beatnik" beret, goatee, and polo-neck sweater.

"To my surprise, the response to the ad was overwhelming, as I got letters from schools, colleges, clubs, businesses, and the media. Not only were there requests for Beatniks, but requests from them. I ran another ad, and before I knew it, I was renting genuine Beatniks."

Fred McDarrah, *Beat Generation: Glory Days in Greenwich Village*, 1996

**Right:** *Mad* magazine's "Rent A Square" ad, published in their 1960 "Beatnik" special.

**Below:** One of the *Village Voice*'s "Rent Genuine Beatniks" ads, which appeared in June 1960.

THE MOST TALKED ABOUT AD IN NEW YORK

Why is The Beat Generation the most significant literary event in our time? Get the real story from the real beats.

**RENT GENUINE BEATNIKS**

BADLY GROOMED BUT BRILLIANT (Male and Female)

FOR FUND RAISING & PRIVATE PARTIES/ TO LECTURE AT YOUR CLUB/MODEL FOR PHOTOGRAPHS/ENTERTAIN OR READ POETRY PLAY BONGO DRUMS / BOX 490 / VOICE / 22 GREENWICH AVE. / N. Y. 11.

RENT A "SQUARE" FOR YOUR NEXT Beatnik Party

I COME COMPLETE WITH:
• White-on-white Shirt
• Polka Dot Bow Tie
• Blue Serge Suit
• Saddle Shoes
AND A GIRL FROM THE BRONX

ADD A NEW WILD KICK TO YOUR EVENING

"SQUARE" SOL

AND HIS STIFF DOLL

"The wild, weird world of the Beatniks! . . . Sullen rebels, defiant chicks . . . searching for a life of their own! The pads . . . the jazz . . . the dives . . . those frantic 'way-out' parties . . . beyond belief!"

Publicity tagline for *The Beatniks*, 1960

Alongside the pulp book publishers, it didn't take long for Hollywood to jump onto the beatnik bandwagon with various exploitation B-movies, most of which bore no relationship to the beat scene as such, some merely alluding to it in an opportunistic choice of title. There's an early hint of what would be regarded as "beatnik" style in *Funny Face*, a 1956 MGM musical starring Audrey Hepburn. She plays a Greenwich Village bookstore clerk discovered by the editor of a fashion magazine and flown to Paris with a photographer (Fred Astaire). Although she thinks the world of fashion is shallow, she takes the trip so that she can hang out with Parisian intellectuals and enjoy their bohemian Left-Bank lifestyle. "We're not inhibited by outmoded social conventions," she declares, as she dances with abandon in a smoky Paris jazz cellar, clothed head to toe in black (except for white socks), in tight pants and a polo-neck sweater. Beatnik chic indeed!

The comedy *Bell, Book and Candle*, released in 1958, had Kim Novak as a member of a coven of very hip Greenwich Village witches, who falls for a square publisher (played by James Stewart). While not a movie about beatniks as such, the witches' lifestyle had some parallels with that of the archetypal hipster. They hang out in an underground jazz bar where one of them (Jack Lemmon) plays the bongos, while Novak's character favors black clothes and prefers not to wear shoes.

Likewise *High School Confidential* (1958) was not directly about beatniks, even though the original trailer trumpeted it as "the story of The Beat Generation." Produced by one of the masters of cheap exploitation pictures, Albert Zugsmith, and featuring rock 'n' roll star Jerry Lee Lewis, the movie has just one "beatnik" scene, in which a girl reads a poem in a coffeeshop—"Tomorrow Is A Drag, Man"—accompanied by a jazz pianist.

Zugsmith was also responsible for *The Beat Generation*, released the following year. Again, though the blurb for the picture promised revelations about "the weird, 'way out' world of the Beatniks!" the movie was in fact a detective drama. Set in a bohemian coffeehouse where beatniks gather to recite poetry, the story revolved around the hunt for a serial rapist, and featured an unlikely cast that included Steve Cochran, blonde bombshell Mamie Van Doren, and jazz legend Louis Armstrong. The beatniks in the film, crude caricatures even by the standard of the media stereotype, are totally unsympathetic characters, and served to reinforce mainstream America's worst suspicions about "beat" culture at the time.

Also known as *Beatsville*, 1959's *The Rebel Set* featured a coffee bar proprietor recruiting three down-and-out beatniks—a writer, an actor, and the jailbird son of an actress—to help him pull off a million-dollar robbery. There was not an honest beatnik in sight. The same year also saw *The Bloody Brood*, with Peter Falk as a drug-dealing gangster who hangs around with beatniks, and *Bucket of Blood*—the latter now acclaimed as a kitsch classic of beatnik cinema. Directed by horror specialist Roger Corman, *Bucket of Blood* concerned a no-hope coffee bar waiter with artistic ambitions. After killing a cat and covering the body in plaster, he's applauded by his fellow beatniks as a potential genius (and it helps pull the chicks, too!). He follows his debut "Dead Cat" artwork with "Murdered Man," "Female Nude," and so on. All the life-like sculptures were modeled from the real thing, for the beatnik artist had killed his subjects to create his artworks.

Undoubtedly the worst example of blatant beatnik exploitation came in 1960 with *The Beatniks*, a tale of teenage hoodlums, who hold up convenience stores for kicks. It may as well have been called "The Delinquents" or whatever, as the hoods—including the central character, who is also a budding rock singer—have absolutely nothing to do with beats, even of the caricature variety.

The British film industry made a foray into beatnikland in 1960 with *Beat Girl* (also known in America as *Wild For Kicks*). It was the tale of a rebellious art student, Jenny, who hangs out at the obligatory underground coffee cellar and dishes the dirt on the stripper background of her new step-mother. With a US

## "The drifters, the hipsters, the hot sisters."

Publicity blurb for *The Rebel Set*, 1959

blurb that read "Hop-Head U.K. School Girls Get in Trouble," the low-budget epic starred Noelle Adam as Jenny, along with leather-jacketed pop star Adam Faith plus Christopher Lee and Oliver Reed in supporting roles.

*The Prime Time* (1960) featured Jo Anne LeCompte as another teenage rebel who gets involved with the beats, posing nude for a local beatnik artist known as "The Beard"—who kills her when she teases him about his masculinity. But the biggest fiasco in Hollywood's attempts to cash in on the beat scene was the screen version of Jack Kerouac's *The Subterraneans*, also released in 1960.

Billed as "Love among the new Bohemians!" it featured Leslie Caron as Mardou, girlfriend of the central character Leo (George Peppard). In the book Mardou was black, but the elfin-like Caron was a far safer choice as far as the studio, MGM, was concerned. Set in San Francisco, the weak script, which bore little semblance to the original novel, was only relieved with some fine atmospheric jazz from West Coast luminaries, including Art Pepper, Shelley Manne, and Gerry Mulligan, the latter also appearing in an acting role. The publicity blurb just about summed it up; it ran—"These are The Subterraneans, Today's Young Rebels—Who live and love in a world of their own, this is their story told to the hot rhythms of fabulous jazz!"

"It is not my fault that certain so-called bohemian elements have found in my writings something to hang their peculiar beatnik theories on."

Jack Kerouac

Released in 1963, after the media spotlight had moved away from the beatniks, *Greenwich Village Story* was far more sympathetic to the realities of the bohemian life than the barefaced exploitation movies. Brian, a struggling novelist, who aspires to be the next Jack Kerouac, lives with his girlfriend Genie (still a radical concept in 1963) in the Village, promising to marry her if his book is a success. After it is panned by the critics he embarks on a weekend affair. Unbeknown to him, Genie is pregnant and subsequently dies having an abortion. The *New York Times* called the film, "A tale of young love and desire . . . roaming the bars, the caverns, the pads, and lofts, and the clangorous confines of the extroverts, introverts, and perverts," while the *New York Herald Tribune* wrote of "marijuana-soaked parties, artists in creative turmoil, and youth in revolt, let alone extra-marital passions."

But in the main the beatnik exploitation movies reinforced the press-created image of the unwashed, dope-addled layabout, often adding their own layer of distortion in presenting the Beats and their followers as actual psychopaths or dangerous criminals, to be discouraged by "straight" society at all costs.

Among the humor and cartoon books, *Suzuki Beane* (published in 1961), by Sandra Scoppettone with Louise Fitzhugh illustrations, was a Bleecker Street beatnik parody of Kay Thompson's Eloise series of illustrated humor books (1956–59). *Suzuki Beane* took a very different angle on caricaturing beatniks. It focused on a little girl who lives with her beatnik parents in Greenwich Village. The one-off almost became a TV series, though only a pilot was ever made. *Suzuki Beane* was set to be revived in an animated film in 2007.

Beatnik "style" first impacted on fashion per se in the gamine look personified by Audrey Hepburn in *Funny Face*—very French, very existentialist, very Juliette Greco. A prime example was Jean Seberg in Jean-Luc Godard's stylish 1960 thriller *À bout de souffle* (*Breathless*), described by one fashion scribe as "the actress who inspired a million pixie cuts." The image of her strolling down the Champs Élysées in Paris in tight black pants and what became an iconic *New York Herald Tribune* sweater reverberated as a fashion statement around the world.

The beatnik stereotype far outlived the media frenzy, and crops up to this day in all manner of contexts—perhaps most ironically when it became once again the inspiration for a women's fashion trend, in 2005. The very idea that the anti-fashion stance of the Beats, or even that suggested by the beatnik caricature, could be appropriated by the style industry over 40 years later says much for the latter's desperation in its constant search for "new" looks in old.

British fashion designer John Galliano initiated the trend with his summer couture collection for the prestigious house of Dior. How the fashionistas managed to get it completely wrong was borne out immediately by the designer citing the mid-60s Andy Warhol muse Edie Sedgwick as a prime inspiration for his black-and-white mohair dresses, black caps, and knee-high black boots. Likewise fellow designer Karl Lagerfeld came up with what the *Daily Telegraph* fashion columnist confidently called a "beatnik look," with black mini-skirt and over-the-knee boots. The striped sweaters and skinny jeans also featured in the various collections were a bit nearer "genuine" beatnik style, if there ever was such a thing, but a press report by UK chain Topshop—enthusing that "Beatle caps and bug-eye sunglasses provide a hip finish"—in many ways said it all.

Despite the media distortion that characterized the short-lived "beatnik" craze—notwithstanding fashion fads four decades on—the fundamental influence of the Beats themselves was more evident than ever as the 50s gave way to the 60s.

SERIOUSLY STYLISH... OUTRAGEOUSLY SEXY

Jean-Luc Godard's

# BREATHLESS

(A Bout de Souffle)

JEAN PAUL
**BELMONDO**

JEAN
**SEBERG**

15

Written and directed by Jean-Luc **GODARD**    from an original treatment by Francois **TRUFFAUT**    Artistic and technical advisor Claude **CHABROL**
Photography by Raoul Coutard    Produced by Georges de Beauregard

# the 60s & beyond

"I was too young to be a beatnik,

and too old to be a hippie."

Ken Kesey

By the end of the 50s, as well as making its mark on new developments in literature and the arts generally, a Beat sensibility made itself felt in the broader field of popular culture. The scenes established by the Beats themselves and their audience— "beatnik" and otherwise—were the basis for the "underground" that was the alternative to mainstream culture for the rest of the decade. The by-products of Beat included little magazines and independent publishers, live poetry circuits, specialist bookstores, experimental theater groups, community arts projects, creative workshops of all kinds, and a burgeoning underground music scene. This emergent Beat-influenced subculture from the early 60s provided a template for the so-called "hippie" counterculture later in the decade. But much of this—except in the case of Allen Ginsberg, who would become a father figure and propagandist for the counterculture—lay outside the province of the original Beats.

Jack Kerouac, in particular, distanced himself from what the Beats had come to represent at the dawn of the 60s. Developments later in the decade, deemed also to have been inspired by them, would distance him further. Yet in 1960 alone, five new books by Kerouac were published (*Lonesome Traveler*, *Book of Dreams*, *Tristessa*, *Visions of Cody*, and *Scripture of the Golden Eternity*). Nonetheless his disillusionment with fame continued, and it was accompanied by a downward spiral into alcoholism, and far less regular (and, in the main, far less satisfactory) bursts of writing.

Kerouac moved house several times, usually accompanied by his mother Gabrielle, and for much of this period the pair lived in Florida. Then in 1966 he surprised everyone by marrying Stella Sampas, the older sister of his childhood friend Sebastian Sampas. The couple settled back in Lowell for a time before moving—along with Gabrielle—to St. Petersberg, Florida.

Somewhere in between the depressingly predictable instances of drinking binges, altercations in bars, and embarrassing press interviews, Kerouac managed to embark on three book projects, the results of which were to prove mixed. In 1965 he flew to Paris with the aim of researching his French ancestry, but after being barred from archive libraries because he wasn't sober, he ended up in a succession of bars and jazz clubs. However, as always, Kerouac found much material there, and his trip became the basis for a slim novel, the poorly-received *Satori In Paris*, which he wrote in a week.

Then, in 1967 he wrote his last full-length book, *Vanity of Duluoz*; this dealt with his early life, as had his *The Town and the*

"I'm bored with the avant-garde and the skyrocketing sensationalism . . . The Beat group dispersed in the early 60s, all went their own way, and this is my home; home life, as in the beginning, with a little toot once in a while in local bars."

Jack Kerouac, interviewed for *Paris Review*, at his home in Lowell, 1968

*City*—but the new book continued the story to after the death of David Kammerer, in the early days of the Beats. Published in 1968, it represented a move from the romanticization of his own myth, in which he previously indulged, to a salutary look at the "vanity" of his and the other Beats' youth. In 1969 Kerouac wrote *Pic*, a short novel that he had started back in 1951, about a black North Carolina farmhand, which was published posthumously in 1971 to no great critical acclaim.

Kerouac died on October 21, 1969, at a hospital in St. Petersberg, Florida. His death, at age 47, was caused by an internal hemorrhage brought on by cirrhosis of the liver, the result of a lifetime of heavy drinking. He was buried in his home town of Lowell, Massachusetts.

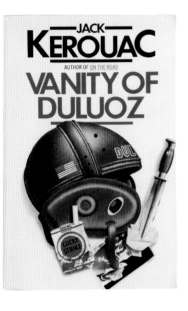

"In the mourners' seats sat Kerouac's middle-class French-Canadian relatives—eyes narrowed, faces florid, arms crossed on their disapproving breasts. Around the casket—dipping, weaving, chanting 'Om'—were Allen Ginsberg, Peter Orlovsky, and Gregory Corso."

Journalist and writer Vivian Gornick

Unlike Kerouac, who rarely ventured out of his beloved America, Bill Burroughs was very much the foreign exile in the first half of the 60s. After *The Naked Lunch* was published in Paris in 1959, it became an instant and much sought-after cult classic in Europe, while Burroughs himself continued to spend his time between Paris, London, and Tangiers.

Burroughs didn't return to the US until 1964, by which time three more of his novels had been published. All had been conceived in the Beat Hotel: *The Soft Machine*, *The Ticket That Exploded*, and *Nova Express*. He'd also become a literary celebrity in his absence, not least after *Naked Lunch* was published in the US by Grove Press in 1962, only to be prosecuted as obscene by the authorities in Massachusetts some months later. Eventually, in 1966, the Massachusetts Supreme Judicial Court declared the work "not obscene," after all, in the wake of what is still the last obscenity trial against a work of literature to have been prosecuted in the US.

Through most of the 60s Burroughs' boyfriend was the mathematician Ian Sommerville, with whom he had first become involved while working with Brion Gysin in Paris. While he and Burroughs were living in London, Sommerville operated a small studio owned by Paul McCartney at 34 Montagu Square, which in 1966 was used by Burroughs for his experimental cut-up sound tapes known as "Hello, Yes, Hello." McCartney and Burroughs met there several times, the Beatle later recalling that "He was very interesting but we never really struck up a huge conversation—I actually felt you had to be a bit of a junkie, which was probably not true." The tapes, featuring a mix of recordings of different radio stations, TV shows, radio static, readings of newspaper bulletins, and Burroughs' own text, were not dissimilar to the tape-collages used by the Beatles in *Sgt. Pepper* (on the cover of which Burroughs' picture appeared) and other recordings made by the band in 1966 and 1967.

Burroughs was also involved in various experimental film projects, one of which was *Chappaqua*, directed in 1966 by Conrad Rooks and featuring Burroughs as "Opium Jones," along with Allen Ginsberg and the musician Ravi Shankar. He was also cited as a seminal influence on the new wave of "inner space"

science fiction, exemplified by writers such as J.G. Ballard and Philip José Farmer. Perhaps most significantly, as well as being considered a founder and icon of the Beat movement, in the 60s Burroughs gained recognition as one of the pop culture "media philosophers" along with Timothy Leary, Marshall McLuan, and others who surfaced at the time.

The Beat scene as such gradually fragmented from the early 60s onward, its other leading players also going their own way, once more unhindered by the gaze of the media.

After his move to San Francisco in 1956, and subsequent sojourn in the Beat Hotel at the end of the decade, Gregory Corso traveled extensively through the 60s, especially in Mexico and Eastern Europe. He earned his living from fees for readings and royalties from books. As well as his best-selling *Gasoline*, published by City Lights in 1958, by the end of the decade these included the poetry collections *The Happy Birthday of Death* (published in 1960), *Long Live Man* (1962), *Elegiac Feelings American* (1970), and the novel *The American Express*, which appeared in 1961. For several summers Corso also taught at the Naropa Institute in Boulder, Colorado, and briefly at the State University of New York in Buffalo. He was dismissed from the latter position in 1965 for refusing to sign an affidavit (shades of Joe McCarthy in the 50s) certifying he was not a Communist.

Following the success in 1958 of his best-known collection of poetry, *A Coney Island of the Mind*, Lawrence Ferlinghetti continued to run the City Lights bookstore in San Francisco; he also continued to publish books under the City Lights imprint. At the same time he was enjoying more and more his rural retreat in the wilder part of California at Big Sur, famously chronicled by Kerouac in his novel of the same name in 1961. The other founding figure in the San Francisco Renaissance, Kenneth Rexroth, lectured as a professor at the University of California in Santa Barbara from the late 60s. Celebrated by the students for his witty and inflammatory remarks on the increasing trend of anti-intellectualism and laziness on the campus, he was also a source of considerable aggravation to the college administration.

Having stimulated an early interest in Zen Buddhism among the emerging Beat scene on the West Coast, in 1956 Gary Snyder confirmed the depth of his commitment to Zen by spending most of his time from then until 1968 studying at Zen monasteries in Japan. When he returned, he had become a seminal figure in the post-Beat hippie counterculture.

The writer and lecturer Allan Watts, too, was increasingly influential in spreading the Zen message through the 60s, during which time he began to experiment with the effects on the meditative process of mind-altering drugs, particularly LSD. He concluded, however, that as an aid to expanding consciousness such drugs could be useful, but once tried had served their purpose—as he put it, "When you've got the message, hang up the phone." Like Snyder, Watts also became a somewhat unintentional spokesperson for the "alternative society" that flourished in the late 60s.

**Far left:** A 1982 UK paperback edition of William Burroughs' supernatural thriller *Cities of the Red Night*, a deliberately disjointed narrative set across vast stretches of time and space which first appeared the previous year.

**Left:** Lawrence Ferlinghetti's best-selling collection *A Coney Island of the Mind*, published in 1958 as #74 in the New Directions Paperback series.

**Above:** William Burroughs in Paris c. 1960.

# the hip humorists

The influence of the Beats was even to be found in a cutting-edge brand of humor. There was a fad for "sick jokes"—most famously translated into print via the cartoons of Jules Feiffer in the *Village Voice*—which was rooted in the stage acts of a new breed of stand-up performers delivering material with a distinctly Beat attitude.

The pioneer of hip humor was undoubtedly Lord Buckley, born Richard Myrle Buckley in 1906, an eccentric character who looked like an old-world aristocrat with a Salvador Dali-style moustache. His language and delivery was equally polyglot—a mixture of upper-class English and Black American street jargon. During the 50s his routines and records featured renditions of stories from the Bible, Shakespeare, classic literature, and history. Laced with his often scandalous sense of humor, they included the story of Jesus ("The Nazz"), the life of Ghandi ("The Hip Gan"), and "Marc Anthony's Funeral Oration." He died in 1960, having been a cult

figure who never had the exposure of subsequent Beat-oriented stand-ups, all of whom acknowledged their debt to him.

Mort Sahl, on the other hand, became very big indeed. The Canadian-born comedian started doing stand-up at San Francisco's trendy "hungry i" club in the mid-50s, where the notoriously hard-to-please audience threw coins and peanuts at him. But they soon got hip to his laconic delivery and satirical approach to politics and the events of the day.

His style of free association, jazz-like improvisation, and stream-of-consciousness delivery had much in common with the Beats' use of language, and his barbed comments on political figures—including US Presidents—were unprecedented at the time. By 1960 he had earned the respect not just of the hipster community, but of the liberal establishment, too. In a rare accolade for a comedian in those days, he was the subject of a cover story in *Time* magazine. Sahl even wrote speeches for his friend, John F. Kennedy, though when JFK was elected President, Sahl wasn't afraid to make jokes critical of Kennedy's policies.

But the most radical of the Beat-inspired comedians was Lenny Bruce. Like Sahl, he honed his craft in the "hungry i" nightclub, through the late 50s developing routines which mocked everything from racism to religion, Judaism to Catholicism, abortion, drugs—no topic was taboo as far as he was concerned. However, it was the language he employed (as opposed to the topics he covered), as was the case with many Beat prosecutions from *Howl* onward, that got him in trouble with the law.

"Hipsters, flipsters and finger-poppin' daddies,

Knock me your lobes!

I came here to lay Caesar out,

Not to hip you to him."

Lord Buckley, "Marc Anthony's Funeral Oration," 1954

"As lords of personal excess, skin-poppin' Bruce and joint-smokin' Buckley were natural nonconformists."

Don Waller in *The Rolling Stone Book of the Beats*

After achieving nationwide TV exposure on the *Steve Allen Show*, and headlining at Carnegie Hall in February 1961, later that year Bruce was arrested for obscenity at the Jazz Workshop in San Francisco. Although acquitted, other arrests followed, and venues began to see him as a liability. While free on bond pending appeal of a Chicago conviction, he attempted to do a show in London, only to be taken to the airport and deported. In April 1964 he was arrested after appearing at the Café Au Go Go venue in Greenwich Village, leading to a widely-publicized six-month trial in which his defense included testimonies from Woody Allen, Norman Mailer, Paul Newman, Bob Dylan, Elizabeth Taylor, Richard Burton, Susan Sontag, Gore Vidal, and many others—to no avail. Bruce was sentenced to four months' imprisonment in December 1964, to be postponed during the appeals process, which was still continuing when he died of a morphine overdose in August 1966.

These radical comics owed much to the Beats in both their style and subject matter, and they in turn influenced generations of humorists to come, from Dick Gregory, Richard Pryor, and Woody Allen, to more recent names such as Bill Hicks and Jerry Seinfeld.

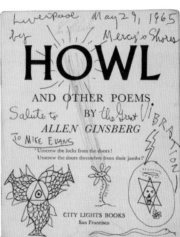

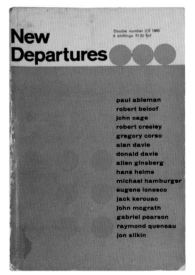

**Left:** Ginsberg during rehearsals for the Royal Albert Hall Poetry International, London, June 11, 1965.

**Below left:** The title page of *Howl*, inscribed to Mike Evans by Allen Ginsberg, during his visit to Liverpool ("by Mercy's shores") in May 1965.

**Below right:** Spearheading the Beat-influenced poetry scene in Britain, *New Departures* was launched by poet Michael Horovitz in 1958. This double issue (# 2/3) from 1960 had a typically impressive line-up of contributors.

Of the major Beat voices, it was Allen Ginsberg who most clearly personified the relationship between the Beat Generation and the new youth-driven counterculture. After extensive travels through South America and India in the early 60s, by the middle of the decade he was touring the nerve-centers of the "new society" like a kaftan-wearing prophet, evangelizing the message of peace, love, and music. As well as speaking at innumerable anti-Vietnam War rallies in the US, he was famously crowned "King of May" before a crowd of 100,000 at a student festival in Communist Prague in 1965. Later the same month he declared Liverpool to be "the center of the consciousness of the human universe."

The focus of his British visit in 1965 was the seminal Poetry International at London's Royal Albert Hall. Featuring Beat and post-Beat writers including Gregory Corso, Lawrence Ferlinghetti, Christopher Logue, Alexander Trocchi, and many others from around the world, this represented the international manifestation of the Beats' literary influence. The worldwide impact of the Beats was particularly evident via a shared language in Britain, where from the late 50s there had been a thriving, Beat-influenced poetry scene. It involved magazines, poetry-and-jazz ensembles, and, most crucially, a "circuit" of live poetry venues stretching northward from London through Liverpool and Newcastle to Edinburgh in Scotland. Back in Britain two years later, Ginsberg headed a landmark "Legalize Pot" rally in London's Hyde Park, before being the main speaker at a "Dialectics of Liberation" conference in the capital. It was July 1967, the so-called "Summer Of Love."

**Right:** Ginsberg as the "King of May" at the May-Day parade in Prague, Czechoslovakia (now the Czech Republic) on May 1, 1965. It was the first time in 20 years that the Communist regime had allowed a May-Day event to be held in the country's capital city.

But the link between a "Beat" and the yet-to-emerge "Hippie" lifestyle was most spectacularly demonstrated in June 1964, when the author Ken Kesey began an odyssey across America, in company with Jack Kerouac's old *On the Road* compadre Neal Cassady. Born in 1935, Kesey enjoyed huge acclaim for his first novel, *One Flew Over The Cuckoo's Nest*, published in 1962 and inspired by his experiences working as an orderly at a mental institution, the Menlo Park Veterans' Hospital in Oregon. There, he volunteered for a government-backed program that involved being administered the same electroconvulsive treatments and drugs as the inmates—the purpose being to acquire a greater understanding of their lives. He took part in experiments that studied the effects of hallucinogenics, particularly the relatively unheard-of LSD. The subsequent novel was a best-seller and a critical success, around which time he first met Cassady.

Following a 1958 arrest for possession of a small amount of marijuana, Neal served a prison sentence in San Quentin and was on parole when he hooked up with Kesey in the summer of 1962. He was having family problems following his release in 1960, and his wife Carolyn finally divorced him in 1963 once his parole expired, a decision she would later have doubts about: "I divorced him because I thought I was going to free him from this burden of having to support a family, and that was the worst thing I could have done, because . . . when he lost the railroad job he lost that pillar, and I took the other one [the family] out . . . and I didn't realize then that this was what it meant to him, so five years later he was dead."

By 1964 Kesey was living in La Honda, just south of San Francisco. He needed to be in New York for the publication of his second novel *Sometimes A Great Notion*, so with part of the book's advance he bought a battered 1939 International Harvester school bus. He lived communally with a group of friends and relatives, who called themselves the Merry Pranksters, most of

whom would form the core of cross-country fellow travelers on his bus, along with Neal Cassady as driver.

Carolyn Cassady was, and still is, convinced Neal would not have taken off with the Pranksters, had he not had some—perhaps subconscious—death wish: "He said he wished nobody would read *On the Road*, because he didn't like Dean Moriarty and all those characteristics that he was trying to overcome. He said he'd wished nobody would read it, but that's what everybody picks up on him . . . So people are always telling me that when he went with Kesey he was trying to live up to the image of Dean Moriarty, which of course is totally untrue. As I say, he didn't like that image, and he was just trying to kill himself . . . but he didn't believe in suicide anymore, so he didn't just do it. But he took any kind of pills, and I heard he was rolling the bus and driving so dangerously. Earlier it was just marijuana and Benzedrine, but then when he got with Kesey—he'd started, I guess, on speed before that—but then he got heavily into that and acid . . . and he told me that he'd take anything anyone would give him. I know he was trying to die."

They named the bus "Further," the name emblazoned on the front and the whole vehicle painted in eye-boggling "psychedelic" patterns with the stars-and-stripes flying from the roof. The seats were replaced by couches and a complex system of sound and movie equipment installed both for entertainment and to record the epic journey.

Fourteen people set out on the bus on June 14, 1964. Passengers could ride on a platform on the top, accessed through a hole cut in the roof, and musical instruments were played, invariably at top volume, as the bus roared south through sleepy towns in Arizona, Texas, and on to New Orleans. A feature of the journey was the "acid test," a group LSD "turn-on," in which the participants were pushed to the edge in terms of how much of the drug they could take, and in how extreme a circumstance.

**Opposite left:** Ken Kesey (center) with a group of Merry Pranksters during their "acid test" period in San Francisco, 1966.

**Opposite right:** LSD guru Timothy Leary (left) with Neal Cassady on board the Pranksters' bus, after they arrived at Leary's Millbrook mansion in 1964.

**Right:** The Pranksters' bus "Further" in October 1966. Before the 1964 trip across America, the name was originally painted as "Furthur" (fusing "further" and "future"), then subsequently changed.

# the neo-beat world of Charles Bukowski

Although not a part of the Beat Generation (his major publications were issued in the 60s and afterward), the work of German-born American writer Charles Bukowski is often considered part of the Beat genre. Over the years, his freeform style, with its rejection of standard structures having much in common with that of Jack Kerouac, Allen Ginsberg, et al., endeared him to Beat readers. His largely autobiographical subject matter—the world of whores, hustlers, and hangovers—is likewise akin to that of the Beats in its street-wise candor.

Bukowski was born in Andernach, Germany, in 1920 and his parents moved to the US when he was three years old. He grew up in Los Angeles, in a poverty-stricken home in which his father was often verbally and physically abusive (as recalled in his novel *Ham On Rye*), and after graduating from High School spent two years at Los Angeles City College taking courses in art, journalism, and literature.

Bukowski began writing during his childhood years, and his first work was published when he was 24. Legend would have it that he then gave up writing for over 20 years. For many of those years he led an itinerant existence, living in cheap rooming houses and spending most of his time in bars across the US, before taking a mind-numbing job as a letter-carrier with the US Postal Service in LA. According to his own later accounts, his life swung between insanity and near-death (two constant themes in his work). He didn't return to writing—so the legend went— until the day he finally left the Postal Service in 1969, encouraged by a $100-a-month "for life" retainer from John Martin of the Black Sparrow Press. In fact, Bukowski's work—both poems and short stories—had been appearing in various small literary journals for a number of years.

He frequently acknowledged Los Angeles to be his favorite subject, its streets and dives grist for the mill in his accounts of bums and barflys: "You live in a town all your life, and you get to know every street-corner," he once said, "You've got the layout of the whole land." He also cited writers as diverse as Chekhov, Kafka, Hemingway, D.H. Lawrence, and Dostoyevsky as influences, though he was clearly also aware of the Beats' more contemporaneous output.

Like the canon of Jack Kerouac, most of Bukowski's prose was autobiographical, with Henry Chinaski his self-based

"My contribution was to loosen and simplify poetry, to make it more human . . . I taught them that you can write a poem the same way you can write a letter, that a poem can even be entertaining, and that there need not be anything necessarily holy about it."

Charles Bukowski, 1974

character in *Ham On Rye* (dealing with his childhood), *Post Office*, and *Factotum*. In *Factotum* we find Chinaski bumming around from town to town, holding down short-term jobs and having even shorter-lived love affairs. It was this image of Bukowski that stuck in the public mind, reinforced when the novel became the inspiration for the 1987 movie *Barfly* with Mickey Rourke playing the (LA-based) alcoholic Chinaski. Bukowski wrote the screenplay for the film, which further perpetuated his self-promoted reputation as a drink-dependent, socially unreliable drop-out.

Bukowski was nothing if not prolific—as well as six novels he eventually had more than 50 books in print, covering hundreds of short stories and thousands of poems. In fact, he is best regarded in literary circles as a poet rather than novelist, even though he considered himself just a writer. He once famously stated, "To say I'm a poet puts me in the company of versifiers, neontasters, fools, clods, and scoundrels masquerading as wise men."

Despite his wild-bachelor image, Bukowski had at least two long-term relationships. In the early 60s he lived for some time with Frances Smith, who bore him a daughter—Marina Louise—and in 1976 he met Linda Lee Beighle, the woman he would marry in 1985. The couple lived in the southern Los Angeles suburb of San Pedro, where Bukowski died of leukemia in 1994, not long after completing the novel *Pulp*. His funeral was conducted by Buddhist monks.

**Left:** Mickey Rourke playing Charles Bukowski's alter ego Henry Chinaski in the 1987 movie *Barfly*.

**Below left:** In a characteristic pose, Bukowski reaches for a six-pack of beer.

**Below right:** Bukowski pictured, glass in hand, in Los Angeles, March 1984.

**Opposite left:** Cassady's Acid Test "pass."

**Opposite right:** Neal Cassady in 1966 performing his party trick—flipping a sledge hammer like a cheerleader's baton—for the amusement of "fans" who had come to see the original Dean Moriarty.

**Far right:** First edition of Tom Wolfe's 1968 account of the Prankster saga, *The Electric Kool-Aid Acid Test*, published by Farrar, Strauss and Giroux.

**Right:** Neal Cassady's only book, the unfinished autobiography *The First Third*, published by City Lights Books in 1971.

"The only thing the filmmakers want to do about him is the last five years with Kesey, when Neal just made an ass of himself."

Carolyn Cassady, 2006

The "Tests" would subsequently be ritualized as mass psychedelic sessions by the Pranksters after they returned to California.

Hitting New York in mid-July, Cassady introduced the Pranksters to Allen Ginsberg and Jack Kerouac. Kerouac was skeptical of their flamboyantly hedonistic attitude, but Ginsberg was more enthusiastic, encouraging them to visit Dr. Timothy Leary, the guru of LSD, who lived in Millbrook, north of the City in New York State. Leary, who had lectured in psychology at Harvard from 1959 to 1963—when he was dismissed for using undergraduates in his drug tests—became the leading advocate of LSD as a medical and spiritual aid. After Harvard he briefly moved to Mexico, where he launched the International Foundation for Internal Freedom (IFIF); later in 1963 he moved to Millbrook. There, he founded the League of Spiritual Discovery, a quasi-religious sect which used LSD as its sacrament.

The Pranksters arrived unannounced, driving up the long driveway to the grand Victorian mansion with rock 'n' roll music blaring from speakers. Occupants of the house wondered what was going on, and they certainly had little in common with

Kesey's motley road crew. Leary and his disciples treated LSD "tripping" as serious therapy and an aid to spiritual enlightenment, while the Pranksters essentially took it simply for kicks.

By the end of August 1964, the Pranksters were back in California, Neal Cassady having returned ahead of the others. His life was to become increasingly chaotic as he lived up to his "wild man of the Beats" reputation, carousing across the US and into Mexico, never in one place for long—and like Jack Kerouac, a victim of his public image. Eventually he was to die in tragic circumstances on February 4, 1968, after he was found in a coma by a railroad track near San Miguel de Allende in Mexico. He'd been to a wedding party in the town the previous night, and started to walk along the track to the next town when he passed out under the influence of drink and drugs, wearing only a T-shirt and jeans despite the cold and rain. He was just 41.

Tom Wolfe describes the whole saga of the Merry Pranksters in his 1968 book, *The Electric Kool-Aid Acid Test*. The trip, and their continuing "acid tests" back in California, would be one of the building blocks of the West Coast psychedelic scene centered on San Francisco. Using the so-called "magic bus" as a traveling base, there were a number of major acid tests staged from November 1965 through 1966—bearing in mind LSD was legal in the US until 1966—involving the Pranksters, Cassady, and a variety of "guests," including Allen Ginsberg and nascent West Coast bands like the Grateful Dead. First staged in various open spaces such as public beaches, they quickly evolved into the embryo "freak outs" characterizing San Francisco rock at venues

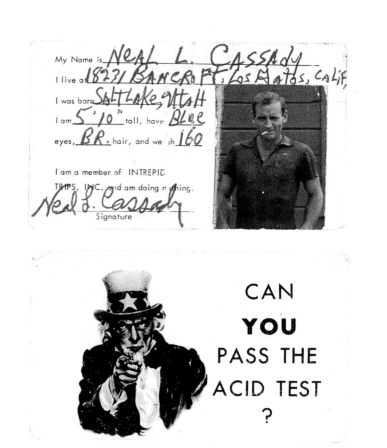

including the Avalon Ballroom and Fillmore Auditorium. That scene, in turn, begat the youth revolution that would soon reverberate across the Western world—and which had many of its roots in the Beat movement of a decade earlier.

The Flower Children's embracing of aspects of Eastern religion, for instance, had its precursor in the Beats' original adoption of Zen Buddhism and meditation. Similarly, with their advocacy of soft drugs—particularly amphetamines and marijuana—which had previously been the province of the jazz world and the Beats, and hallucinogenics (primarily LSD) that achieved the psychedelic mind-expansion sought by Bill Burroughs, Allen Ginsberg, and others in their experimentation with everything from the mystic yage to Brion Gysin's Dreamachine. While the Beats had their soundtrack in the jazz of the 50s and early 60s, so the counterculture was even more closely linked to the rock revolution that by the late 60s had evolved from mere pop music to the anthemic rallying call of the alternative society.

And the Beats' apolitical stance, seeing art and creativity as "above" social considerations, had its parallels in the hippies' espousal of "dropping out" rather than being socially engaged with the existing status quo. In their anti-war stance during the years of the Vietnam conflict, the peace-and-love generation generally made their voices felt *outside* conventional politics, just as Beat-era attitudes under the shadow of the H-bomb had been similarly distanced (and often dismissive of) the established channels of protest.

"Someone handed me *Mexico City Blues* in St. Paul [Minnesota] in 1959 and it blew my mind. It was the first poetry that spoke my own language."

Bob Dylan

But the impact of the Beat Generation, which has far outlived its immediate influence in the late 60s, would be felt for decades to come, and it continues to reverberate throughout modern culture even though few of the leading protagonists are still alive.

Although he died in 1969—at the height of the hippie movement which he derided to the end—Jack Kerouac's legacy has been immense. There was the direct influence of his writing style, particularly on the "New Journalism" of Tom Wolfe, Norman Mailer, and others who moved away from conventional "objective" reporting to a more personal and intuitive style. Also, the so-called "Gonzo journalism" of Hunter S. Thompson, exemplified in his best known work *Fear And Loathing In Las Vegas*, published in 1971. Blurring the boundaries between fiction and non-fiction, Thompson's approach—usually written in the first person—was deliberately humorous and bizarre, with the truth shamelessly embellished to achieve more impact.

And, largely thanks to Kerouac, there has been the perception of a "Beat" attitude, real or imagined, and personified in *On the Road*. It has inspired not just the boho romanticism of the likes of Bob Dylan and Tom Waits, but succeeding generations of disaffected youth whose lifestyles Kerouac would, nevertheless, have generally despised.

After the death of his widow Stella Sampas in 1990, administration of the Kerouac Estate (which Sampas had inherited) passed to her brother, John. With his son Tony, Sampas continues to look after the Kerouac archive and, over the years, he has released a good deal of previously unpublished material.

Similarly posthumous was the only book written by Neal Cassady, an unfinished autobiography titled *The First Third*, published by City Lights Books in 1971. Cassady's greatest literary contribution, however, was undoubtedly his letters, many of which had a direct influence on Jack Kerouac's own "spontaneous prose" style in the early 50s. They, too, would eventually be published, years after Neal's death, in *Grace Beats Karma: Letters from Prison*, which appeared in 1993, and *Neal Cassady: Collected Letters, 1944–1967*, published by Penguin in 2004.

By the time of his death on April 5, 1997, at age 70, Allen Ginsberg had become a much-respected figure in a new literary establishment. In later life he was the recipient of many honors and awards, including the Woodbury Poetry Prize, a Guggenheim fellowship, the National Book Award for Poetry, and the French Government's Order of Arts and Letters. Ginsberg continued to campaign for civil rights, gay liberation, and world peace to the end of his life.

After forging a link between the Beats and the late 60s' hippies, his influence was acknowledged in numerous areas of popular culture, from the songs of his friend Bob Dylan to collaborations with musical voices as disparate as Dylan, Philip Glass, Paul McCartney, and The Clash. In 1996 he played a leading role in an opera by John Moran, *Mathew in the School of Life*, and was featured as a supporting character in the science fiction novel *Patton's Spaceship* by John Barnes, and even referenced in at least two episodes of *The Simpsons*.

Ginsberg died, surrounded by family and friends, in the East Village loft in New York City which had been his home for many years. He succumbed to liver cancer via complications of hepatitis, and continued to write through his final illness, with his last poem "Things I'll Not Do (Nostalgias)" written just six days before his death.

Bill Burroughs died four months after Allen Ginsberg, on August 2, 1997, at his home in Lawrence, Kansas, following a heart attack the previous day. Though his work seems to be the least "accessible" of that produced by the leading Beat writers, by the 80s he had become a revered giant of the counterculture. He collaborated with performers ranging from avant-garde musicians Bill Laswell and Laurie Anderson to singer/songwriter Tom Waits and alt-rock band Sonic Youth, and appeared in the 1989 Gus Van Sant movie *Drugstore Cowboy* as a character based largely on

himself. In addition, he was cited as a major influence by "punk poetess" Patti Smith, the British indie rock band Joy Division, and Nirvana's Kurt Cobain.

As well as being associated with other movers and shakers in the arts such as Andy Warhol, Dennis Hopper, Susan Sontag, and Terry Southern, his literary admirers included the British critic Peter Ackroyd and authors J.G. Ballard, Angela Carter, and Jean Genet. In 1984 he was inducted into the American Academy and Institute of Arts and Letters, a prestigious institution which at any one time only has a maximum of 250 living US citizens as members.

In 1991 the film director David Cronenberg released the movie that many said was impossible to make, an adaptation (with Burroughs' approval) of *The Naked Lunch*. In fact, the film wasn't strictly an adaptation at all, but a semi-biography mixed into a paranoid fantasy exploring Burroughs' writing process through his personal demons and nightmares. The leading character (played by Peter Weller) was called Bill Lee, the pseudonym "William Lee" which Burroughs had used on the first publication of his debut book *Junkie*.

A few months after his death, *Word Virus*, an anthology of writings covering Burroughs' entire career, was published, as was a collection of journal entries written during the final months of his life, published under the title *Last Words*. A long-awaited memoir by Burroughs called *Evil River* was published by Viking early in 2007, having initially been earmarked for a 2005 release.

After half a century since the first publication of *On the Road*, many more key Beat names have left the stage. West Coast poetry-and-jazz pioneers Kenneth Patchen and Kenneth Rexroth died, ten years apart, in 1972 and 1982 respectively. The man who first popularized the notion of a "Beat Generation," John Clellon Holmes, made his exit in 1988, while Gregory Corso passed on, aged 70, in 2001—he was buried exactly where he wanted, next to the grave of the English romantic poet Percy Bysshe Shelley in Rome. Robert Creeley bade the world farewell in Odessa, Texas, just as the sun came up on March 3, 2005. Ironically, Lucien Carr, once called a "catalyst for the Beat Generation," outlived all three of the major Beat writers—Bill Burroughs, Allen Ginsberg, and Jack Kerouac—that he had been instrumental in introducing to each other, dying from bone cancer in January 2005, a month short of his 80th birthday.

The impact of the men and women of the Beat Generation was not just in terms of their role as poets and novelists, though the revolution they represented in the world of letters was important enough in itself. Nowadays, many of the radical positions taken by the Beats, in enlightened sexual mores and liberal social attitudes, as well as literary style and convention, are taken for granted as part of the cultural status quo. But during the relatively short time of their heyday they played a crucial role in the pivotal decade of the 50s, irrevocably influencing the changes wrought then and in the tumultuous years that followed, the lasting significance of which is still felt today.

# chronology

**1914**
February 5: William Burroughs born in St. Louis, Missouri.

**1922**
March 12: Jack Kerouac born in Lowell, Massachusetts. Burroughs, aged eight, produces first fiction, *Autobiography of a Wolf*.

**1926**
June 3: Allen Ginsberg born in Newark, New Jersey.

**1939**
Fall: Jack Kerouac arrives in New York City to attend Horace Mann School for Boys.

**1940**
September: Jack Kerouac begins as a freshman at Columbia University.

**1941**
Spring: Ginsberg's first work appears in the Paterson Central High magazine, the *Spectator*.
September: Ginsberg transferred to Paterson East Side High, where he is introduced to the work of Walt Whitman.

**1943**
January: Kerouac meets Edie Parker through old Horace Mann friend Henri Cru.
Spring: Burroughs moves to New York.
September: Ginsberg enrolls in pre-law course at Columbia University.
October: Returning from sea, Kerouac moves in with Parker who shares an apartment with Joan Vollmer-Adams at 421 West 118th Street.
December: Via Parker, Kerouac meets Lucien Carr. Ginsberg meets Lucien Carr. Through Carr, Ginsberg meets Burroughs and Kammerer.

**1944**
Ginsberg writes for Columbia *Jester* magazine.
c. January/February: Kerouac meets Ginsberg.
February: Kerouac meets Burroughs. *Circle* magazine is launched, heralding San Francisco Renaissance.
Spring/summer: The "New Vision" develops via discussions between Ginsberg, Carr, Burroughs, Kerouac, Vollmer.

Summer: Joan Vollmer moves to apartment 35 at 419 W 115th Street.
August 14: Carr fatally stabs David Kammerer.
August 22: Kerouac marries Edie Parker, the couple briefly moving to her home town of Grosse Pointe, Michigan.
October 6: Lucien Carr sentenced to an "indeterminate term" in the Elmira Reformatory.

**1945**
January: Ginsberg begins writing his first serious poetry.
March: Ginsberg moves into West 115th Street.
September: Kerouac moves into West 115th Street.
Late summer: Burroughs moves into West 115th Street.
October: Herbert Huncke introduced to West 115th Street, moves in soon after.
November: The "Night of the Wolfeans."

**1946**
Summer: West 115th apartment vacated.
December: Neal Cassady arrives in New York, meets Kerouac.

**1947**
*Ark* magazine launched in San Francisco.
January 10: Cassady meets Ginsberg.
May: Cassady returns to Denver, followed by Ginsberg.
July 17: Kerouac leaves New York on first "road" trip.

**1948**
Spring: Kerouac, back in New York, finishes first novel *The Town and the City*.
April 1: Cassady marries Carolyn Robinson in San Francisco.
June: "Portrait of a Hipster," an essay by Anatole Broyard, in *Partisan Review*.
July 4: John Clellon Holmes meets Kerouac at a party thrown by Ginsberg.
December: Cassady drives to New York with ex-wife LuAnne Henderson and Al Hinkle.

**1949**
January 19: Kerouac, Cassady, and LuAnne Henderson set off from New York for San Francisco, the trip that would form the centerpiece of *On the Road*.
March 29: Back in New York, Kerouac is offered $1,000 advance for *The Town and the City*.
June 29: Ginsberg admitted to Columbia Psychiatric Institute, where he meets Carl Solomon.

Summer: Kerouac heads back for San Francisco, from where he drives to New York with Cassady via Denver, Chicago, and Grosse Pointe.

September: Burroughs and Joan Vollmer move to Mexico City.

Fall: Kerouac first uses the term "Beat Generation" in discussion with John Clellon Holmes.

## 1950

February 27: Ginsberg discharged from CPI.

March: Ginsberg makes contact with William Carlos Williams.

Early March: Kerouac's first novel *The Town and the City* is published.

Spring: Carl Solomon article "Report from the Asylum" is published in *Neurotica*.

May: Kerouac travels to Denver, then, with Cassady, to Mexico City.

August: Kerouac returns to New York, resuming work on *On the Road*.

November 3: Kerouac marries Joan Haverty.

December 27: Kerouac receives letter from Cassady which he calls (claiming it was up to 40,000 words long) "a masterpiece."

Winter: Ginsberg meets Gregory Corso.

## 1951

Winter–spring: Cassady works on autobiographical memoir, published in 1971 as *The First Third*.

April: Over three weeks, Kerouac completes 86,000 words of *On the Road* on nearly 120 feet of continuous manuscript.

July: Burroughs goes to Ecuador in search of yage.

August: Ginsberg and Lucien Carr visit Joan Vollmer-Burroughs.

September 6: Burroughs shoots and kills his common-law wife, Joan Vollmer-Burroughs.

## 1952

Spring: Kerouac begins affair with Carolyn Cassady.

July: Peter D. Martin launches *City Lights* magazine, featuring work by new San Francisco writers.

August: First ever Happening, *Theater Piece No. 1*, staged at Black Mountain College.

Fall: John Clellon Holmes' *Go* is published, the first novel about the Beat Generation.

November 16: Holmes' article "This is the Beat Generation" appears in the *New York Times Magazine*.

## 1953

January to June: Burroughs embarks on second search for the drug yage.

May: William Burroughs' first novel *Junkie* is published by Ace Books.

June: Lawrence Ferlinghetti and Peter D. Martin open the City Lights bookstore in San Francisco.

July: Viking editor Malcolm Cowley expresses interest in *On the Road*.

December: Ginsberg travels to Mexico.

## 1954

January: Burroughs settles in Tangiers. Kerouac begins to study Buddhism.

Spring: First edition of *Black Mountain Review*, edited by Robert Creeley.

December: Ginsberg meets Peter Orlovsky in San Francisco.

## 1955

August 10: Ferlinghetti launches City Lights' "Pocket Poets" series with his own collection, *Pictures of the Gone World*.

Fall: Kerouac and Ginsberg meet Gary Snyder in San Francisco.

October 7: The seminal "Six Poets" reading at San Francisco's Six Gallery, at which Ginsberg first reads from (the still incomplete) "Howl."

October 26: First edition of *The Village Voice*.

End October: Kerouac and Snyder climb the Matterhorn mountain in Yosemite National Park, inspiring Kerouac's *The Dharma Bums*.

## 1956

March: Robert Creeley arrives in San Francisco.

March 18: Ginsberg premiers the entire "Howl" at the University of California, Berkeley.

May 5: Gary Snyder leaves for Japan to study Zen.

Fall: Black Mountain College closes.

September: *New York Times Book Review* reports favorably on "Pacific Coast upstarts" in a piece titled "West Coast Rhythms."

October: City Lights publish Ginsberg's *Howl and Other Poems*.

## 1957

February: Burroughs joined in Tangiers by Kerouac.

March: Burroughs joined in Tangiers by Ginsberg and Orlovsky.

March 25: 520 copies of *Howl* seized by US Customs.

Spring: *Evergreen Review* first appears. Early poetry-and-jazz experiment by Kenneth Rexroth and Lawrence Ferlinghetti at The Cellar, San Francisco.

April 5: Kerouac leaves Tangiers for Paris and London.

June 1: City Lights bookstore raided.

Summer: The "Howl" trial opens in San Francisco. "The White Negro" by Norman Mailer appears in *Dissent* magazine. *Evergreen Review* #2 devoted to "The San Francisco Scene."

August: Final issue of *Black Mountain Review* (#7) co-edited by Robert Creeley and Ginsberg.

September 5: Kerouac's *On the Road* published by Viking, soon makes #7 in best-sellers.

October: Kerouac, Philip Lamantia, Howard Hart, and David Amram stage first New York poetry-and-jazz reading at the Brata Art Gallery.

October 3: Judge Clayton Horn rules "Howl" not obscene.

October 15: Ginsberg, Orlovsky, and Corso check into the "Beat Hotel" in Paris.

November 13: Ginsberg begins writing "Kaddish" in Paris.

## 1958

Gregory Corso's *Gasoline* published by City Lights.

January 16: Burroughs arrives in Paris from Tangiers, checking into the Beat Hotel.

February: Grove Press publishes Kerouac's *The Subterraneans*.

March: LeRoi and Hettie Jones publish *Yugen* magazine.

April 2: The word "beatnik" appears for the first time, in the *San Francisco Chronicle*.

June 14: Neal Cassady sentenced to "five years to life" in San Quentin for possession of three marijuana "reefers."

July: Ginsberg leaves Paris for New York. Brion Gysin moves into the Beat Hotel.

October: Viking publish Kerouac's *The Dharma Bums*.

November: Kerouac performs disastrous week-long season at the Village Vanguard jazz club in New York.

December: An excerpt from *The Naked Lunch* appears in the *Chicago Review* and is subsequently censored. *Playboy* magazine prints excerpt from Kerouac lecture on "The Origins of the Beat Generation."

## 1959

At the Beat Hotel, Brion Gysin and Ian Sommerville construct the first Dreamachine.

March: *Big Table* magazine publishes excerpts from *The Naked Lunch*, 499 copies then impounded by the US Post Office.

May 9: *Beatitude* launched by Ginsberg, Bob Kaufman, and others in San Francisco.

June: *Poetry For The Beat Generation*, an album of Kerouac reading with Steve Allen on piano, is released. The movie *Pull My Daisy*, including Ginsberg, Kerouac, Orlovsky, and Corso is released.

July: Burroughs' *The Naked Lunch* is published by Olympia Press, Paris. *Playboy* publishes Beat article with poems by Kerouac, Ginsberg, and Corso.

September: "Squaresville USA vs Beatsville" article in *Life* magazine. In Paris, Brion Gysin and Burroughs discover the possibilities of cut-ups.

September 29: *The Many Loves of Dobie Gillis* launches on US television, introducing archetypal Beatnik character Maynard G. Krebs.

November: Kerouac appears on the Steve Allen TV show with an audience of 35 million.

December: First "Rent-A-Beatnik" ad appears in the *Village Voice*.

## 1960

First-ever cut-up book, *Minutes To Go*, by Burroughs, Gysin, Corso, and Sinclair Beiles, published in Paris.

June 14: Cassady released from San Quentin.

July 5: Judge Julius J. Hoffman sets aside ban on *Big Table* that featured *The Naked Lunch* excerpts.

August: Kerouac stays at Ferlinghetti's retreat at Big Sur, inspiring book of same name.

September: *Mad* magazine includes "Beatnik: The Magazine for Hipsters."

## 1961

Diane Di Prima and LeRoi Jones launch the *Floating Bear* newsletter.

## 1962

*The Naked Lunch* published in the US by Grove Press, subsequently prosecuted by Massachusetts authorities as obscene.

December: Burroughs leaves the Beat Hotel.

## 1963

Ginsberg receives a Guggenheim Fellowship award.

Ginsberg is awarded the prestigious Woodbury Poetry prize.

Spring: The Beat Hotel closes.

## 1964

Burroughs returns to the US.

June 14: Ken Kesey and Neal Cassady begin Merry Pranksters' "Acid Test" road trip across America.

**1965**

Gregory Corso dismissed from teaching post at the State University of New York in Buffalo for refusing to certify he was not a member of the Communist Party.
May 1: Ginsberg declared "King of May" in Prague.
June 11: Poetry International staged at London's Royal Albert Hall, including Ginsberg, Ferlinghetti, and Corso.
November: Kesey and Pranksters stage first of the California-based Acid Tests.

**1966**

Massachusetts Supreme Judicial Court declares *The Naked Lunch* "not obscene." Burroughs in role of "Opium Jones" in the movie *Chappaqua*.
November: Kerouac marries Stella Sampas.

**1967**

Kerouac writes his last full-length book, *Vanity of Duluoz*.
July: Ginsberg appears at "Legalize Pot" rally in London's Hyde Park.

**1968**

February 4: Neal Cassady dies by a railroad track near San Miguel de Allende, Mexico.

**1969**

Ginsberg receives a National Institute of Arts and Letters award.
October 21: Jack Kerouac dies at a hospital in St. Petersberg, Florida.

**1971**

Charles Bukowski's first novel *Post Office* is published by Black Sparrow Press. Neal Cassady's autobiographical *The First Third* published by City Lights.

**1973**

Ginsberg wins the National Book Award for *The Fall of America: Poems of These States*, published by City Lights.

**1974**

Burroughs relocates to the US permanently, having spent most of the late 60s in London.

**1979**

Ginsberg is awarded the National Arts Club Medal of Honor for Literature.

**1981**

Burroughs' *Cities of the Red Night* is published.

**1983**

May: Burroughs inducted into the American Academy and Institute of Arts and Letters.

**1986**

April: Allen Ginsberg is named winner of the Frost Medal for distinguished poetic achievement by the Poetry Society of America.

**1988**

August 6/7: Ginsberg involved in the Tompkins Square Park Police Riot, providing an eyewitness account to the *New York Times*.

**1989**

Burroughs appears in the movie *Drugstore Cowboy*.

**1990**

Burroughs releases spoken-word album *Dead City Radio*.
Burroughs collaborates with director Robert Wilson and singer Tom Waits on the play *The Black Rider*, which opens in Hamburg.

**1991**

With Burroughs' sanction, *The Naked Lunch* is adapted as a film by David Cronenberg.

**1993**

The French Minister of Culture awards Allen Ginsberg the medal of the *Chevalier des Arts et des Lettres* (the Order of Arts and Letters).

**1997**

April 5: Allen Ginsberg dies at his home in New York City.
August 2: William Burroughs dies at his home in Lawrence, Kansas.

# selected works

**Willam Burroughs**
Junkie (1953)
The Naked Lunch (1959)
The Soft Machine (1961)
The Ticket That Exploded (1962)
Dead Fingers Talk (1963)
Nova Express (1964)
Exterminator! (1973)
Letters to Allen Ginsberg 1953–1957 (1976)
Cities of the Red Night (1981)
Interzone (1987)
Tornado Alley (1989)
Last Words (1997)

**Allen Ginsberg**
Howl and Other Poems (1956)
The Yage Letters (with William S. Burroughs) (1960)
Kaddish and Other Poems (1961)
Reality Sandwiches (1963)
Planet News (1968)
The Fall of America: Poems of These States (1972)
First Blues: Rags, Ballads & Harmonium Songs (1975)
White Shroud, Poems 1980–1985 (1986)
Visiting Father and Friends (1993)
Death and Fame: Poems (1999)
Collected Poems 1947–1997 (2006)

**Jack Kerouac**
The Town and the City (1950)
On the Road (1957)
The Dharma Bums (1958)
The Subterraneans (1958)
Doctor Sax (1959)
Maggie Cassidy (1959)
Mexico City Blues (1959)
Visions of Cody (1960)
Big Sur (1962)
Vanity of Duluoz (1968)
Book of Blues (1995)
Some of the Dharma (1997)
Book of Haikus (2003)

**Neal Cassady**
The First Third (1971)
Grace Beats Karma: Letters from Prison (1993)
Neal Cassady: Collected Letters, 1944–1967 (2004)

**Lawrence Ferlinghetti**
Pictures of the Gone World (1955)
A Coney Island of the Mind (1958)
Starting from San Francisco (1967)
The Secret Meaning of Things (1970)
Landscapes of Living and Dying (1980)
Americus: Part I (2004)

**Gregory Corso**
The Vestal Lady and Other Poems (1955)
Gasoline (1958)
Bomb (1958)
The Happy Birthday of Death (1960)
Minutes to Go (with Sinclair Beiles, William Burroughs, and Brion Gysin) (1960)
The American Express (1961)
Mindfield: New and Selected Poems (1989)

**Kenneth Rexroth**
The Phoenix and the Tortoise (1944)
In Defense of the Earth (1956)
Bird in the Bush: Obvious Essays (1959)
World Outside the Window: Selected Essays (1987)

**Kenneth Patchen**
The Journal of Albion Moonlight (1941)
The Memoirs of a Shy Pornographer (1945)
Poems of Humor and Protest (1954)
When We Were Here Together (1957)
The Love Poems of Kenneth Patchen (1960)

**Gary Snyder**
Riprap (1959)
Six Sections from Mountains and Rivers Without End (1965–1970)
Turtle Island (1974)
Back on the Fire: Essays (2007)

**Diane di Prima**
This Kind of Bird Flies Backward (1958)
Memoirs of a Beatnik (1969)
Selected Poems: 1956–1975 (1975)

**John Clellon Holmes**
Go (1952)
The Horn (1958)
Gone In October: Last Reflections on Jack Kerouac (1985)

# bibliography

**Herbert Huncke**
Huncke's Journal (1965)

**LeRoi Jones**
Preface to a Twenty Volume Suicide Note (1961)

**Bob Kaufman**
Solitudes Crowded with Loneliness (1965)
Golden Sardine (1967)
Cranial Guitar: Selected Poems by Bob Kaufman (1996)

**Michael McClure**
For Artaud (1959)
The Beard (1965)
The Sermons of Jean Harlow and the Curses of Billy the Kid (1968)

**Ted Joans**
The Hipsters (1961)
Black Pow-Wow (1969)

**Philip Lamantia**
Erotic Poems (1946)
Ekstasis (1959)
Selected Poems 1943–1966 (1967)

**Philip Whalen**
Heavy Breathing: Poems, 1967–1980 (1983)
Canoeing up Cabarga Creek: Buddhist Poems 1955–1986 (1995)
Overtime: Selected Poems (1999)

**Charles Bukowski**
Post Office (1971)
Burning in Water, Drowning in Flame: Selected Poems
1955–1973 (1974)

James Campbell, *This is the Beat Generation,* Vintage (UK) 2000
Carolyn Cassady, *Off the Road,* Black Spring Press (US) 1990
Ann Charters, *Kerouac,* Andre Deutsch (UK) 1974
Ann Charters (Ed), *The Penguin Book of the Beats,* Penguin (UK) 1993
Ann Charters (Ed), *The Portable Beat Reader,* Penguin (US) 1992
Tom Clark, *Jack Kerouac,* Paragon House (US) 1990
Holly George-Warren (Ed), *The Rolling Stone Book of the Beats,*
    Hyperion (US) 1999
Barry Gifford and Lawrence Lee, *Jack's Book,* St Martin's Press
    (US) 1978
Michael Hrebeniak, *Action Writing: Jack Kerouac's Wild Form,*
    Southern Illinois University Press (US) 2006
Joyce Johnson, *Minor Characters,* Harvill Press (UK) 1983
Hettie Jones, *How I Became Hettie Jones,* E.P. Dutton (US) 1990
Arthur Winfield Knight (Ed), *The Beat Vision,* Paragon House (US) 1987
Brenda Knight, *Women of the Beat Generation,* Conari Press (US) 1996
John Leland, *Hip: The History,* Ecco (US) 2004
Lawrence Lipton, *The Holy Barbarians,* Messner (US) 1959
Lewis MacAdams, *Birth of the Cool,* Scribner (UK) 2002
Fred McDarrah/Gloria S. McDarrah, *Beat Generation:*
    *Glory Days in Greenwich Village,* Schirmer (US) 1996
Dennis McNally, *Desolate Angel: Jack Kerouac, the Beat Generation*
    *and America,* Random House (US) 1979
Barry Miles, *Allen Ginsberg: A Biography,* Virgin (UK) 2000
Barry Miles, *The Beat Hotel,* Grove Press (US) 2000
Barry Miles, *Jack Kerouac King of the Beats: A Portrait,* Virgin
    (UK) 1998
Barry Miles, *William Burroughs: El Hombre Invisible,* Hyperion
    (UK) 1993
Bill Morgan, *The Beat Generation In New York,* City Lights (US) 1997
Ted Morgan, *Literary Outlaw: The Life and Times of William S.*
    *Burroughs,* Henry Holt (US) 1988
Gerald Nicosia, *Memory Babe: A Critical Biography of Jack Kerouac,*
    Grove Press (US) 1983
Lisa Phillips (Ed), *Beat Culture and the New America 1950–1965,*
    Flammarion/Whitney Museum of Modern Art (US) 1995
Ed Sanders, *Tales of Beatnik Glory,* Stonehill (US) 1975
David Sandison, *Jack Kerouac,* Hamlyn (UK) 1999
David Sandison/Graham Vickers, *Neal Cassady: The Fast Life*
    *of a Beat Hero,* Chicago Review Press (US) 2006
Steve Turner, *Jack Kerouac Angelheaded Hipster,* Bloomsbury
    (UK) 1996
Steven Watson, *The Birth of the Beat Generation,* Pantheon (US) 1995

# index

Figures in **bold** refer to
illustration captions

# picture credits

# quotes: sources

p. 10: Walt Whitman, from "Song Of The Open Road," first published in Leaves of Grass, 1855

p. 14: Burroughs quoted in Patrick Joubert, *An American Nightmare: William Burroughs*, bornagainredneck.blogspot.com, 2005

p. 18: Leo Kerouac in Dennis McNally, *Desolate Angel: Jack Kerouac, the Beat Generation and America*, Random House (US) 1979

p. 22: Edith Parker, 1988 interviewed for BBC *Arena*, "Kerouac"

p. 26: Ginsberg, in "The School Day I Remember Most", *Instructor* magazine, May 1979 (piece dated September 21, 1978)

p. 28: Hal Chase, interview with Ted Morgan 15/3/1985, the Morgan Archives, Arizona State University

p. 33: Ginsberg, in Ted Morgan, *Literary Outlaw: The Life and Times of William S. Burroughs*, Holy (US) 1988

p. 34: Ginsberg, interview with Stephen Watson March 27, 1995, *The Birth of the Beat Generation*, Pantheon (US) 1995

p. 41: *New York Times*, August 18, 1944

p. 42: Thomas Wolfe, original source unknown, widely quoted including quotationsbook.com

p. 46: John Clellon Holmes in William Plummer, *The Holy Goof: A Biography of Neal Cassady*, Paragon (US) 1981

p. 47: Herbert Huncke in *Jack's Book*, St Martin's Press (US) 1978

p. 48 (top): Letter to Ginsberg from Herbert Huncke in prison, September 23, 1946

p. 48 (bottom): Thomas Wolfe quoted in D.G. Kehl, "Writing the Long Desire: The Function of *Sehnsucht* in *The Great Gatsby* and *Look Homeward, Angel*," *Journal of Modern Literature*, Vol. 24, #2, Winter 2000/2001, Indiana University Press

p. 50: Kenneth Rexroth, "Disengagement: The Art of the Beat Generation," *New World Writing*, 1957

p. 56: Walt Whitmnan quoted in Ted Morgan, *Literay Outlaw: The Life and Times of William S. Burroughs*, Holy (US) 1988

p. 65: LuAnne Henderson in *Jack's Book*, St Martin's Press (US) 1978

p. 66: James Elmont, "The Scroll of Jack Kerouac," literarytraveler.com, 2002

p. 74: John Clellon Holmes quoted in John Tytell, *Naked Angels: The Classic Account of Three Who Changed America's Literature*, Grove Press (US) 1976

p. 76: Jackson Pollock quoted in *Possibilities I, Winter 1947–48* contemporary art review, New York 1947.

p. 80: Gerry Mulligan 1971, quoted in liner notes to 1989 CD reissue of *Birth Of The Cool*

p. 83: Kerouac interview with Ted Berrigan, "The Art of Fiction XLI: Jack Kerouac," *Paris Review* #43, 1968

p. 84: Ted Joans, interviewed on National Public Radio, June 1, 2001

p. 86: Ginsberg interview by Steve Yun and Henry Flesh, "Ginsberg: From Howl to Shout!" c.1996

p. 88: John Clellon Holmes to Kerouac, 1950 from *Jack Kerouac, Selected letters 1940–1956*, Viking (US) 1993

p. 90: John Clellon Holmes, "This is the Beat Generation," *New York Times Magazine*, November 16, 1952

p. 93: Burroughs, *Excelsior* newspaper (Mexico City), September 8, 1951

p. 95: Corso in Ronald Sukenick, *Down and In: Life In The Underground*, Macmillan (US) 1987

p. 97: Burroughs to Ginsberg, quoted in "Word Virus," lucaspickford.com

p. 98: Michael McLure in *Scratching The Beat Surface*, North Point Press (US) 1982

p. 100: Ferlinghetti quoted in *San Francisco Chronicle*, September 1, 2005

p. 103: Kenneth Rexroth, in court statement in support of "Howl."

p. 104: Ken Kesey interviewed for digitalinterviews.com, posted September 2000

p. 109: D.T. Suzuki, *An Introduction to Zen Buddhism* (1949), Grove Atlantic (US) edition 1991

p. 112: Burroughs, original source unknown, widely quoted including "Beat Quotes," angelfire.com

p. 114: Burroughs interviewed by Lee Ranaldo for "Literary Kicks" (litkicks.com), April 9, 1997

p. 117 (bottom): Burroughs to Ginsberg, October 29, 1956, in *The Letters of Willam Burroughs 1945–1959*, Ed. Oliver Harris, Viking (US) 1993

p. 117 (top): Gilbert Millstein, *New York Times*, September 5, 1957

p. 118: Burroughs to Ginsberg, October 29, 1956, in *The Letters of Willam Burroughs 1945–1959*, Ed. Oliver Harris, Viking (US) 1993

p. 120: Jean-Jacques Lebel, interviewed by Barry Miles, 2000, in *The Beat Hotel*, Grove Press (US) 2001

p. 123: Mike Zwerin, *International Herald Tribune*, Paris, May 25, 2001

p. 126: Brion Gysin, *Dreamachine Plans*, Temple Press (US) 1994

p. 129: Brion Gysin, *The Third Mind*, Grove Press (US) 1978

p. 130: John Cage, *Silence: Lectures and Writings by John Cage*, Wesleyan University Press (US) 1973

p. 132: Allan Kaprow, *Untitled Guidelines for Happenings*, 1965

p. 135: Jonas Mekas, *Film Culture* magazine, 1959

p. 136: Louis Adamic in *Black Mountain College, Sprouted Seeds: An Anthology of Personal Accounts*, University of Tennessee Press (US) 1990

p. 140: Dan Wakefield, interviewed by Richard F. Shepard, the *New York Times*, 1999

p. 142: Gilbert Sorrentino, in *The Little Magazine in America: A Modern Documentary History*, The Pushcart Press (US) 1978

p. 144: Ed Sanders, interview with Billy Bog Hargus, June 1997, www.furious.com

p. 146: Tom Paxton talking to author Robbie Woliver in *Hoot!—A 25-Year History of the Greenwich Village Music Scene*, St. Martin's Press (US) 1986

p. 148: Diane di Prima (with Leroi Jones), *The Floating Bear: a newsletter*, Laurence McGilvery, (US) 1973

p. 152: Gregory Corso, talking to Art Buchwald in "The Upbeat Beatnik," *New York Herald Tribune*, January 4, 1960

p. 154: Herbert Gold 1960, quoted in Glen Burns, *Great Poets Howl: A Study of Allen Ginsberg's Poetry*, Peter Long (US) 1983

p. 158: Fred McDarrah, *Beat Generation: Glory Days in Greenwich Village*, Schirmer (US) 1996

p. 162: Kerouac quoted in *New York Journal American*, December 8, 1960

p. 164: Ken Kesey, interview with Robert K. Elder, *The Bronc Express* (Billings Senior High School newspaper, Billings, Montana), 1999

p. 166: Kerouac interview with Ted Berrigan, "The Art of Fiction XLI: Jack Kerouac," *Paris Review* #43, 1968

p. 168: Vivian Gornick, in essay "Wild At Heart" in *The Poem That Changed America: "Howl" Fifty Years Later* (Ed. Jason Shinder), Farrar, Straus & Giroux (US) 2006

p. 170: Lord Buckley, "Marc Anthony's Funeral Oration," 1954

p. 171: Don Waller, "Hipsters, Flipsters and Skin-Poppin' Daddies," *The Rolling Stone Book of the Beats*, Hyperion (US) 1999

p. 176: Charles Bukowsky in *Second Coming* magazine (US) 1974

p. 179: Bob Dylan to Ginsberg, while shooting scene for *Renaldo and Clara* (1975) at Kerouac's grave, Lowell, 1975